Evelyn Waugh

★

PORTRAIT OF AN ARTIST

EVELYN WAUGH AGED 26

from the portrait by HENRY LAMB in the collection of LORD MOYNE, by
whose kind permission it is here reproduced.

Frederick J. Stopp

EVELYN WAUGH

Portrait of an Artist

LITTLE, BROWN AND COMPANY

Boston   Toronto

First published 1958

Contents

5

APPENDICES

Illustrations

Preface

EVELYN WAUGH's first novel, *Decline and Fall*, was pub-lished thirty years ago, in 1928. During that time much has been written on the author and his works, but no general study of the kind attempted in the present book has appeared. For this there are, I think, two reasons. One is the common assumption that the comic genius is a freakish gift of nature, which neither calls for nor repays lengthy examination by the literary critic. The second is that Mr Waugh holds, and does not hesitate to express, many opinions which provoke opposition. Irritation is a poor guide to insight.

This is a pity. The novels are so subtle in technique and structure, and so rich in allusion, that there is no end to the fascinating task of exploring them. Several quite different books could be written on them; I have selected one possible approach. At the same time I do not think that the novels should be studied in isolation from Mr Waugh's life and other works. Hence the division of this work into Part One, on the life and works in general; Part Two, in which I have given a formal analysis of each novel separately; and Part Three, in which I have drawn together the threads of my critical interpretation. I should not have been able to write the first two chapters at all without generous assistance from Mr Waugh. But I believe also that the later chapters would have lost much had I not had the pri-vilege of knowing him.

To have related my views to those of other critics in detail would have increased the size of the book unduly. But I have read them and learnt from them. I have not given specific references in the text to the critical and biographical sources from which I quote, but they are all to be found in the Biblio-graphy.

A number of people were kind enough to provide me with information on Mr Waugh's life; they include especially Mr C. L. Chamberlin, Father Martin D'Arcy, S.J., Mr C. Hollis, Mr J. Pick, and Mr D. Woodruff. I remember with gratitude an afternoon's conversation with the late Mgr R. A. Knox. I wish also to thank the Editors of *The Month* and of *Renascence* for permission to use material already published in their pages.

Finally, I am deeply indebted to my wife for her constant help and criticism at all stages of the work.

31 January 1958   F.J.S.

Part One

THE WRITER

CHAPTER 1

Youth and Travel

Affectionate, high-spirited and busy in childhood; dissipated and often despairing in youth – EVELYN WAUGH on Gilbert Pinfold

EVELYN ARTHUR ST JOHN WAUGH was born on 28 October 1903, the feast of SS Simon and Jude, the second son of Arthur Waugh, publisher, editor, and man of letters. On his father's side he descended from a family which had been farmer proprietors for centuries in the village of East Gordon, in Berwickshire, until, at the end of the eighteenth century, Alexander Waugh, a Minister, came south and established himself in London. His son, the Rev. James Hay Waugh, then moved to the West Country to become Rector of Corsley, near Frome. Evelyn Waugh's grandfather was a popular and well-known doctor, sportsman, and keen amateur actor, in Midsomer Norton, and although Arthur Waugh moved to London in 1890, it was natural that his son, Evelyn, when he married into a West Country family in 1937, should return to that area and re-establish the West Country line of Waughs. His mother, coming from a family with antecedents in the Army and the Indian Civil Service, was also from the West Country.

Arthur Waugh was a fairly good poet, with many critical interests, the author of an excellent book on Tennyson, and of editions of others of the English masters. After twelve years spent in gaining literary experience in the capital, he became, in 1902, at the age of thirty-five, chairman and managing director of the old-established publishing firm of Chapman and Hall, then in the doldrums and relying too heavily on the profitable but diminishing asset of the Dickens copyright. He directed the firm with his combination of literary sympathy and business aptitude until his retirement in 1929.

11

The two sons of the marriage, Alec (born 1898) and Evelyn, soon created independent literary reputations for themselves, and there does not seem to have been any presage of the second son's remarkable satirical gifts in the talents or career of this good and worthy late Victorian, with his capacity for 'keeping young' by periodical visits to Sherborne, which he himself had left thirty years before. A man who could still see the motor-car as the symbol of modern change and restlessness, he is reported by Dudley Carew to have said that 'if a man knows the Bible, Shakespeare and Wisden he won't go far wrong'. It has been observed that there is little of what may be termed family life in the novels of Evelyn Waugh; Brideshead is the only family group that springs to mind, and that, in its Catholic faith and manorial setting, is clearly a highly imaginative product. The one child with his guardian or eccentric father is, however, a group which constantly recurs, from *Decline and Fall* to *Brideshead*. There is seldom a mother figure in the group.

When the time came for Evelyn to enter a public school, family tradition would have indicated Sherborne, had not Alec Waugh's precocious novel of public school life, *The Loom of Youth*, published in 1917, caused a considerable stir, and made the choice of some other school advisable for the younger son. Lancing was chosen, and later appeared in the works as 'a school of ecclesiastical temper on the South Downs'. Indeed, its strong religious life was one of the factors which led to its choice, since, as the father noted, the young Evelyn had always shown a deeply religious temperament. His memories of the first two years are not happy: coming up in the bye-term of 1917, he experienced the loneliness of falling between two year-groups. This and the absence of good masters and other war-time privations made the first two years hungry and dark, and the memory of chilblains loom large, even after forty years. The Lancing Register records his career laconically: 'Evelyn Waugh, May 1917 – December 1921. Head's. House Captain, Editor L.C.M., President L.C.D.S., in 1921.' The last two entries, relating to the College Magazine and Debating Society, were a source of satisfaction to the father, who records that Evelyn was the third of the family to edit his School Magazine and to win a prize for English verse. For Evelyn, this improvement revolved largely round the figure of J. F. Roxburgh, Classics master and general form master for the Upper Sixth, and later the first Headmaster of Stowe School. Roxburgh combined with his brilliant gifts as a teacher enough personal idiosyncrasy and a touch of the grand manner to make him a prominent figure in any company; it was not surprising, therefore, that his weekly period on general and classical culture fascinated the seventeen-year-old pupil, who regarded him as an absolute model and paragon of form in all matters, including speech, handwriting, and clothes.

The immediate postwar years were, at Lancing as elsewhere, something of a time of burgeoning; at Lancing, 'J.F.' seems to have been the most pervasive leavening influence. The greatly increased freedom within the existing public school tradition, and the absence of unnecessary restraints through which he made his mark at Stowe was for several years in evidence at Lancing, and must have influenced the young Waugh towards the generally subversive attitude to authority for which he is still remembered. A contemporary, Dudley Carew, has left us a picture of the activities of the future satirist and of his influence on his contemporaries. We hear of iconoclastic attacks on established reputations, especially of those enshrined within the covers of the Oxford Books of English and of Victorian verse; of duels with authority, carried out with 'the same impassive exterior, the same innocence of the intent to be amusing as later characterized his books'. An entry in a diary of 1921 predicts that he will be the Max Beerbohm of his generation, if not something greater, records a parody of an epigram by Landor, and ends, significantly, 'J.F. likes it a lot'. Another contemporary, C. L. Chamberlin, recalls how Waugh, though without any status in his House, decided to contrive that Head's won a House Drill Competition, and organized the whole House to this end behind the back of authority, so as later to make a mockery of the whole affair. The plot was discovered and the same authority made sure that Head's did not win.

Roxburgh's influence was especially strong in the Lancing

13

College Debating Society. On his departure, in 1923, for Stowe, the Lancing College Magazine recorded that 'nowhere were his varying gifts so manifest as at the Debater's table. Faulty arguments he destroyed in the flash of an epigram and truth he established for all time within an impregnable fortress of reinforced polysyllables.' Waugh was a regular debater, and, in his last term at Lancing, President of the Society. Proposing a motion recommending re-incarnation as the best solution to the problem of immortality, 'Mr E. A. St J. Waugh besought us to put away both pride and prejudice, and not to reject his doctrine because it was also Mrs Besant's, or because we feared to see a family portrait in every Landseer print'. The chronicler of a debate on a motion deploring the disrespect shown by the youth of today to its elders, restricted himself – perhaps wisely – to saying that Waugh, opposing, made what was perhaps the best speech of the evening, and 'several most controversial statements'. On the proposition that 'science is the root of all evil', E. A. St J. Waugh 'would have nothing to do with science'. On a motion that the House of Commons should be abolished, 'Mr E. A. St J. Waugh, proposing, looked on politics as a profession – a profession of breach of faith – in which foresworn majorities might represent minorities in the country at large. It was not representative, it was not admirable, it was not useful.' On institutional religion, 'the President was conventional; religion was the focus for all that was finest and best in man' – and 'Mr J. F. Roxburgh was devout; religion was the focus for all that was finest and best in man'.

Arthur Waugh has recorded his impression that 'the Lancing Prefect after the War was an extremely grown-up and sophisticated type of schoolboy'. This was probably not then true, nor has it ever been true. But some justification may be found for the view in the special circumstances of Head's at that time. Through Canon Bowlby, Headmaster from 1909 to 1925, who had been an assistant master at Eton, Lancing had for many years attracted boys with an Eton connexion. These naturally entered the Headmaster's House, giving it something of a special tone – and, incidentally, beginning for Waugh a long personal associa-

14

tion with Etonians through the Oxford years and since. To such men a certain panache and an assumption of fastidious sophistication seemed natural – it might even be expected of them. This was the tone of the recorded occasion when one member of Head's, repelled by the institution of the communal lavatory, had his own personal lavatory seat made in red plush, and carried it across the quadrangle each morning. The pattern of this incident was to find artistic shape many years later in Apthorpe's Thunder-Box.

This note of sophisticated boredom is present in the two societies which Waugh – with others, such as Roger Fulford, Hugh Molson, Tom Driberg, and Dudley Carew – founded at Lancing: the Dilettanti Society, a literary and artistic society for those below Sixth Form level, and, later, the Corpse Club. This latter, as recorded by C. L. Chamberlin many years later, was 'a short-lived society that caused a great stir, since its avowed object was to discourage any form of enthusiasm, its uniform a black tie and a black tassel, its ritual funereal, and its attitude provocative'. There were thirteen members; of these, eleven were corporeal (with Evelyn Waugh, the Undertaker, heading the list), and two were 'spiritual presences', one of these being the second grave-digger in Hamlet. Mr Chamberlin quotes the terms of his own reception into the Club: 'The Undertaker finds a mournful pleasure in announcing the interment of the late Mr C. L. Chamberlin.' This capacity for extracting humour from the macabre and from subjects normally taboo links the Corpse Club, over a period of nearly thirty years, with *The Loved One*.

Another schooltime production, described by Arthur Waugh, was a skit on public school life, called *Conversion*, in three contrasted acts: Act I – as our maiden aunts believe it to be; Act II – as some of our novelists represent it, a travesty of Alec Waugh's *Loom of Youth*; and Act III – as we all know it really is, a satire of Lancing manners.

Evelyn's tenure of the office of Editor of the Lancing College Magazine lasted only for a term, being cut short by his departure for Oxford; but the two numbers for which he was responsible were graced by Editorials which contrasted sharply with

the stolid tone of those preceding and following. The one was
an attempt to define 'The Youngest Generation', immediately
following the War. Among the more obvious qualities of clear-
sightedness, reticence, and lack of ideals we read: 'They will
watch themselves with, probably, a greater egotism than did the
young men of the nineties, but it will be with a cynical smile. . . .
They will not be a happy generation.' The other was a piece of
social observation called 'The Community Spirit'. An unsuspecting foreigner is taken round a public school, and learns with
astonishment that, instead of the companionship of three hundred friends, his cicerone, through the operation of the complex
rules of house association, seniority, and differing taste, is
restricted to the intimacy of a mere handful – and those known
only in the most superficial manner.

As a University, Oxford was clearly indicated by his father's
career at New College, but Evelyn's decision was governed by
his winning a Senior Scholarship in History at Hertford, a respectable but not otherwise notable College. His attainments in
History were, by his own description, modest, and the scholarship awarded on the journalistic points of his answers. However
this may be, the decisive College figure for men reading History, Cruttwell, then Tutor and Dean and later Principal of the
College, suffered perhaps too much by comparison with the incomparable Roxburgh. A historian of the Rhineland, he was dis-
mayed to find that Waugh thought the Rhine flowed into the
Black Sea, and appears thereafter to have punctured any pretensions which the new scholar may have had to genuine historical
knowledge. Whether this incident alone earned him his Tutor's
'immediate and implacable disapproval' (*Ninety-two Days*, pp.
15–16) is uncertain; it is, however, significant that in a number
of the novels the name 'Cruttwell' graces a gallery of quite un-
attractive characters.

This lack of sympathy with Hertford and History, whatever
its reason, certainly prevented Evelyn from playing any role in
College life, and led him to seek his friends outside the College
community, in literary and artistic groups connected with the
Cherwell, *Isis*, and *Broom*. To the last-named he contributed

some cover designs and wood-engravings which continued a taste
and aptitude already indulged at Lancing. When, after taking a
Third Class in final examinations in 1924, he discovered that he
would have to wait one more term to take his degree (he came
up a term late, in the Lent term 1922, the Lancing experience
repeated), the natural course seemed to him to go down without
taking a degree.

For Evelyn Waugh, Oxford has always meant less a respected
scholastic foundation (he has penned more impressive and moving words about Campion Hall under its Rector Fr D'Arcy, S.J.,
than about any other Oxford institution) than a place where he
met many friends, mainly of literary inclinations, with whom he
has remained on terms of friendship for many years: Christopher
Sykes, Peter Quennell, Cyril Connolly, Anthony Powell, Henry
Green (Henry York), Douglas Woodruff, Patrick Balfour (Lord
Kinross), Frank (Lord) Pakenham, Alfred Duggan. It is impossible for one who did not experience at first hand the Oxford
of those years, the early twenties, to see the currents of aesthetic
life except through the medium of Harold Acton's *Memoirs*, or
the general tone of elegant undergraduate manners other than in
terms of the nostalgic backward glance of *Brideshead*. Nor need
the reader assume that the joint picture afforded by the *Memoirs*
and *Brideshead* is essentially false. Christopher Sykes tells us in
his *Four Studies* (p. 80, on Robert Byron): 'Attempts have been
made to evoke the fusion of ancient tradition and what was then
ultra-modernity, which made the quality of mid-twenty Oxford,
of which Harold Acton was the Arbiter Elegantiarum, and
Robert one of the prime movers, but the only truly successful
description of this remarkable phase of University life is to be
found in the opening chapters of Evelyn Waugh's novel *Brideshead Revisited*. People may believe that in this book he cannot be
attempting a serious picture of that ancient seat of learning, but
the picture is true'. Sykes continues, however, to remind us that
its nature completely changed in 1926, the year in which Robert
Byron went down, and he himself came up. We must also remember that the element of ultra-modernity, magnificently
evoked by Acton in his passage (*Memoirs*, p. 148) on the saxo-

phone and Gershwin's 'Rhapsody in Blue', with its concomitants of new drinks, and fast cars making the journey to London possible in an evening, is entirely omitted in *Brideshead*; and further, that the stamp which a small group of gifted young men can leave upon an institution or a decade is itself due in some degree to a foreshortening of perspective. Waugh himself has made strenuous and caustic attacks on the association of the Oxford of the thirties with a small group of 'progressive' writers and with the famous Union resolution of 1937 not to fight for King and Country.

In fact, Evelyn Waugh's activities were much like those of many another undergraduate of marked personality and artistic gifts: membership of the Hypocrites Club (so-called because their motto was the Greek for 'water is best'), a place for both highbrow and lowbrow tastes, poetry and folk-dancing or corduroys, beer and bawdiness; membership of the Conservative party, the Chatham and Carlton Clubs, and speeches at the Union in the Conservative interest; the production of black and white drawings and an occasional short story for the literary magazines; association with a circle of Chestertonian friends of Catholic sympathies, who gathered in his rooms for what they called 'offal'. But the combined impression of the *Memoirs* and of *Brideshead* on the general reader is that of an elegant and highbrow eccentricity fittingly symbolized by the one event which they have in common: Anthony Blanche, the aesthete *par excellence*, reciting the 'Waste Land' through a megaphone to the muffled and sweatered oarsmen on their way to the river, as Acton recited *Aquarium*, his first volume of poems, to the passing groups on Christ Church Meadows.

And yet Acton supplies also the corrective to a superficial view of the literary atmosphere in the early twenties at Oxford. Three close friends of his, and characteristic members of his generation, published after going down the matured product of their Oxford enthusiasm in solid literary and critical works: Robert Byron, *The Station* (1928), Peter Quennell, *Baudelaire* (1929), and Evelyn Waugh, *Rossetti* (1928). 'Neither Peter, nor Robert, nor Evelyn, were butterflies, and all three were characteristic members of my own generation. The butterfly never settles on any flower for long. Robert, Peter, and Evelyn settled on any subject that aroused them like grim death and clung to it tenaciously until they had extracted every drop of essence. Robert clung to Byzantium; Peter to Baudelaire's *dandyisme*; Evelyn to Rossetti and social satire and, eventually, to Rome.'

If Waugh's memorial to the Acton of the Oxford days is that to an aesthete, Acton's description of Waugh is in the spirit of the role which so impressed his friends at Lancing, and an anticipation of the future satirist: 'Though others assure me that he has changed beyond recognition, I still see him as a prancing faun, thinly disguised by conventional apparel. His wide-apart eyes, always ready to be startled under raised eyebrows, the curved sensual lips, the hyacinthine locks of hair, I had seen in marble and bronze at Naples, in the Vatican Museum, and on fountainheads all over Italy.' Though here seen through the idiosyncratic eyes of one person, this impression is borne out by the remarkable portrait by Henry Lamb, painted a few years later (see Frontispiece).

But these are hardly the qualifications needed by an ex-Oxford man, without the title of a degree, and with no more definite intentions for a career than of becoming something in the arts and crafts, possibly a painter or a printer. A short period of study at Heatherleys, an Art School, living at his parents' home, and mixing with a wide circle of Bohemian friends, drinking, making debts, and generally causing his family much anxiety, ended in a debt settlement conference with the father, and an undertaking to pay his own way. 'In those days schoolmastering was to the educated classes what domestic service was to the uneducated classes. It was the one job open to those who had failed or got into disgrace.' So for a short time Waugh tried his hand as a schoolmaster at two successive private schools. The story of this, 'one of the more absurd escapades of my youth', has often been told to inquirers. The two schools have become one – identified, in fact, with the second, a mushroom establishment at Aston Clinton, Bucks, calculated to pay with thirty pupils, but liable to instant closure, as indeed happened soon after, as soon as numbers fell to twenty-eight. The end of the story is a fine example of stylized under-statement: 'It is no use pretending I was involved in any way in Education. – I enjoyed it very much. . . . I left when I was expelled. For drunkenness. There were no hard feelings on either side.' No more is needed, for the story – perhaps only slightly enhancing the reality – has been told in *Decline and Fall*.

A fortnight as a reporter on the staff of the *Daily Express*, nothing he wrote being printed, concludes the account of two more years, with no apparent advance in discovering a suitable career.

A fresh start was made in the autumn of 1926, this time on a carpentry course at a School of Arts and Crafts, with the intention of becoming a cabinet-maker. In a wireless interview in 1953, Waugh admitted that he had always wanted to be a man of action – soldiering, exploring, being a carpenter or making things – and few successful writers can have come to the practice of the craft of writing in a more indirect way. Characteristically, it was a practical motive which led him to undertake his first book. He became engaged to the Hon. Evelyn Gardner, the youngest daughter of the first Lord Burghclere; not surprisingly, the future parents-in-law did not approve of carpentry as a career, but the writing of books was the next most suitable occupation. So social requirements were satisfied when Waugh obtained a commission from Duckworth for a book on Rossetti, published in 1928, and the marriage took place in conditions of semi-secrecy in June 1928. The young couple set up in Islington with Waugh (again according to Acton) devoting infinite care to a variety of domestic arts and crafts, such as buying 2d. and 3d. packets of foreign stamps and sticking them onto an ugly old coal-scuttle, which was then varnished.

As soon as *Rossetti* was finished, Waugh wrote his first hilarious novel of many, *Decline and Fall, An Illustrated Novelette*, published in 1928. This also brought him his first brush with more conventional ideas of propriety, since Duckworth's requested considerable cutting, on grounds of obscenity, before publication; Waugh thereupon took the complete unbowdlerized MS. to Chapman and Hall, thus beginning his long and successful association with the publishing house with which the family name had long been linked. *Decline and Fall* made his name known widely in the literary world, though it did not immediately (in spite of Mr Winston Churchill's choosing it for his personal Christmas present) achieve a wide sale. For this, and for the disappearance of serious financial worries, Waugh had to wait till *Vile Bodies* appeared in 1930. Less purely autobiographical than *Decline and Fall*, and placed in the easily recognized milieu of Mayfair society, its success was both literary and social: a dramatized version, by H. Dennis Bradley, in twelve episodic scenes, was produced by Nigel Playfair in the autumn of 1931, at the Arts Theatre Club, and given twelve performances. Much of the original dialogue was used, but anything that savoured of a risqué situation was developed, so that the result contained more scandal than sparkle.

It was while he was writing *Vile Bodies* that Mr Waugh's first marriage, having lasted almost exactly one year, broke up; and it is perhaps this which is reflected obliquely, but with great poignancy, in the latter part of the novel. A civil divorce was obtained, and the marriage was later (1936) annulled by decree of the Catholic Church. There then began a period of some seven years during which Mr Waugh spent as much time travelling abroad as he spent at home writing up the results in the form of travel books. Not that travel books were uncommon in those days; many young authors were discovering that an advance from a publisher followed by a trip abroad (even the area might be chosen according to the requirements of the London book market), and a few months in the country writing up the results, followed by a repetition of the same cycle, was as good a way as any of maintaining oneself while gaining experience and maturity.

These journeys and their literary outcome may be briefly summarized. The winter of 1929–30 was spent in the Mediterranean voyage which resulted in *Labels* (1930). The next winter, from October 1930 to March 1931, saw Waugh at the Coronation of

Haile Selassie in Abyssinia (nominally for *The Times*), and then making a brief visit to Aden, East Central Africa, and South Africa; these journeys were described in *Remote People* (1931). During the winter of 1932–3, Waugh visited British Guiana and the West Indies, and wrote, on his return, *Ninety-two Days* (1934). The winter of 1933–4 was spent in Fez (cp. *Work Suspended* and *Brideshead Revisited*). At the end of 1935 he was in Abyssinia with a commission to report the Italo-Abyssinian conflict for the *Daily Mail*; leaving before the war had properly developed he spent Christmas on his first visit to Jerusalem. His report on the war was entitled (though not by his own choice) *Waugh in Abyssinia* (1936). Finally, late in 1938, soon after his second marriage, he visited Mexico and published (in 1939) *Robbery under Law*. Between the major journeys there were many of smaller scope such as one with an exploring party to Spitzbergen in 1934 and many visits to Paris and Venice.

Travel books are a mirror of civilized man's constantly changing sensibility. Compounded equally of fact and fiction, the staid currency of instruction and the gold-dust of fable, they are a shell into which is poured a mixture suited to the desires of the age; the mixture hardens and no longer satisfies, so a new artificer shatters the old pot and mixes the ingredients anew. After the first World War, the mood of the age required and was given a new deal: the sophisticated travel book. It was devised by Evelyn Waugh, with *Labels*, *Remote People*, and *Ninety-two Days*, and by Peter Fleming, with *Brazilian Adventure* (1933). One survey of modern English literature dates the new epoch actually from 1930, the year of *Labels* – 'an extremely sophisticated chronicle', with a blend of self-mockery, cocksureness, beauty and comedy. Robert Graves, in a survey of English domestic life between the wars, describes the age as one of disguise. 'Old period pieces were "vandalized", as the antique-dealers called it, by being converted to modern uses: a William-and-Mary commode would be gutted to house a gramophone and records. . . .' Evelyn Waugh and his confederates gutted an ancient form of European literature and converted it to a new content – entertainment – to meet a new taste – 'a growing taste in the semi-literate public for vicarious locomotion'. The dominant note may be described in the pet-words of the period: sophistication, even maliciousness; but above all the new-style travel-book had to be bright. If anyone was to be bored, it had to be the traveller, not the reader. Journeys might – indeed they had better – begin, continue, and end with a fair dash of pointlessness, boredom, discomfort, that form of heroic hardship in a minor key which is most attuned to subsequent relaxation in an armchair.

A country is selected because it is absurdly remote: Guiana because he knew so little about it, and because it had always seemed to him odd that 'those three little gobs of empire should survive in the general explosion of South American self-government'. Indeed, he admits to knowing no geography, and later, as a reviewer, commends an author who 'enjoys idling over an atlas and speculating on the reality behind the symbols'. From 1935, when his books were commissioned, and he went to Abyssinia as a reporter, he felt himself to be 'in the livery of a new age'. Most journeys begin, and all end, with a sense of unreality. You start with a visit to a tropical outfitters, and a mountain of kit rises in the hall of your club, most of which you discard *en route*; or you are transported, in a week or so, from a house in Ireland 'where chinoiserie and Victorian gothic contend for a mastery over a Georgian structure' to 'the familiar depressing spectacle of French colonial domesticity' on the decks of a Messagerie vessel bound for Djibouti, and thence to the Alice in Wonderland scene of Addis Ababa, administrative centre of a barbarous Empire, an anachronism in colonial, partitioned Africa. You have a keen eye for contrasts between the exotic and the familiar, the brash, fragmentary European culture of the Jeunesse d'Éthiopie, the contrast between a great occasion of the Abyssinian Church and the Western medieval tradition of ancient and organically developing culture, learning, liturgy, and craftsmanship. You are struck by the scenic similarities between Palestine and Scotland, so that the sight of Arab families with camels raises a curious confusion in the mind 'by this association of Bonny Prince Charlie with the glamour of the

23

inscrutable East'. You are haunted by certain images: Harar, with its fringe of empty and ruinous houses is like the lepers which throng its streets; Harar, also, might be dead and decaying at its extremities. Mexico is another waste land, plague-stricken by politics, the sign of a civilization which is beginning to rot at *its* extremities. Everywhere you note the borderline of jungle and civilization, never stable, an uneasy no man's land between two destructive and predatory forces. You may hope to notice things accepted as commonplace by those more experienced, and so convey to a distant public something of the aspect and feel of a place. You may be commended for a good historical summary, as was Mr Waugh for Chapter One of *Waugh in Abyssinia*, or for some perceptive comment on the historical role of the British Empire overseas, in Malta or in Zanzibar – clean, blazered young Englishmen, by a quirk of colonial trusteeship, making the place safe for the immigrant Indian.

But this is not the ambulant writer's only role. For the traveller's eye is directed both outwards and inwards; and his comments on his own reactions serve to establish the link between writer and reader which is the note of these new works. The traveller is on guard against being taken in by what he sees, and cultivates an ironic and independent eye; but he is also on the watch against being humbugged by himself, and so a subtle game of hide and seek goes on between the zest and restlessness which drives him on and the instinct which causes him to play down each new experience in his own mind, between the traveller and the writer. One reviewer of *Ninety-two Days* seeks a word for this peculiar state of mind, and would like to describe Mr Waugh's colic welcome of the 'asperities' of travelling in Guiana as 'disgusto', the opposite of the 'gusto' of another type of traveller.

Above all, though hardships realistically told are not likely to stir an answering movement in the breast of the armchair explorer, futility and boredom are aesthetically pleasing. The reviewer who commented that it was not by accident that the title *Ninety-two Days* suggested a penal sentence of three months had entered into the spirit of this intention. *Remote People*, between extended sections on the Ethiopian Empire and the British Empire in Africa, heads its interludes of real travel 'First Nightmare', 'Second Nightmare,' 'Third Nightmare'. Above all the first nightmare contains an impassioned disquisition on boredom during travel in the tropics: 'No one can have any conception of what boredom really means until he has been in the tropics. The boredom of civilized life is trivial and terminable, a puny thing to be strangled between finger and thumb. The blackest things in European life . . . the very terrors, indeed, which drive one to refuge in the still-remote regions of the earth, are mere pansies and pimpernels to the rank flowers which flame grossly in those dark and steaming sanctuaries.' And the one-time Undertaker of the Corpse Club at Lancing goes on to suggest, in lighter vein, an anthology of bored verse, with Richard Sickert's 'Ennui' as a frontispiece, and an appendix of the letters and notes left behind by suicides. And when all is over and the traveller steps off the boat, there awaits him the final boredom, the labour of composition, 'an attempt to revive artificially under the iron lung of rhythmic, day to day observations, the revelation of first acquaintance' – and the imperative need to conceal from one's equally bored friends that one has been anywhere at all. ' "Why Evelyn, where *have* you been? I haven't seen you about anywhere for days." ' – ' " *Basil.* Once and for all, we don't want to hear travel experiences". . . . "That's the way to deal with him," said Alastair from his armchair. "Keep a stopper on the far-flung stuff." '

'From 1928 until 1937 I had no fixed home and no possessions which would not conveniently go on a porter's barrow. I travelled continuously, in England and abroad'. In 1946 Mr Waugh preserved all that he considered still to be of interest – omitting entirely the Mexican work – in the collection entitled *When the Going was Good*. But the writer in Mr Waugh stored up, in these nine years of locomotion by choice, followed very soon by six years of locomotion by movement order, enough copy for several lifetimes of writing. The journeys brought their immediate harvest of works, in which regularly a novel balanced a travel book: the two Abyssinian visits gave *Black Mischief*

(1932) and *Scoop* (1938), and the trip to Guiana *A Handful of Dust* (1934) as years later other journeys produced *The Loved One* and *Scott-King's Modern Europe*. The author's gallery of memorable types had been permanently enriched by M. Besse, of Aden, the wealthy shipowner and later munificent benefactor of Oxford, who was delighted by his portrait as Mr Baldwin, in *Scoop*; and by Mr Christie, the coloured rancher in Guiana, whose personal brand of religious belief was almost certainly certifiable, and whose opinion of his transformation into the grimly memorable Mr Todd almost certainly unrecorded. But the retentive memory also stored many impressions which re-appear in more distant analogies in the later works, from *Brideshead* to *Pinfold*. Thus Mr Pinfold, walking the promenade deck of the S.S. *Caliban*, 'as though he were a noteworthy, unaccompanied female, newly appearing in the evening promenade of some stagnant South American town', re-echoes after twenty-five years a fantasy once indulged in Boa Vista, British Guiana.

A porter's barrow is a very restricted platform from which to develop a wide range of literary activities, and Mr Waugh's writing, apart from the travel books and novels, was in these years limited mainly to occasional reviewing. But after he had settled in England in 1937, he reviewed regularly for the *Spectator*, and also for *Night and Day*. This latter was a bright journal rather on the model of the *New Yorker*, which ran through its short life in the one year of 1937. A collection of short stories published in 1936 called, after the first piece, *Mr Loveday's Little Outing*, combined the polished style and the social setting of Wodehouse with the grim undertone of Mr Waugh. Two were fragments of novels already published – *Black Mischief* and *A Handful of Dust* – and were not later reprinted. Others found their way, in more developed form, into later novels: Beckthorpe, the ingenuous clubman in *On Guard*, became Atwater in *Work Suspended*; the discreet racket which is the subject of *An Englishman's Home* was later written up, in *Put out more Flags*, with the much more effective cast of Basil Seal and the Connolly kids. The tone varies between the frivolous and the cynical, the theme between the slightly scandalous and the macabre; but mostly these stories are derivative from assorted literary models, and lack the gusto and depth of experience which give even the slighter of the novels their extra bite.

There remains therefore little direct evidence of the internal process by which, during these years, the unsuccessful undergraduate matured into the successful novelist and writer. Mr Waugh has never indulged in deliberate self-revelation, and any internal struggles which may have taken place have always been given formal, external shape in the literary works, whether novels or travel books. But some of the products of these years – particularly *Ninety-two Days* and *A Handful of Dust* – contain a loneliness as near to despair as Waugh has ever revealed, and it is clear that the constant, restless travel of these years was more than a continued publishing project. *A Handful of Dust* he regarded as his best work till *Brideshead Revisited*. A social novel, dealing with the behaviour of human savages in England and Brazil, it 'was humanist and contained all I had to say about humanism'. Certainly *Brideshead*, if not greater in achievement, has a theme which is vastly more ambitious. But the critic, judging purely from the works before him, will perhaps conclude that the earlier novel is the result of as deep and bitter an experience as has ever been transmuted by Mr Waugh into a work of fiction, and moreover, the experience has been transmuted into an integral work of art. Others went to the Gobi Desert and to Iceland in couples; Mr Waugh was always alone. The circumstances of these years certainly exacerbated his dislike of anything like cliques in literary production, and a special edge was given to his opposition to certain 'progressive' writers who (with many others) claimed to speak for the decade – at least for its social conscience – by 'their chumminess. They clung together. They collaborated. It seemed always to take at least two of them to generate any literary work however modest.' Mr Waugh was always ferociously alone.

The last two travel books, on Abyssinia and Mexico, were reportage with a political flavour, and deeply changed Mr Waugh's status in English educated opinion. A writer later described by Mr Robert Graves as 'Evelyn Waugh, the Oxford and Mayfair arch-playboy and most gifted novelist of the new Disillusion', was now revealed as a propagator of the Fascist Illusion, or, in the form to which the criticism has now mellowed, as 'the outstanding diehard of the intellectual Right'. At Oxford he had been a member of the Conservative Party; he regarded, and still regards himself as an old-fashioned Tory. This was at least respectable, but the report from Abyssinia changed all that. The book which had started with a chapter praised by all as an admirably succinct and balanced account of the political history of Abyssinia ended with a chapter called 'The Road'. The great engineering feat of the new trunk road which the Italians were building from Massawa on the coast to Addis Ababa provided the theme for an account of their progress in settling the country. It was a rhapsody, somewhat in the Belloc-Chesterton tradition, of the civilized settlement of an uncivilized country. '. . . and along the roads will pass the eagles of ancient Rome, as they came to our savage ancestors in France and Britain and Germany, bringing . . . the inestimable gifts of fine workmanship and clear judgement – the two determining qualities of the human spirit, by which alone, under God, man grows and flourishes.' Read after the lapse of twenty years, and a second World War, it seems innocuous – indeed there are some excellent comments on the reaction to Imperial power on the part of the Abyssinian master race, the English colonizer, and the Italian settler. But in the days of the League of Nations and of Sanctions, of the first major use of air power since the first World War, and the disturbing employment of poison gas, it read, no doubt, quite differently. Dame Rose Macaulay pronounced it, in 1948, a Fascist tract. It led on, naturally, to further provocation over Franco: in a manifesto called *From the Ivory Tower*, in which a number of writers expressed their views on the Spanish War, Mr Waugh was the only one not against Franco. And it completed the process started by the work on *Campion* (1935), by bringing him into an odour of partisanship with a considerable part of the public, and with perhaps an even larger proportion of the critics. We must therefore return to what was undoubtedly the greatest single personal event of these

28

early years, his reception into the Catholic Church on 29 September (St Michael's Day) 1930.

Here again, we must expect no autobiography of conversion or spiritual diary. Almost all he has to say on his conversion was written, on request, for an American work called *The Road to Damascus*, in three pages; nothing could be more precise and, within this compass, more complete. A childish enthusiasm for things ecclesiastical was succeeded by loss of faith at sixteen through the influence of a Modern Churchman temporarily seconded to Lancing during World War I. His first contact with Catholics was with Oxford friends, who in turn put him in touch with the Jesuit Fathers of Mount Street, and with Father Martin D'Arcy, who instructed and received him. So, at twenty-six, he relinquished unregretted the remnants of an earlier shallow piety for adhesion to a universal Christian faith, and 'on firm intellectual conviction but with little emotion I was admitted into the Church'. Asked what kind of spiritual reading came his way in the earlier period of indecision, he will point to Gwendoline Plunkett-Greene's *Mount Zion* – a work of spiritual reflections of mystical temper but otherwise undistinguished, by a niece and spiritual child of Baron von Hügel – as having as much to do with his final step as any other work. Father D'Arcy has said that he has seldom had anyone to instruct whose approach was so objective, factual, and unemotional. And the firm intellectual conviction was not, it would appear, concerned primarily with the vanquishing of philosophical doubts about the existence of God, or with considerations on the nature of authority Waugh's one significant statement of motive in *The Road to Damascus* is the one appropriate to the former historian: a realization of the undeniable historical presence and continuity of the Church. 'England was Catholic for nine hundred years, then Protestant for three hundred, then agnostic for a century. The Catholic structure still lies lightly buried beneath every phase of English life; history, topography, law, archaeology everywhere reveal Catholic origins. Foreign travel anywhere (in Europe) reveals the local, temporary character of the heresies and schisms and the universal, eternal character of the

Church. It was self-evident to me that no heresy or schism could be right and the Church wrong. It was possible that all were wrong, that the whole Christian revelation was an imposture or a misconception. But if the Christian revelation were true, then the Church was the society founded by Christ and all other bodies were only good so far as they had salvaged something from the wrecks of the Great Schism and the Reformation. This proposition seemed so plain to me that it admitted of no discussion. It only remained to examine the historical and philosophical ground for supposing the Christian revelation to be genuine.'

No statement could be clearer, no position more definite. His advice to friends outside the Church, attracted by certain features, but puzzled and repelled by others, has always been practical and personal; there is no attempt to enter into their conflict of feeling. 'Come inside. You cannot know what the Church is like from outside. However learned you are in theology, nothing you know amounts to anything in comparison with the knowledge of the simplest actual member of the Communion of Saints.'

For Mr Waugh, therefore, the acceptance of the Catholic faith is both a personal matter, for private rejoicing, and a public matter, resting on incontrovertible evidence. So, in the three decades since that date, he has constantly returned to subjects connected with the faith, whether directly, as in his Campion biography, in *Brideshead Revisited* and *Helena*, or indirectly, by allowing his religion to suggest an unobtrusive background setting, as in the war books *Men at Arms* and *Officers and Gentlemen*. Further, he has pleaded eloquently for a more Christian and active approach to the problem of the preservation of the Holy Places; and his occasional writings, especially in *The Tablet* and *The Month*, have left no doubt about the uncompromising nature of his principles on this matter. He holds, indeed, that man's nature is not understood wholly unless it is seen from the religious point of view. 'So in my future books there will be two things to make them unpopular: a preoccupation with style and the attempt to represent man more fully, which, to me, means only one thing, man in his relation to God' (1946). But he is neither a purveyor of the *drame intérieur spirituel*, nor has he become a sectarian writer, writing as a Catholic for Catholics. His Catholicism is expansionist, practical, and inspired by a vivid sense of the continuity of history in living tradition; not cloistered, reflective, and fed by the communication of the spark of pious belief between choice souls, outside age and clime. Nor is his attitude dependent on a facile assumption of man's capacity to recover true belief, or his mood elated by statistics of yearly conversions. On the contrary, he refers frequently, and almost with zest, to a not improbable return of the catacomb age.

Mr Waugh had early occasion to take stock of his own personal position on the relation between his writing and his faith, and did not hesitate to reject the assumption that the novelist of Catholic belief need apply any principles other than a few purely negative safeguards of prudence in his writing. For the appearance of *Black Mischief* gave rise to one of the earliest of many adverse comments on the author's readiness to express himself in terms and incidents which give shocked offence to some readers; this one was given added point in coming from a co-religionist, Mr E. J. Oldmeadow, in an editorial notice in *The Tablet*. The notice (7 January 1933) was in the stern and righteous tone of an older generation. 'Whether Mr Waugh still considers himself a Catholic, *The Tablet* does not know; but, in case he is so regarded by booksellers, librarians, and novel-readers in general, we hereby state that his latest novel would be a disgrace to anybody professing the Catholic name.' No specific incidents were mentioned and, indeed, the Editor's principles prevented him even from printing the title of the book or the name of the publisher. A brief and dignified letter from twelve leading Catholics, priests and laymen, pointed out that this and similar editorial comments 'exceed the bounds of legitimate criticism and are in fact an imputation of bad faith', and stimulated the Editor to a specific listing of certain allegedly obscene and irreligious incidents and passages. A trail of letters, and a lengthy recapitulation and defence by the Editor, in which the latter had, at least in amount of paper covered, the best of the argument, graced some later numbers.

The author himself, being out of the country, was silent through all this. But, on his return, he expressed his views in an 'Open Letter to the Archbishop of Westminster' (then the legal owner of *The Tablet*). Though this was never published (MS. dated May 1933) two arguments there developed are of considerable general interest. After refuting the accusation of irreligion by pointing out some misconceptions of the Editor of *The Tablet*, Waugh addresses himself to the accusation of 'coarseness and foulness . . . outrageous lapses . . . following vile fashions', i.e. the accusation of obscenity. This, he says, is a matter of tone, age, and temperament. So in the bedroom scene between Prudence and William there is nothing to excite prurience; what Oldmeadow in fact objected to was, 'the unsavoury room (the soapy water unemptied)' and such suggestive crudities of tone. Secondly, however, there remains the climax of the novel, the eating of Prudence at a cannibal feast; and here, Oldmeadow is seen to have missed the point of this 'foul invention', which was to display the emergence of barbarism in a setting for which the author was not morally responsible, but which he was describing with artistically shaped indignation. 'Several writers whose opinion I respect . . . have told me that they regard this as a disagreeable incident. It was meant to be. . . . The story deals with the conflict of civilization, with all its attendant and deplorable ills, and barbarism. The plan of my book throughout was to keep the darker aspects of barbarism continually and unobtrusively present, a black and mischievous background against which the civilized and semi-civilized characters performed their parts; I wished it to be like the continuous, remote throbbing of the hand drums, constantly audible, never visible, which any traveller in Africa will remember as one of his most haunting impressions. I introduced the cannibal theme in the first chapter and repeated it in another key in the incident of the soldiers eating their boots, thus hoping to prepare the reader for the sudden tragedy when barbarism at last emerges from the shadows and usurps the stage. It is not un-

GENERAL CONNOLLY AT UKAKA
(From the painting of a native artist)
Black Mischief

likely that I failed in this; that the transition was too rapid, the
catastrophe too large.' But at any rate, if this were so, it was an
artistic failure, not a moral one.

The whole conflict was a classic demonstration of the confusion between ends and means, or, in literary terms, between
medium and result. The writer may, in pursuing a moral aim,
use means which seem to an observer untouched by aesthetic
considerations to be conducive to some immorality of imagination or behaviour with which the artist, his gaze bent on his
inner vision, is not even remotely concerned. If Oldmeadow had
seen the limited edition of *Black Mischief*, with illustrations by
the author, he might have absorbed a little of the light-hearted
spirit in which the work had been written. Mr Waugh had
earlier produced six line-illustrations for *Decline and Fall*, and a
frontispiece drawing for *Labels* and for *Vile Bodies*. The four
in *Black Mischief* included two of excellent spirit 'after native
artists', one showing the Emperor Seth of Azania (a pastiche of
the plate of Haile Selassie in *Remote People*), and one of General
Connolly at the Battle of Ukaka (*v.* page 33).

A more auspicious occasion for association with the public life
of the Catholic Church in England came when the Jesuit Fathers
at Oxford, in 1934, rebuilt Campion Hall on a new site. 'I wished
to do something to mark my joy in the occasion and·my gratitude
to the then Master (Father Martin D'Arcy, S.J.), to whom,
under God, I owe my faith.' A short life of Edmund Campion
himself was an obvious, and in the event a happy choice, and
Edmund Campion appeared in 1935, all financial return from the
book being donated to the building fund. The work claimed no
more than to be 'a simple, perfectly true story of heroism and
holiness'; the authorities were mastered, help received from
literary records at Farm Street, and the skill of the novelist did
the rest. In the event, the book, which received the Hawthornden
Prize, revealed that Mr Waugh, if he had so wished, could have
made a career for himself as a writer of readable, effective narrative in the Catholic cause and thus have taken over some part of
the Chesterton-Belloc role. The story is told with imagination,
sympathy, a brilliant disposition of light and shade, and the

author's unfailing verbal skill. Reviewers, even those unsympathetic to its general intention and thesis, praised it for its mastery of the sources and gift of expression. Cricitism, apart from matters of historical detail, was drawn, by the ineluctable force of gravity, to the central problem of constancy in the faith versus treason to the State, and the whole question of the claim to historical continuity by the new Church and the new political order. Here no compromise is possible; in any case Mr Waugh was only lending his gifts as a novelist to a cause to which he had already adhered on other grounds.

But, controversy apart – and the case against *Campion* has seldom been put so penetratingly as by Dame Rose Macaulay – there is surely no basis for her assertion that partisanship is inimical to art: 'in art so naturally ironic and detached as his, this is a serious loss; it undermines his best gifts.' Even if Mr Waugh's version of history had been, as Edmund Wilson asserted, 'in the vein of 1066 and All That', his literary skill need not have deserted him. In Dame Rose's comment we see an example of the view that would detach the artist from his intuitions, the craftsman from the creator, and disturb the interplay of style and belief, of sense and sensibility. The work opens with a vivid intuition of historical continuity: the martyrdom of Father Pro in Mexico, mentioned in the Preface, sets the tone – 'the haunted, trapped, murdered priest is our contemporary'; it is March 1603, Queen Elizabeth is on her death bed, there is a brief review of the profit and loss of her reign, a glance forward to 1688 and beyond – and then the dying queen's thoughts move back to a summer's afternoon in 1586, in the heyday of her reign, when she held her court among the scholars in Oxford – and the hero of the book steps quietly on to the stage. This sense of historical continuity was criticized by the reviewer in the *Times Literary Supplement*, as going beyond the idea of a short biography. But it is a credible view of history, at the least, to say that 'the new, rich families who were to introduce the House of Hanover were already in the second stage of their metamorphosis from the freebooters of Edward IV's reign to the conspirators of 1688 and the sceptical, cultured oligarchs of the eighteenth century'; and if so, then it is permissible for the novelist to draw on such glimpses of historical continuity for the colours of his palette. In the same sense, the last three pages represent an epilogue to the brutal details of the martyrdom in which light and shade, past and present, are admirably balanced: the crowd turns to gentler pleasures – two Dutchmen, a giant, and a dwarf; but one man, Henry Walpole, was irrevocably changed by a spot of the martyr's blood, and died the same death thirteen years later; and so the work of the martyrs continues, through the times of Challoner and the early nineteenth century, the Catholic minority lost to the nation, down to the present day, when the site of Tyburn is marked by a chapel, and a noble structure has risen in Campion's Oxford, and in his name.

CHAPTER 2

War and the Settled Years

. . . his long, lonely, tranquil days at Lychpole . . .
    — EVELYN WAUGH on Gilbert Pinfold

IN APRIL 1937 Evelyn Waugh married Laura, youngest
daughter of the late the Hon. Aubrey Herbert, M.P., and
grand-daughter of the fourth Earl of Carnarvon. They settled
down at Piers Court, an old Gloucestershire Manor dating in
part from the sixteenth century, which was to be their home for
the next twenty years, though during the second World War the
property was let, the house to a convent, the fields to a grazier.
The pattern of the comparatively secluded country existence
which then began for the writer who, for the previous ten years,
had been almost constantly on the move, is described in the first
chapter of *The Ordeal of Gilbert Pinfold*. In the same year he took
the coat-of-arms of 'Waugh of Midsomer Norton', which with
the motto 'Industria ditat' (Hard Work Pays) had been used,
without licence, by his ancestor, Alexander Waugh, from about
1780, and by his descendants. Before the outbreak of war there
was just time for the young couple to make a visit to Mexico,
which resulted in the only overtly political work Waugh has
ever written, *Robbery under Law*, published in 1939.

It was clear from the theme and the setting of the next novel
to be taken in hand – an expatriate writer returning home to set
up a new existence free from the support of the parental home –
that Mr Waugh's new status would have its effect on his writing,
This change of theme was accompanied by a radical change in
technique; the circular pattern of order succeeded by disorder
and then by order regained, which had worked so well from
Decline and Fall to *Scoop*, was no longer adequate. The parental

link having broken, John Plant is deprived of his bolt-hole –
Scone College or Boot Magna – and is cast on the waters of life.
His future can only be one of development and integration, in
conflict with his grotesque double, Atwater. But when war came,
the novel was broken off, to remain 'a heap of neglected fools-
cap at the back of a drawer', till it was published in fragmentary
form, in 1942, under the appropriate title *Work Suspended*. In
the character of the hero, John Plant, the author says in a postscript: 'And so an epoch, my epoch, came to an end. . . . My
friends were dispersed. . . . Roger (Simmonds) rose from department to department in the office of Political Warfare. Basil
(Seal) sought and found a series of irregular adventures. For
myself, plain regimental soldiering proved an orderly and not
disagreeable way of life.' Political warfare and some of Basil's
irregular adventures form the staple of *Put out more Flags*,
written on a troopship, and published in 1942. The formulation
of Mr Waugh's war experiences had to wait till the publication
of *Men at Arms*, in 1952. Apart from this, the only major work
of the war years was *Brideshead Revisited*, 1945, where Charles
Ryder is the plain regimental soldier, whose lot was very much
that of Mr Waugh.

Burke's *Landed Gentry* records Mr Waugh's Army service in
World War II in the following compressed terms: 1939–45,
commissioned in the Royal Marines 1939; with No. 8 Commando in Middle East 1941; transferred to the Royal Horse
Guards (the Blues) 1942; British Military Mission to Jugoslavia 1944 – to which may be added: demobilized June 1945,
and returned to Piers Court. In a sense, little need be added,
since Mr Waugh, with notable logic and clear-sightedness,
adopted neither of the two courses of action which presented
themselves to many men of the educated professions: either to
seek a 'reserved' post which would enable them to continue in
some measure their intellectual routine; or to seek to make of
the Army a temporary alternative profession, by entering into
and rising through the recognized chain of command. Both of
these actions he would have considered to be a betrayal of the
vocation of the writer. His unpublished essay on 'Writers at

War' starts off with the characteristic and uncompromising statement: 'The organized dispossession, capture, and killing of his own species are among the activities which, like husbandry, distinguish civilized man from brute creation.' This being so, 'it is the writer's function to aim at the heart of the matter and in war that lies at the extremity of the vast conveyor belt that puts the soldier into action, at the little ridge ahead at the end of his sights'. The writer's presence in the firing line is not an enforced change of jobs for the worse, but one for the better, since it gives him access to the source of his strength. 'He has no duty to glorify the cause of his rulers. He is their natural enemy. He is immune from the emotions of the crowd. But he battens on the individual lives of his fellow-men.' Thus, 'Army life with its humour, surprises and loyalties, its ferocious internal dissensions and its lack of all hate for the ostensible enemy, comprises the very essence of human intercourse and in an age of scant opportunity for adventure serves to dissipate literary vapours.'

Thus it is that the wartime reminiscences of this man who was an exemplary regimental soldier, showing great courage and coolness in conditions of great danger, volunteering at thirty-seven for service with the Special Service Brigade, normally considered only for the youngest and fittest, at Dakar, in Crete, and North Africa, are commonly but a series of names of those friends with whom he served: Bob (Lieutenant-Colonel, later Major-General Robert) Laycock, Randolph Churchill, and others. 'The war is going to be a long one,' says Tommy Backhouse in *Men at Arms*, 'the best thing one can do is to spend it with friends.' The quintessence of 'Army life with its humour, surprises and loyalties', is in *Men at Arms* and *Officers and Gentlemen*, and, for all the author's disclaimer that he has nothing in common with his observer-hero, Guy Crouchback, beyond their common faith and age, the sequence of events follows roughly the author's own experiences till after the fall of Crete.

When the forces under Combined Operations Headquarters in London were reorganized for parachuting behind the enemy's lines in the Normandy stage of the invasion, Mr Waugh was pronounced too old, and was given indefinite leave of absence, which he used to write *Brideshead Revisited*. Anyone who has known the tension involved in being a spare staff officer at a time when a major operation is afoot, will be startled at the degree of detachment which enabled Mr Waugh to write, at this time, his retrospective account of the vanished beauty of Oxford life of twenty years before, and of the characters and foibles of a very Catholic family. Was it an instinct that the postwar world was on the threshold, and would allow the author no further backward glance to the memories of youth? Or was it disillusion with the progress of the war, which had at this stage, in Europe, grown so vast, so confused in its aims? Perhaps something of both. Certainly disillusion was the experience of both Crouchback and Scott-King. And Scott-King, 'as the face of Europe coarsened and the war . . . cast its heroic and chivalrous disguise and became a sweaty tug-of-war between teams of indistinguishable louts . . . became Neutralian in his loyalty and as an act of homage resumed with fervour the task on which he had intermittently worked, the translation of Bellorius into Spenserian stanzas.' This improbable task, we are told, was finished at the time of the Normandy landings. So was *Brideshead Revisited*; the footnote to the manuscript reads: Chagford (Devon), Feb. – June 1944.

But the war was not finished, and at this moment Randolph Churchill rescued Waugh from his state of military inanimation to join Brigadier MacLean's mission to the Jugoslav partisans. They were together at Topusco, near Zagreb, for the autumn and winter 1944–5, and it was there that Waugh dealt with the proofs of *Brideshead*, before moving to Dubrovnik, where he saw out the war. It was only later that he saw the operations of which his force had there formed part within the perspective of the general war strategy. He wrote, in 1947, in an introduction to *Irregular Adventure*, by Christie Lawrence, a fellow officer of No. 8 Commando: 'The black decision to abandon the Allied landings and to leave the decisive invasion to the Russians and Bulgarians meant the surrender of all who looked west for salvation to Communist domination and punishment.' By way of personal reparation for the part he himself had played, he sought for a time to arouse public opinion on the matter, through letters and articles to the press. When Tito ('our guest of dishonour') visited this country in March 1953, this action led to a cartoon by Low in the *Manchester Guardian* in which a mixed group of Roman Catholic laymen and ecclesiastics, only Graham Greene and Evelyn Waugh being named, look on as scaffolding and seating is prepared for the Government's guest. The caption is: *Shame! Now if it were for some sturdy upholder of democracy – like Franco. . . .* A short story, 'Compassion', was the only piece of writing which came out of the Jugoslav episode.

The post-war years saw a steady output of writing interspersed by journeys abroad, few of which failed to provide the stimulus, and in some cases almost the whole material, for new work. In June 1945 Mr Waugh attended the celebrations held at Salamanca, Spain, in connexion with the tercentenary of the birth of Vittoria, the international lawyer; this was his first experience of official hospitality in the new Modern World, in which previously he had travelled as a free man. When *Scott-King's Modern Europe* appeared in 1947, the critics were not slow to notice that, though some details of the setting might suggest Jugoslavia, the direction of the resources of the State to the official sponsoring of select foreign guests was as much within the ambit of the New Spain.

But the more important new trend of these years was Mr Waugh's connexion with America. His works had, of course, been well known in America for years before, having appeared in American editions; *A Handful of Dust*, when printed as a magazine serial, had even been provided with an alternative ending (happy or cynical, according to the taste), later reprinted in *Mr Loveday's Little Outing*. *Brideshead Revisited* had even been serialized (November 1944 to February 1945), in *Town and Country*, with illustrations by Alajálov, before its appearance in either country in book form. In January 1946 it was there chosen as the American Book of the Month, which was the main factor in the enormous figure of nearly three-quarters of a million American sales. Later, the author would have liked to bring out a new edition, cutting the text; but he was dissuaded from doing this by the argument that it was the element of 'glossiness' in its present form which was to the taste of the American public.

The 'American honeymoon' proper began with a request from *Life* for a general account of his career, which was published late in 1946 as *Fan-Fare*. This was followed, in 1947, by a trip to Hollywood to discuss the filming of *Brideshead*. The project came to nothing because of disagreements on the cutting of the plot; Mr Waugh turned down 150,000 dollars in film rights rather than concede what one headline described as 'Molotov veto rights' over the script. But almost more time was spent in Whispering Glades, the great commercialized cemetery of Los Angeles, than in the studios; and on his return he carried back with him, if not a lucrative film contract, at least 'the artist's load, a great shapeless chunk of experience' which, given shape in the summer of 1947, became *The Loved One* (1948). A whole number of *Horizon* (February 1948) was devoted to this work, before its appearance in book form. It was the greatest success of the post-war years in his pre-war satirical vein – both a *succès d'estime* and *de scandale*. The following winter of 1948–9 saw two further visits to the United States, this time to the centres of Catholic intellectual life, including Notre Dame, Indiana, and Loyola, Baltimore, lecturing on R. A. Knox, G. K. Chesterton, and Graham Greene, as three contrasted converts to Catholicism; Loyola College had already, in 1947, awarded him an honorary degree, accepted on his behalf by Father Martin D'Arcy. This in its turn led to two further articles in *Life*, one on 'The American Epoch in the Catholic Church', the second on the Holy Places. A journey to Jerusalem in 1951 in connexion with the last-named article resulted in an essay on 'The Defence of the Holy Places', which, together with an article on 'St Helena, Empress', was published in 1953, in a limited edition, as *The Holy Places*.

Since 1935, his first visit to Jerusalem, Mr Waugh had been drawn to the figure of St Helena, the mother of Constantine the

Great (one tradition, to which Waugh adhered, giving her a British parentage), and discoverer of the baulks of timber acclaimed as and traditionally held to be the True Cross. Work had begun on a fictional life and account of her discovery after the war, but had involved Waugh in more labour than he had had to spend on any other book. The imaginative fusion of the historical tradition and the author's own basic view of Helena's sanctity, the extreme artistry with which, after intensive pruning and shaping, the main threads of spiritual symbolism were drawn throughout the apparently exiguous material, makes this one of the most subtle and chiselled of his novels. Reception was and has since continued to be disappointing, though in England some critics reported favourably; but in America the work completely failed to meet the public's taste.

Among Mr Waugh's jottings for his American lecture on Mgr Ronald Knox, a cryptic phrase stands out: 'the Esquimaux and his igloos rather than child welfare and nuclear fission.' The contrast is more in the vein of Evelyn Waugh than of Mgr Knox, but no doubt it drew the audience's attention to the latter writer's most striking, though little known work of controversy, *God and the Atom*, published in 1945, which Mr Waugh has described as an outstanding work of Christian inspiration, and to which he devoted a considerable part of his summary of Mgr Knox's writing published in *Horizon*, in May 1948. Here Mr Waugh analyses his subject's mastery in the three fields of controversy, Biblical translation, and the sermon. He has restored the sermon to its place as a classic form of literary art, for in every Knox sermon there is 'that sudden flash and fusion of ideas and observed fact which corresponds to the process known as literary "creation"'. Mr Waugh followed up this argument by making his own selection of eleven from among his subject's more formal set-piece sermons, and publishing them, in a limited edition, in 1949.

The *Horizon* article was one of a series which required the contributor to point out 'The Best and the Worst' in his chosen writer. Dame Rose Macaulay had written in this manner on Evelyn Waugh in the issue of December 1946, producing the most penetrating criticism yet written of Mr Waugh's own romantic other-self which, in *Brideshead*, had temporarily seized the pen – 'an unhappy and quite unsuitable partnership, overdue for dissolution'. Coming to the later article, many a reader of *Horizon* must have asked himself what on earth he would find there as 'the worst' of Mgr Knox. Mr Waugh was not at a loss, and deftly inverted the terms of his commission, making Mgr Knox's limitations redound largely to his credit. Mgr Knox used the language of a generation which, in intercourse, could assume a general background of humane letters with which to express its ideas. Being the least didactic of men, it is when he is seeking to make plain in non-technical terms a metaphysical distinction, that he draws on this fund of allusive knowledge, 'courteously assuming that we all remember our Virgil and Matthew Arnold'. The reader of *Horizon* finds the mote in Mgr Knox's eye turned most gracefully into a beam in his own eye. It was felt to be very appropriate when it become known that before his death Mgr Knox had appointed Mr Waugh to be his literary executor, and had approved his proposal to make a *Life* of his friend his first commitment. There is every reason to expect that the combination of author and subject will lead to an outstanding literary work of our time.

By 1950, Mr Waugh may be said to have become a public figure in the world of literature. Both his own publisher, Chapman and Hall, and Penguin Books, had produced cheap reprints of some of the works from 1937, but the post-war years provided the opportunity to extend this range. Chapman and Hall produced eight more volumes in the Uniform Edition (1947–9), and Penguin Books issued, in 1951, ten works in cheap reprints, an honour which had previously fallen to the lot only of Bernard Shaw and H. G. Wells. Since then the small Penguin Waughs have been a ubiquitous element on the bookstalls, new and second-hand, and the earlier works, from *Decline and Fall* to *Scoop*, were given a chance to show how little their polish had tarnished by the lapse of almost a generation.

Mr Waugh's experience of wireless broadcasting has been less encouraging. Two novels have been broadcast in adaptations: *Helena*, adapted by Christopher Sykes, in 1951 (with Flora Robson as the Empress Helena and John Gielgud as the Emperor Constantine), and *Brideshead Revisited*, adapted by Lance Sieveking, in 1956. But otherwise the works have probably had less than their fair share of sensible radio comment. A broadcast interview of 1953, in the series 'Frankly Speaking', did not improve matters; the author was not complaisant enough to do violence to his dislike of the medium and the occasion. The whole affair was much more successful as one of the irritants which stimulated the experience and the book which received the title *The Ordeal of Gilbert Pinfold.*

This was one of the less welcome results of the pressures which public literary status entailed. Between Easter 1949 and 1950 Mr Waugh decided to celebrate his own private Holy Year, and resolved to accept all invitations to speak in public; fortunately this resolve only became generally known towards the end of the year, so that he was spared the more distressing results of his zeal. But in 1951 – the Penguin Year – Mr Waugh was invited to stand as a candidate for the Lord Rectorship of Edinburgh University. With characteristic frankness he admitted, in his Electoral Address, that his claims to the suffrage of the Electors – apart from being a Scot of the Diaspora – were meagre and mainly negative, but turned this to good advantage by inveighing against men in public life: 'I have never gone into public life. Most of the ills we suffer are caused by people going into public life. I have never voted in a Parliamentary Election. I believe a man's chief civic duty consists in fighting for his King when the men in public life have put the realm in danger. This I have done. I have raised a family and paid such taxes as I find unavoidable. I have learned and practised a very difficult trade with some fair success.' Among Mr Waugh's opponents were the Scottish poet Hugh McDiarmid, the late Aga Khan, the Persian Moussadek – now hardly remembered – and the late Sir Alexander Fleming. Whether it was because the support of the senior members was given to an eminent academic man, or because the junior members rallied to one who admitted to fourteen years as a private in the London Scottish and an

Honorary Chieftainship of the Doy-gei-taun of Kiowa tribe – Sir Alexander Fleming was elected by a comfortable majority.

The last major works of this post-war period were the two war novels, *Men at Arms* (1952) and *Officers and Gentlemen* (1955), and *The Ordeal of Gilbert Pinfold* (1957). Work on the life of Mgr Knox will presumably prevent any further novels being written for the moment. The war novels were announced first as a trilogy, then, tentatively, as a tetralogy. But on publication of the second, Mr Waugh announced that the two works would, for the moment, constitute the whole. 'If I keep my faculties I hope to follow the fortunes of the characters through the whole of the war.' Themes still outstanding included, he said, 'Crouchback in Jugoslavia'. 'I shall deal with Crouchback's realization that no good comes from public causes; only private causes of the soul.' Between the two war novels came *Love among the Ruins* (1953). Begun some time before, under the stimulus of his dislike of the constructions – the Dome of Discovery and others – which rose on the South Bank for Festival Year, it was finished off and offered to the public as the author's Coronation Year effort. It is a slight, melancholy, and not too well assembled glimpse into an unhappy future, and could not have been less suited to the mood of that year. As a further incongruous touch, Mr Waugh had his own personal copy bound in a sheet of the special Coronation stamps. *Love among the Ruins* is especially notable for its illustrations. Mr Waugh has always devoted care to the external appearance of his books, but had not always been happy with his illustrators. This time, he returned to his earlier practice of producing his own whimsical line illustrations. They are adapted from the reproductions of Canova's classical statuary engraved by Henry Moses in 1876 – an ironical comment on the incapacity of the Welfare State to produce anything of beauty on its own.

Indeed, no writer of comparable status in present-day England has expressed so consistently, pointedly, and sardonically, his opposition to all those aspects of social and public life which may be summed up under the terms 'Welfare State', or even, in a wider sense, 'Progress'. Many examples will be given in their proper place; here one small but characteristic marginal gloss by Mr Waugh may be mentioned. In the person of Mr Pinfold he tells of his shabby old house which, over the years, 'he had filled with pictures and books and furniture of the kind he relished'. The significant word here is 'relished'. Mr Waugh happened to acquire two pictures by the Victorian artist Robert Musgrave Joy on 'The Pleasures of Travel'. In each case the scene is from the inside of a travelling carriage. A bearded figure appears at the door: in 1751 it is a highwayman, in 1851 a ticket-collector. How inevitable is progress! So Mr Waugh then commissioned a third picture by Richard Eurich, A.R.A., with the theme of the Pleasures of Travel, 1951. The scene is from the passenger cabin of an aircraft as it crashes; the details may be imagined.

The mixed reception accorded to the last works, as indeed to most of the works since the war, with the exception perhaps of *The Loved One*, suggests that Mr Waugh has not even yet found a public for his writing completely in sympathy with all aspects of his work. While the earlier works, from *Decline and Fall* to *Put out more Flags*, were, through the Penguin reprints, reaching and delighting an unusually wide public, his post-war work seems to have aroused sectarian passions which have not been allayed by his undoubted standing in the world of letters. Given his position as a satirist of the first order and an incomparable stylist, there are still many, from critics to unknown readers, who dislike his politics (*Scott-King*, *Love among the Ruins*), his religion (*Helena*, *Men at Arms*), the accompanying rush of romanticism which welled up in *Brideshead*, or the occasional grotesquerie which has been present in his writing from the first. They would prefer the author to reserve the more 'serious' aspects of his convictions for private airing, and continue to give his delighted public the inspired fooling, which, they say (though with a few unhappy lapses from taste) was the secret of the success of his earlier works.

Brideshead Revisited, appearing immediately after the war, set the tone for this line of criticism. Mr Waugh seemed to have become an acolyte swinging the incense-burner at the foot of

altar and throne. 'I sought inspiration among gutted palaces and
cloisters embowered in weed', says Charles Ryder of his American journey. A pity Mr Waugh did not do the same, thought
some; we might then have had a macabre fantasy in the manner
of Mr Charles Addams, of the *New Yorker*. Mr Waugh's *Brideshead* and its art nouveau chapel are very much in use. And what
had become of the cool, sober style of *Work Suspended*? Was the
style of *Brideshead* to be Mr Waugh's 'art nouveau'? 'Love, the
English aristocracy and the Roman Catholic Church combine to
liquefy a style that should be dry,' said Dame Rose Macaulay.
Her selection of passages to show the lushness which came over
the author when writing of these hallowed subjects – and of
food – drove the point home. It is hardly an exaggeration to say
that Mr Waugh's reputation among the critics has hardly yet
recovered from the blow dealt by *Brideshead*. The charge is that
Mr Waugh has abandoned his old detachment, and has declared
his loyalties – excellent things, loyalties, comments Mr O'Faolain, but fatal for an artist. 'A religious theme given institutional
treatment is always liable to get lost in the embroidered folds of
ecclesiasticism', is his comment on *Brideshead*. In stylistic terms
the charge is that he has abandoned the stringency of satire for
the sweetness of romanticism. Mr Waugh, says Mr Mikes, is 'a
powerful satirist but only a mediocre missionary. . . . In *Edmund
Campion* and *Helena* he stands on a pair of spiritual buskins
and can be incredibly dull.' 'Even Saint Helena is made
tolerable only by being represented as a Miserere Mei in
her youth and a bit of a fool in her old age', says Mr O'Faolain
again.

Reviewing the earlier works in the light of this apparent
decline, critics have commonly gone on to describe Mr Waugh's
genius as 'brainless'; the note varies from approval to downright condemnation. Mr O'Faolain's summing up is sympathetic: 'Waugh is a writer of purely brainless genius, which
he has amplified by the possession or development of enormous
technical skill.' But whether the term is used in praise or in
blame, the inference is always that Mr Waugh should stick to
satire, since he is not equipped to speak in his own person.

As Mr McCormick says: 'Basically an anti-intellectual, he is now in a position where he must propose intellectual positions.'

But the antitheses set up by these and similar critical judgements are altogether too easy. True, Mr Waugh has constantly rejected the idea that the novel is a medium for the propagation of views, Though keenly interested in the social scene, he is more inclined to distinguish than to unite; his assertion, in the U-language discussion, that 'everyone draws the line of' (social) 'demarcation immediately below his heels', is more the comment of a satirist than of a social theorist. One remembers the Lancing Editorial of 1921, making it plain that the whole school is knit by a bond of comradeship, except – the whole school. He is not a theological writer, in spite of his known decided attitude on questions of faith, morals, and dogma; his intermittent excursions into public controversy are probably due as much to a desire to provoke people, as to an urge to propagate his own views. The religious themes in his works are momentous, but structurally simple, and are not accompanied by introspective analysis: in *Brideshead* the reconversion of a lapsed Catholic family, in *Helena* the reassertion of the historical reality of the Cross, in the war novels the problem of a just cause in war. Any subtlety of treatment called for will be one of novelistic technique, not of theological casuistry.

But on this showing, surely one might expect rather less than more speaking in his own person; certainly we should not expect to find him setting about anything so ill-defined as 'proposing intellectual positions'. And must he be called 'anti-intellectual' if he considers the vocation and equipment of a novelist to be quite different from that of a journalist, critic or scholar? Holding the writing of novels to be a full-time task, Mr Waugh has never wasted much time explaining them, but he has said a little more about his work than 'writing should be like clockmaking', and that little is quite revealing. In 1938, for instance – in the full flood of his 'brainless' period – he said that the common opposition of 'creative' and 'critical' writer seemed to him to imply an invidious distinction; a better word for 'creative' would be 'architectural'. 'I believe that what makes a writer, as distinct from a clever and cultured man who can write, is an added energy and breadth of vision which enables him to complete a structure.' Can one have this added breadth of vision and yet be just a brainless anti-intellectual? Can enormous technical skill exist in a vacuum? Is there not here something of the fallacy that the comic genius is – just a born comedian? One critic even speaks of Mr Waugh's 'freak talent'. But there is a long and rich tradition of interest in freaks of nature – theologians, philosophers, astrologers, biologists, pathologists, and creative artists have never failed to find in them food for thought.

Again, when reviewing a work of Mr Connolly in 1938, Mr Waugh wrote: 'Writing is an art which exists in a time sequence; each sentence and each page is dependent on its predecessors and successors; a sentence which he admires may owe its significance to one fifty pages distant. I beg Mr Connolly to believe that even quite popular writers take great trouble sometimes in this matter.' The crassly unjust treatment meted out, even by normally sympathetic critics, to *Helena*, is an extreme case of failure to take heed of this warning; it was the intervening fifty pages which defeated them. Fellow novelists have been more percipient; Miss Elizabeth Bowen and Mr Anthony Powell have written with discernment of his work. In some degree Mr Waugh has created his own adverse publicity by his reticence about his works. His manner of writing demands periodical bouts of intense creative effort, with long intervening periods of outer emptiness during which the internal dynamism is recharged. During twenty years at Piers Court the tedium of life sent him on innumerable afternoons to the Dursley Cinema. But every few years Mr Waugh has thrown off something quite different, showing the intervening growth; his work includes three or four quite distinct modes of writing. To attempt to restrict him to something between *Decline and Fall* and *The Loved One* is a disservice to a writer whose genius, though fundamentally consistent, is in its outward manifestations quite unpredictable.

His standing in the world of critical journalism has, however, perhaps suffered most by his readiness to provoke his critics, and his resolute refusal to graduate from the status of writer to that of 'man of letters'. An outline of his life, habits, and opinions, since his settled years, may now be found in Chapter One of *The Ordeal of Gilbert Pinfold*. In relation to public affairs, his views are largely negative. In art they are, for many people, retrograde. In music and 'thought' they are non-existent. What, then, is one to make of a man who writes of himself that 'since the end of the war his life had been strictly private'; who asserts that 'lots of the ills we suffer are caused by people going into public life'; who is thankful to a fellow writer for paying with enthusiasm 'all the penalties of eminence which real writers shirk', so that 'in middle age he forms a valuable dummy who draws off the bores while they get on with their work'?

There is quite a simple key to Mr Waugh's attitude to the complexities of literary and public life. It is that the writer is a man who has set up to sell the products of his craftsmanship in writing the English language; all other aspects of his life are as inviolate as if he were selling boots, and his opinions on matters far removed from the technicalities of his trade are unimportant. He himself has not refrained from judging adversely the work of writers and literary groups whose approach to their trade is distasteful to him. Thus in criticizing the lack of fine writing at the Universities – by which Mr Waugh means Oxford – he comments: 'Sir Maurice Bowra is learned and lucid, but dull; Lord David Cecil has grace but no grammar; Mr Isaiah Berlin is diffuse and voluble; Mr Trevor Roper vulgar.' A review of Mr C. B. Cochran's *Cock-a-doodle-do* begins: 'It is an incorrigibly boastful work and it is completely shapeless.' His private feud against the group of 'progressive' writers associated, in the thirties, with Mr Auden and Mr Isherwood, has lasted so long as to have become a familiar aspect of the literary scene. But he has always taken great care to restrict himself to comment on their activity as writers. Public comment on an author's work may not disregard the law of libel. Mr Waugh himself, in two successive law-suits in 1957, secured verdicts against the Beaverbrook-owned *Daily Express*, with damages to the total sum of £5,000, for printing statements on his books which were held to go beyond legitimate critical comment.

The products of the writer's craft are associated, in Mr Waugh's mind, with other products of the skilled craftsman, furniture, clocks, hats, rather than with 'ideas', 'opinions', 'points of view', or – worst of all – 'programmes'. The labour involved is seen as physical as much as mental. 'It is so well written that I sweated at every word' (1937). Making and selling a book is like any other mutually profitable exchange of products. For an American audience, he writes (1949): 'The writer sweats to write well; the reader sweats to make dollars; writer and reader exchange books for dollars.' One reads Mr Maugham's works with a feeling of increasing respect for his mastery of his trade: 'one has the same delight as in watching a first-class cabinet maker cutting dovetails; in the days of bakelite this is a rare and bewitching experience.'

In his own writing, Mr Waugh practises what he preaches – and with an assiduity the greater for his having few other intellectual interests. When a book is in progress, each day's draft is corrected with meticulous care, so that, if the author fell dead, there would be nothing on the desk which he would not want to be published. Hardly a single day passes without some exploration in the pages of the Oxford Dictionary. He uses words rarely to be found elsewhere – 'somewhere in the ultimate curlicues of his mind . . .' Thomas Merton was sent a copy of Fowler's *Modern English Usage*, to assist him in cleaning up his prose style. As a test of the above statement that Lord David Cecil has 'grace but no grammar', Mr Waugh was sent a copy of his Inaugural Lecture on Pater; a postcard arrived by return with a half-dozen infelicities and one howler gathered from the first two pages.

Mr Waugh sees his own period as a silver age; the criteria of good writing are mainly the formal ones of lucidity, elegance and individuality, and reticence. The writers he most admires are those noted for their verbal skill and dexterity: Sir Max Beerbohm, Mgr Ronald Knox, Mr P. G. Wodehouse, Mr Somerset Maugham. Among contemporary novelists respected for their

TO THE LITERARY EDITOR

This book will be published on

JAN - 6 1958 PRICE $ 4.00

Do not review before publication date.

Tear sheets or clippings of your review are requested.

Please do not quote more than 500 words without special permission

Little, Brown & Company, 34 Beacon St., Boston 6

attractive and distinctive styles are Mr Anthony Powell, Mr Graham Greene, Miss Compton-Burnett, Miss Elizabeth Bowen, and Mr Henry Green. There is room for splendour and magnificence in writing, though few writers now attempt it. Sir Osbert Sitwell's five-volume autobiography stands alone in this respect. Sir Winston Churchill's historical studies, 'though highly creditable for a man with so much else to occupy him, do not really survive close attention'. In most forms of literature, indeed, fine writing is out of keeping with the age. 'The majority of English speakers muddle through with a minute vocabulary. To them any words not in vulgar use, are "fancy", and it is, perhaps, in ignoble deference to their susceptibilities that there has been a notable flight from magnificence in English writing.' Apart from Sir Osbert Sitwell, Mr Waugh, surveying the literary scene, sees only Mgr Knox's set-piece sermons and panegyrics, 'rich carpets spread for the feet of prelates and scholars.'

The quality of its writing is the touchstone of the life and vigour of a civilization. 'This is the century of the common man; let him write as he speaks and let him speak as he pleases.' So the present scene is full of the signs of decadence. 'Microphone and magazine have largely usurped the place of the pulpit . . .' – 'Father D'Arcy has among his many gifts the supreme art of conducting a conversation, the rare, almost extinct craft that has today grossly descended to the "question-masters" of the B.B.C.' The outlook for the future is gloomy indeed. Society is changing in a way which makes it increasingly difficult for the writer – or indeed for any artist – to live at his ease. A few will, no doubt, submit to the new era and hire out their talents to the State in one of the numerous fields of public relations. 'For the more vigorous, however, the choice lies in the two extremes of anarchic bohemianism and ascetic seclusion. Each provides a refuge from the State' (1943). In the days of the new barbarism, the earliest pattern of our era is re-asserting itself: a small but vital sphere in catacomb and cloister, where all is light and sanity, surrounded by a world of darkness and savagery; the picture is the same for religion as it is for literature. Practical applications in the field of culture follow from this view. A knowledge of Latin, the medium through which a basic sense of the structure of language is acquired, is becoming rare; the tradition of English prose is endangered. The Bible, in the Authorized Version, has been for three hundred years the greatest formative influence on English prose style. That time is now over. 'When the Bible ceases, as it is ceasing, to be accepted as a sacred text it will not long survive for its fine writing.'

It is clear that what concerns Mr Waugh all the time is not just art, but art in society. Technical proficiency is not likely to fail, but it is the spirit that matters; literature, art, the spoken word are all threatened by the same erosion of substance. 'The present generation of Englishmen inherited some of the finest town architecture in Europe, the very finest country houses, and a landscape of immense variety and charm. In fifty years half of it has gone and the rest is going' (review, 1938). In one art, however, that of painting, the very conditions of our vision have changed; the artist's vision has atrophied owing to the invention of photography. Painting has an unbroken tradition from the great days of Velasquez, Veronese, and Titian, down to the English nineteenth-century subject painters, the pre-Raphael-ites, and their descendants in this century. Painting in England decayed from about 1850, and generally with the French impressionists, whose style ruined English painting as soon as it crossed the channel. (An exception is made only for modern portraiture; Mr Waugh has great respect, for instance, for Augustus John.) Now that the function of recording visual impressions has been taken over by the machine, painters have had to start all kinds of silly by-products. The final attack on the visual arts was carried out in the twenties, by a small cosmopolitan set in Paris round Gertrude Stein, the first collector of Picasso. It succeeded, but that on literature, by the first writer of absolute gibberish, failed.

The question arises, what was the nature of this great art of the past, and what were the conditions of its existence. The answers are simple: its nature was the recording of a noble experience, its condition the enlightened patronage of the individual. The visual artist must be impassioned with a visual image, which means being 'obsessed by the nobility of his subject, the beauty of his subject, or by the technique of recording his impression'. As for the conditions of its flourishing, it is worth recording in full the most considered defence which Mr Waugh has written, in 1943, of the system of private patronage: 'Aristocracy saved the artist in many ways. By its patronage it offered him rewards more coveted than the mere cash value of its purchases; in its security it invited him to share its own personal freedom of thought and movement; it provided the leisured reader whom alone it is worth addressing; it curbed the vanity of the publicist and drew a sharp line between fame and notoriety; by its caprices it encouraged experiment; its scepticism exposed the humbug. These and countless other benefits are now forgotten or denied. Its particular service to literature was that it maintained the delicate and unstable balance between the spoken and the written word. Only a continuous tradition of gentle speech, with all its implications – the avoidance of boredom and vulgarity, the exchange of complicated ideas, the observance of subtle *nuances* of word and phrase – can preserve the written tongue from death, and lifelong habitude to such speech alone schools a man to write his own tongue.'

Nor is Mr Waugh inclined to permit the claim that support by the people or by enlightened groups acting in its name can ever replace the patronage of the enlightened individual. The 'Art of the People' is a term which has no sense in his language. If you point, in the history of the drama, to religious drama and popular farce, he will bring to your attention the court masque and the royal pageant. If you point to evidence of the willingness of the public 'to shoulder some of that burden of support formerly borne by individuals of wealth and taste' (Secretary-General of the Arts Council, in *The Times*) he will counter that artists have no claim to support similar to that which society admits, as a moral obligation, in the case of paupers or lunatics; but vast numbers of artists, in the past, strove to give delight, and patrons were and still are prepared to buy their works for the pleasure they afford. We are back at the beginning: dollars

for boots, shillings for books. The only thing to do for the writer
is to leave him alone, and not to encourage him to see himself as
part of a Movement or a Group.

All these views are arguable, of course; our concern here is
not to discuss them on their merits, but to use them as pointers
to the understanding of the works. Several points of view may
be and have been taken up by critics and others.

To some the emphasis on tradition in religion and society will
be frankly distasteful; they will cry snobbery, reaction, popery.
One may remonstrate gently with such people. One may remind them that Mr Waugh's praise of aristocracy in the past
does not extend to all members of the aristocracy in the present,
indeed that he positively smacks his lips over the detection of
decay in the ranks of the Lords. One may remind them that it is
less to the person of the aristocrat that his esteem is directed
than to the manner of life of the great country house. Architecture is one of his chief sources of delight; books on this subject,
and especially those of the eighteenth-century builders, he collects and reads gluttonously – not books on their occupants, on
heraldry, genealogy, family history. Nor does what has been
described as his 'anti-Hooperism' ('These men must die to
make a world for Hooper' – Charles Ryder) without further
qualification fit him for the function of Tory apologist. 'He (Mr
Pinfold) had never voted in a parliamentary election, maintaining an idiosyncratic toryism which was quite unrepresented in
the political parties of his time.' Surely Mr Pinfold would not
maintain these views if they *were* represented in Parliament?

Those, again, who deprecate this complete withdrawal from
public life, may be reminded that Mr Waugh claims the right
to be concerned, deeply, with only two things: his faith and his
writing; that his detachment from forms of activism includes
also an avoidance of the public action increasingly enjoined on
the faithful by his own Church. This withdrawal is, however,
balanced by many acts of kindness and self-denying charity of
which one only learns by questioning his closest friends, just as
in his many reviews he has never failed to give encouragement,
criticism, and advice to other, and especially younger novelists.

Lastly, one should ask such critics whether possibly their irritation with Mr Waugh's views is not in some small measure due to his complete lack of false deference. Especially in religion, he asserts his views without seeking to propagate them; and it is with delight that he tastefully arranges the skull among the roses. A review of Father Devlin's *Life of Robert Southwell* (1956) began: 'The century following Cranmer's consecration is unique in our history as being the only period in which any considerable numbers of English had the will and the opportunity to die for their religious beliefs.'

To others, the sum of Mr Waugh's reported opinions – religious convictions apart – amounts to a pose. He is, they say, by his own admission, often bored. So, for the amusement of his friends, to the annoyance of his enemies, and to occupy the public imagination between novels, he has elaborated and maintained a stylized attitude. He is by nature a romantic, with a fastidious personal temperament which he has allowed increasingly to dictate his mode of life and recorded opinions. He has constructed a personal myth which is something between that of a Knight of the Round Table and an English eighteenth-century squire. They might support this by argument that even the gusto with which he studies and collects Victoriana does not prevent him from harking back constantly to the great classical tradition in art and the tradition of the universal Church. Mr Pinfold records the gift from a friend (James Lance, *alias* John Betjeman) of a massive wash-hand stand, fancifully elaborated, by an English architect of the 1860s (William Burges), 'a man not universally honoured, but of magisterial status to Mr Pinfold and his friends'. This was on the occasion of his fiftieth birthday, in 1953. But very shortly before, in December 1952, Mr Waugh had reviewed his friend Mr Betjeman's *First and Last Loves*, and had written an incisive condemnation of 'Betjemanism' as conducive to that mediocrity and vulgarity which the author himself deplores. The final criterion of taste is what can only be defined as the 'Grand Tradition'. 'He (Mr Betjeman) denounces suburban mediocrity, while he himself has been the leader and sole instigator of the fashionable flight from Greatness, away from the traditional hierarchy of classic genius, away from the library to the threepenny-box of the second-hand book-seller, away from the Mediterranean to the Isle of Man, away from the Universal Church into odd sects and schisms, away from historic places into odd corners of Aberdeen.' The turn of phrase is characteristic, so the argument which we are considering would continue, but how many of these criteria of taste and culture can be accurately identified? The Grand Tradition is defined more by those agencies through which it is betrayed, than in its proper nature. Mr Waugh's tastes, continue such judges, are nothing but the expression of a conscious but uninformed desire for what is best in everything, a desire which is ultimately less potent to establish or to continue a tradition than it is useful for castigating the surrounding decay.

Both these contrasting views are stated here for what they are worth – and, indeed, they are worth much, since they probably express, suitably simplified, the views of nine-tenths of the readers of Mr Waugh's novels who do not just go to him for pure entertainment. To neither can a satisfying answer be given without reference to the works. If Mr Waugh's views are retrograde, they are at least views which he has shaped for himself throughout years of writing; they express the vision of the artist, as well as the views of the man. If they are a pose, then no one, including Mr Waugh himself, can say where the pose ends and settled opinion begins; to attempt to do so would be to make an entirely artificial distinction between the man and his work.

The most telling argument for the 'pose theory' is, though this may seem paradoxical, the success of his novels with the reading public. One might assume that a writer professing the opinions described above would attract a small and esoteric band of readers, but not a vast audience. How strange that a writer who has sold over four million copies of his books, in nearly thirty years of writing, should never ride in a bus or in the undergound, and should claim that he has never met 'the man in the street'. How strange that a popular novelist in this, the century of the common man, should be such an 'uncommon man'. It is not quite enough to say that the author has developed his attitudes with the increasing years, that before the war they were much less distinct and extreme. It is not even the whole story that the common man has no desire to be entertained at the common level, any more than *Brideshead Revisited*, which sold over 700,000 copies in the United States, has anything to do with the 'American way of life'; or that Mr Waugh has an outstanding comic genius and an astonishing technique. All these things are true, and yet they are not all. Mr Connolly has said that Evelyn Waugh seems never to be so happy as when he is writing a drawing of Mr Osbert Lancaster. It would certainly be as true to say that he is never more successful than when exploiting either the reality or the myth of the personality of Evelyn Waugh. For, apart from his wit and satire, he has consistently exploited a simple pattern of story-telling deeply in harmony with instinctive human desires and ways of thought. This is why the terms 'myth' and 'fantasy', and even 'fairy story' and 'symbol', occur from time to time in this study. The common reader is little concerned with the Evelyn Waugh who asserts that 'the cloister offers a saner and more civilized life than "the world"'; nor need he know anything about the writer's motives. But he can appreciate the underlying contrast between a haven of peace and the surrounding bedlam, between sanity and insanity. '. . . most men harbour the germs of one or two books only,' thinks Mr Pinfold; 'all else is professional trickery.' He is quite right. Mr Waugh has, perhaps, two books in his armoury; with one or other he has never ceased to give pleasure to millions. The first is this contrast between sanity and insanity; it has been used, with variations, from *Decline and Fall* to *Scott-King*, and beyond. The second, a simple development from the first, is the spectacle of sanity venturing out into the surrounding sphere of insanity, and defeating it at its own game. This pattern is tentatively worked out in several of the earlier and the later works, but with complete succe ss – though in widely differing modes – only in *The Loved One*, *Helena*, and *The Ordeal of Gilbert Pinfold*.

Part Two

THE NOVELS

CHAPTER 3

Four Entertainments, 1928-38

'. . . you cannot help being struck by an amazing cohesiveness of events.'
— AUGUSTUS FAGAN, M.D.

A YOUNG MAN from Oxford, student of theology, is drawn, partly comprehending, into a fantastic world. Debagged by College rowdies, he is sent down for indecent behaviour. He is then successively hired by a mushroom private school, rescued and seduced by an elegant woman of the world, involved by her – again innocent – in white slave dealings, charged, sentenced, and imprisoned. Again the lady comes to his rescue, and by a faked release and change of personality he is returned, much relieved, to College and the continuance of his studies. Such is the improbable sequence of settings on which Mr Waugh's mordant wit and satire here exercises itself. His first novel is, appropriately, a fantasy of the impact of the lawless outside world on one brought up to academic seclusion. Scone College and the Bollinger Club, Church and Gargoyle the Scholastic Agents, the seedy incompetence of Llanabba Castle, the succession of improbable life-stories related by the irrepressible Philbrick – a series of hilarious and sardonic scenes pass before the mind's eye. Three worlds are juxtaposed: the serious and unworldly sphere of an academic community; the frivolous, worldly sphere of Society, with its criminal fringe, where traffic in prostitution goes on; and a transitional sphere by which Paul enters and withdraws from the world of Margot Beste-Chetwynde – that of the minor public school, Llanabba Castle, and the prison, Blackstone Gaol. There are some strange creatures who, provided with the appropriate breathing organs, inhabit College or Society. Paul Pennyfeather is not one of these. For him the one is a limbo, the other a madhouse; for him the Lessons of Life can only be learnt in their respective grotesque reflections, the school, and the prison.

The whole is uproarious, scandalous, delightfully 'malicious' (a popular expression at the time), a comic extravaganza whipped up from a few personal experiences. The style is crisp and spare, with more than a suggestion, in some of the dialogue, of P. G. Wodehouse and his Drones. ' "Old boy," said Grimes, "you're in love." – "Nonsense?" – "Smitten?" said Grimes. – "No, no." – "The tender passion?" – "No." – "Spring fancies, love's young dream?" – "Nonsense!" . . .' The brisk sequence of dialogue and events is only interrupted for the musings of Paul and an occasional bravura passage of burlesque pastiche. Take, for instance, the lament of Captain Grimes on his last beano before his marriage to Flossie Fagan. It starts with an echo of the Lament of Dr Faustus (' "Oh why did nobody warn me? . . . about Flossie, not about the fires of hell" '), continues with Shakespeare (' "Our life is lived between two homes. We emerge for a little into the light, and then the front door closes" '), and ends with a tirade in the mood of Schopenhauer from Samuel Butler's *Notebooks* (' "What is this impulse of two people to build their beastly homes? It's you and me, unborn, asserting our presence" '). A great future awaits this type of effect in Mr Waugh's later novels.

In short, this first novel is an excellent sample of Mr Waugh's method of mixing farce, comedy of character and satire, and telling his story with that studied understatement of the shocking which relates him more closely to the 'dead-pan' manner of Damon Runyon than to the self-conscious seaminess of the early Huxley or the mannered violence of Hemingway. The fate of little Lord Tangent (surely an unconscious, sardonic echo of 'little Lord Fauntleroy'), for instance, is told in four asides widely separated one from another. They may be summarized as: Tangent shot through foot at school sports – foot swollen and black – foot amputated – Tangent dies. Mr Linklater has summed up this attitude as 'a bland assumption . . . that the most monstrous injustice is as much a part of life as the early morning cup of tea', and a 'calm acceptance of an irrational, glittering, unjust and determined sequence of events'.

Admirably put, but is it correct? 'Irrational, glittering', no doubt. But 'unjust and determined'? Or rather, if the fate of Pennyfeather, Tangent, and of Prendergast – whose head is sawn off by a criminal lunatic – is unjust, how then *is* it determined? Monstrous injustice by itself is neither satisfying nor funny. Surely there must be here some higher justice, a more satisfying form of unreason than we normally expect and find in life. His first book shows Mr Waugh already as a master of what has been described as 'the higher lunacy'; what are the laws of this strange world? To find them, we must look more carefully at the sequence of events.

Paul Pennyfeather is a theological student well advanced towards ordination. He has that combination of personal innocence and theoretically progressive views which is the blessed patrimony of nine-tenths of English undergraduates. 'Paul had no particular objection to drunkenness – he had read a rather daring paper to the Thomas More Society on the subject – but he was consumedly shy of drunkards.' This is the position in a nutshell. Into this life irrupt the disordered revels of the Bollinger Club, acting, like the Dionysiac revels of ancient Greece, as an orgiastic transition to the world of irrationalism, of disturbing vital desires (Margot) and fundamental intellectual doubt (Prendergast). The Bollinger is the epitome of the world into which Paul is about to be plunged. The emissary of this world of irrationalism is Alastair Digby-Vane-Trumpington – a P. G. Wodehouse name if ever there was one, but how different is the role – half satyr, half messenger of the gods. He is associated with Paul's debagging and consequent rustication, is cast for the role of best man at Paul's wedding with Margot (since, 'however indirectly, Paul owed him a great deal of his present fortune'); much later he assists in the events by which Paul sloughs off his past personality and assumes a new identity ('Sir Alastair, like Sir Bedivere, watched him out of sight') – and, finally, he is Paul's successor in Margot's amours.

The world of unreason itself is peopled by figures embodying

E   65

various of its aspects: Fagan the impostor, Philbrick the impersonator, Grimes the life-force, Prendergast the personification of fundamental doubt, and finally, Lucas-Dockery, the personification of that even more corroding element, fundamental
rational optimism. Fagan presides over Paul's two changes of
personality – as Dr Fagan ('Esq., Ph.D.'), proprietor and headmaster of Llanabba School, and as Augustus Fagan ('M.D.'),
proprietor and director of Cliff Place, Worthing, 'High-Class
Nursing and Private Sanatorium'. Philbrick receives him as a
butler to Llanabba (' "Yes," said the butler, "I know all about
you" '), and later as 'reception bath cleaner' supervising the
transformation of citizen into convict at Blackstone Gaol
(' "Thought I'd be seeing you soon," he said'). Grimes is the
life-force, hunted, and constantly escaping from the domesticity
of the home and the regimentation of the prison, an agent of
catalysis fostering Paul's love for Margot (as in the dialogue
after the school sports); while Prendergast, in every respect the
antithesis of Grimes – Prendergast always in Doubt, Grimes
always in the Soup – exhibits as a deterrent the basic anarchy
which breaks in when firm beliefs are corroded. The theological
student is being invited to savour the vitality of life, and to contemplate the necessity of faith; Grimes is a shadow figure of the
natural man, Prendergast of the spiritual man.

So Fagan as the magician Merlin (this is especially evident in
his physical description), Philbrick as Charon, Grimes as a kind
of Loki, and Prendergast as the unhappy shade from the comfortable world of chintz curtains in the rectory drawing-room,
are the inhabitants of Paul's dream world. And in their various
capacities these shadow figures preside over or accompany the
various metamorphoses suffered by the comparatively passive
hero. Philbrick, Grimes and Paul disappear in rapid succession
and for various adequate reasons from Llanabba. Grimes reappears at King's Thursday as soon as Paul has, in his night of
love with Margot ('Pervigilium Veneris') paid his tribute to the
life-force. And the same three are in the end spirited away from
prison, Grimes to continue his immortal adventures, Philbrick to
return to his accustomed affluence, and Paul to face again Scone

and ordination. Prendergast also makes his exit – but for him is reserved a signal fate at the hands of a blood-crazed inmate of Blackstone Gaol. And here, at this first example of a series of painful deaths (Prudence in *Black Mischief*, Fausta in *Helena*) which have distressed critics in all Mr Waugh's books, we must understand the fundamentally fantastic nature of his writing, or close the book in incomprehension.

The mask of the social satirist in Mr Waugh only partly conceals the features of the moralist. In human affairs, whether moral and religious or purely social and secular, there is a certain order, which, whatever its origins, cannot be disturbed with impunity. Disorder may, however, originate as much with the rationalist as with the lunatic – Mr Waugh would no doubt agree with the view of Chesterton that the lunatic is a man who has lost, not his reason, but everything except his reason. Here it is Lucas-Dockery, with his rationalist dogmatism, who bears the responsibility for unleashing the force which destroys Prendergast. And yet events cannot deny their Providential origin, though in such cases it is a queer, distorted, grotesque view of Providence which emerges. At the surface level the episode of the murder of Prendergast is a satire on the loss of fundamental sanity in Church and State: on the Modern Churchman who 'draws the full salary of a beneficed clergyman and need not commit himself to any religious belief', and on the officer of the Executive who believes that 'almost all crime is due to the repressed desire for aesthetic expression'. But the link between these two is the carpenter, who, in his blood-crazed mind, sees himself as 'the sword of Israel', and smites the Philistine in the name of the Lord of Hosts. With such rational lunacy prevalent in Church and State, Providence itself, in its divine task, can only go about its business in a grotesque fashion.

And yet, in this dream world, it is not for the abstract demonstration of a principle of order that Prendergast dies, but for the concrete benefit of the hero Paul. So the laying of the ghost of incipient generalized doubt, that perennial problem of the student of theology, is finally made manifest when in the end Paul reflects how right the Church has been to condemn the

67

second century heretical Bishop, who denied almost all the fundamentals of Christianity, and to suppress the ascetic Ebionites who turned towards Jerusalem when they prayed. Prendergast has not died in vain.

Last among the major figures of Paul's dream world is Margot. Elegant, attractive, and rich, she is an appropriate dream-figure, an *anima*, for any theological student, or for that matter the appropriate *dea ex machina* for anyone's desire for 'sudden elevation from schoolmaster to millionaire'. In her relation with her own son, Peter Pastmaster, she is timeless, and defies the succession of the generations; she has something of the andro-gynous nature of the brother-sister pairs in later Waugh books. Most important of all, she appears as sinless – there is no guilt in the unconscious, but only liberation or frustration. And so Paul comes to the conclusion that, since he is a visitor and no denizen of the dreamworld, there is no meeting ground between him and her where normal morality applies. Judged morally, his action in going to prison for her had been chivalrous, but sense-less, since it protected her from the consequences of her own crimes. Judged personally, as a matter of Boy Scout honour, she had jolly well let him down. She is the feminine aspect of the life-force which is Grimes. 'It was impossible to imprison the Margot who had committed the crime.' Grimes suffered con-striction both at Llanabba and at Egdon Heath, and made his escape; Margot made an incursion into both these worlds with the specific purpose of liberating Paul, for whom, being only a mortal and no original expression of the life-force, stone walls do indeed (apart from such interventions) a prison make.

There is no need to adopt the presumably callow views of the undergraduate Stiggins, reading a paper to the O.S.C.U. on 'Sex Repression and Religious Experience', to see the relation-ship in this book between the vital and the spiritual fields, and the extent to which the release of repression in both spheres is the passport to new experiences of the mind. The capacity shown by Fagan, Grimes, and Philbrick for becoming involved with the opposite sex are uncomplicated and, on their more burlesque level, overshadowed by the problems of domesticity. For Paul, this sphere is both more fundamental and more liberating. The irrational world twice draws Paul into its sphere by the imputation of indecent behaviour: once when he is debagged by the Bollinger, and again when he is involved in the activities of the Latin-American Entertainment Co. Ltd. But in each case the imputation of an unreal guilt is the key to an experience of real value. His 'indecent behaviour' leads him to Llanabba, where he learns (both in relation to his own qualifications, and in the problem of dealing with the boys), Life Lesson No. 1, to 'temper discretion with deceit'. The imputed crime of white slave trafficking gains him entry to Blackstone Gaol, where, through quiet reflection on his relations with Margot, he learns Life Lesson No. 2, that 'there was something radically inapplicable about the whole code of ready-made honour . . . of the Englishman all the world over.' The rigid moral code has suffered shipwreck in his mind – in that shadow sphere of learning which is the English public school, and in that shadow of Society which is the English prison. (Appropriately enough these are both institutions in which, in the view of the community, right thinking and moral principles are instilled.) Potts, that alter ego of Paul at Scone, who plays the role of the shadowing Censor (on behalf of the League of Nations) throughout the King's Thursday sequence – Potts, whose abstract interest in schools, brothels, and prisons and all 'progressive' matters accompanies Paul's real, if only imaginative experience of them, is laid to rest with Prendergast. The rigid moral code engenders general doubt, Potts conjures up Prendergast; true belief drives out both.

True, the Paul Pennyfeather of the Prelude seems to have emerged almost unchanged from his Ordeal by Life. The Potts of his earlier existence is succeeded by another monosyllabic name in Stubbs, a theological student with whom Paul goes through the identical motions of joining the League of Nations Union and the O.S.C.U., and of prison-visiting. The recurrent dinner of the Bollinger, celebrating in Peter Pastmaster's rooms as they did once in Alastair Digby-Vane-Trumpington's, brings Paul a visit from his former pupil, once almost his stepson, during which the world of people is neatly – though a little Teutonically – divided into those who are static and those who are dynamic. 'You're dynamic, I'm static,' said Paul Penny-feather to his counterpart Peter Pastmaster. Paul seems finally to have thrown in his lot with Scone and the Church – a Church now preserved from the dry-rot of Prendergast's universal doubt – rather than with the various aspects of change brought about by the Modern Age – the letting of Llanabba, with its combination of medieval and Georgian, to a cinema company, the rebuilding of the pure domestic Tudor of King's Thursday in the functional style ('something clean and square', as Margot said), the adaptation of Blackstone Gaol to the spirit of the time working through Lucas-Dockery. But the static romanticism of Paul's mental picture of King's Thursday before he came upon its horrid reality ('"English spring," thought Paul, "In the dreaming ancestral beauty of the English country",') is only one side of a complex personality which is basically as much in flux as these more superficial manifestations of change. The extremes of rational doubt and of rational dogmatism have indeed been eliminated by the simple and efficacious process of being fused and consumed in the white-hot flame of their joint lunacy. But, within those extremes, who shall say that Grimes, Philbrick, and Fagan, and the androgynous pair Margot and Peter, will not once again find entry into the spiritual world of Paul Pennyfeather?

Vile Bodies appeared in 1930. It was and has since again been hailed as the brilliant epitome of a decade just over, and a har-binger of one just beginning. Mr Waugh appears here, even more than in *Decline and Fall*, which was both more personal and more timeless, as the chronicler and satirist, or even, as has often been said, as the laureate of the gay twenties. The laureate be it noted not of the solemn twenties of Locarno and Geneva or, except by implication, of the grim twenties of the General Strike, but of that small yet highly vocal Mayfair set which became known throughout the popular press of the capital as the Bright Young People. They seemed to sum up the twenties, as the aesthetic movement had seemed to sum up post-war Oxford, and as a small group of left-wing poets (the expression is Mr Waugh's) 'ganged up and captured the decade' that followed. No one doubts that decades cannot thus be captured, and that the illusion that they can is due to a trick of historical perspective. But the work of the satirist is to register, like a seismograph, the initial shock—it is for others much later to measure how much the rocks have shifted.

It is remarkable with what fidelity Mr Waugh has, with the needle of his incisive style, traced the outline of the social disturbance which was then taking its rather hectic course between Bond Street and Park Lane. Anyone curious enough to dip into contemporary memoirs, such as Patrick Balfour's *Society Racket*, will find the original raw material of this change, the instrument readings and day-to-day recordings, so to speak, of the breaking down of the taboos and traditional barriers of English social life. For the Bright Young People are not alone in this book. They are only the Younger Generation, whose doings, when raised as a topic of conversation at the Anchorage House gatherings, among their elders and betters, 'spread through the company like a yawn'. But they reflect in their lives and affairs all the social problems of the 'Society Racket': the attempt by the newly rich society of the Archie Schwerts to gatecrash the barriers of the old; the degeneracy of the offspring of the older generation of Balcairns, Throbbings, Blackwaters, and Chasms; the eccentricity of Colonel Blount, who, in letting out Doubting Hall to the Wonderfilm Company of Great Britain, puts on the biggest charade of the whole book; the hectic activities of the Bright Young People themselves, their parties, disguises, slang, imitation Cockney, love affairs, and their refusal to take themselves or anyone else seriously; their exploitation, as gossip-writers and impecunious patrons, by editors of newspapers and owners of restaurants, pandering to the insatiable social curiosity of middle-class readers; the uncertain demarcation of public and private life in the world of entertainment, and the mixed welcome accorded to a notorious gossip-writer; even the uncertainty about the identity of one's own guests, the gatecrashers, the lawsuits, the permitted and non-permitted lists, the system of payment for information from venial servants, out for their pickings.

All these things the socially curious reader will find sketched in with the lightest of acid points. He may even be amused to draw parallels to the activities of known persons. Lord Kinross (Patrick Balfour) asserts that Lady Eleanor Smith – the sister of Lord Birkenhead – and the two Jungmann sisters were the first 'Bright Young People' before the term became current. Lord Birkenhead, in a memoir of his sister, mentions her writing for a newspaper a series of 'startling comparisons, written and pictorial, between great Englishmen of the past and the contemporary representatives of their line.' This has become, in *Vile Bodies*, Mr Chatterbox's series of gossip-paragraphs on 'Titled Eccentrics'.

It is the age of promiscuity which announces itself in these pages, and the symbol of social promiscuity is the party. The decline and fall of English social institutions is, indeed, here mirrored in a series of parties, each appropriate to a different milieu. The old brigade, still maintaining its frowstiness and its distance, musters at Anchorage House, the Bright Young People flock to Archie Schwert. Alone among Mayfair hostesses, Margot Metroland can invite both sets and get away with it; her party for Mrs Ape is a highlight of the book. Significantly, at the gatherings paid for by Archie Schwert, or by Miss Moss, with futuristic invitations by Johnnie Hoop, class livery is thrown overboard with class distinctions, and fancy dress becomes the rage. '. . . the chief artistic product of the twenties, when all is said and done,' states our guide Patrick Balfour, 'was the fancy-dress party.' In the much-quoted words of the novelist and his hero Adam: ' "Oh, Nina, *what a lot of parties*." – (. . . Masked parties, Savage parties, Victorian parties, Greek parties, Wild West parties, Russian parties . . . all that succession and repetition of massed humanity. . . . Those vile bodies . . .).' As a courtly literature will find its apotheosis in the court, the picaresque its natural setting in the thieves' kitchen, and as some woman novelists are said to make everything happen round the tea-table in the Vicarage garden, so *Vile Bodies* is the apotheosis of the party, preserved, so to speak, in the acid spirit of the author's satire, like something both curious and short-lived.

Into the lightest of narratives, or rather into a kaleidoscope of scenes loosely associated with Adam's efforts to earn, borrow or win by chance, skill or sleight of hand, enough money to redeem honourably his engagement to marry Nina Blount, Mr Waugh has woven certain contemporary phenomena, and some minor themes representing his own preoccupations at the time. There is Mrs Melrose Ape (Aimée Macpherson, the American Revivalist) attended by her Angels (with their distinctly 'worn wings' as one of them declares at the Customs), and prepared to carry all before her to the strains of 'There ain't no flies on the Lamb of God'. There is a hard-hearted publisher, straight out of Dickens, whom we shall meet again in *Put out more Flags*. And there is an omniscient and incessantly active Jesuit, Father Rothschild, who can only be described, in the idiom of the book, as 'too, too bogus'.

The total effect is one of crazy inconsequence, like Colonel Blount's film of the life of Wesley (though at no stage is the spool put in wrongly, so that the action positively goes backwards), or like the vision of the English countryside presented to the terrified eyes of Miss Runcible at the wheel of racing-car No. 13 (too sick-making). Straight descriptions of parties, a race-meeting, and of accidental deaths and not so accidental hangovers are interspersed with passages where the wandering film camera picks up snatches of dialogue from one person or group after another; a bad Channel crossing becomes thereby even more ill-making, and Lady Metroland's party for Mrs Ape even more shaming. Everywhere pastiche keeps raising its irrepressible head, as in the constant intrusions of the language of the gossip-column, the superbly bogus conversations between middle-class matrons in a train to Aylesbury, and the stream of technical commentary overheard in the pits at the motor-race. The whole produces a patchwork impression which conceals the cunning with which the pasteboard figures have been mounted. It might well have been one of the Wonderfilm Company's more flighty scenarios: 'Subject, the Naughty Twenties. Actors, the Bright Young People. Continuity (if any), Mr Evelyn Waugh.' And, when reading Chapter Eleven, which consists entirely of staccato telephone exchanges between Nina and Adam on the perennial subject of their marriage (' "We aren't going to be married today?" – "No." – "I see." – "Well?" – "I said, I see." – "Is that all?" . . .'), we are reminded of Mr Isaacs' principle: 'A hundred feet or so of galloping horses is always useful.' The freshness with which it all comes over to the reader after a generation has elapsed is a tribute to the author's power of registering, heightening, and speeding up the contemporary scene so that there is none of that slight yellowing of the edges which marks the period piece. There are passages which have a Wodehouse ring, but the genuine Waugh sting is in the tail. Thus, when Chapter Four opens:

'At Archie Schwert's party the fifteenth Marquess Vanburgh, Earl Vanburgh de Brendon, Baron Brendon, Lord of the Five Isles and Hereditary Grand Falconer to the Kingdom of Connaught, said to the Eighth Earl of Balcairn, Viscount Erdinge, Baron Cairn of Balcairn, Red Knight of Lancaster, Count of the Holy Roman Empire, and Chenonceaux Herald to the Duchy of Aquitaine, "Hullo," he said.'

we are in the world of Bertie Wooster and Lord Blandings of Blandings Castle; but the next two lines:

' "Isn't this a repulsive party? What are you going to say about it?" for they were both of them, as it happened, gossip writers for the daily papers'

bring us back to the less innocent world of bottle-parties and one-room flatlets.

It is, in fact, a doomed world, not one perennially rejuvenated by the approach of the London publishing season, as was the analogous world of the Drones Club. And there are some who have written disapprovingly of *Vile Bodies* being 'rich in unregarded death'. Death certainly, but hardly unregarded. For sudden, unanticipated death is part of the hectic undertone of this whole series of events, and claims its victims in a gradually increasing crescendo of painfulness: Florrie, the kept ex-chorus girl ('Miss Florence Ducane, of independent means . . . and well known in business circles'), Balcairn, the failed gossip-writer (the last Earl, who put his head into a gas-oven and was thus gathered to his fathers who had fallen at Acre and Agincourt), and, finally and most poignantly, Miss Runcible ('the Hon. Agatha Runcible' . . . 'Society Beauty' . . . 'Lord Chasm's lovely daughter'). But the chandelier, the gas-oven and the gramophone records played in a nursing home, the lethal properties in this modern Grand Guignol, are as much a feature of the party as the hangover, that 'ninetyish feeling', when 'the momentary illusion of well-being and exhilaration gives place to melancholy, indigestion and moral decay'. 'Death at the Party' is as much the theme of this novel as of any detective novel, and more so in one sense than the smart jargon and the dressing up in Hawaiian costume.

In the book as a whole the hangover precedes the party as well as following it; events are preluded by that most 'spirit-crushing' of all experiences, a rough Channel crossing, and the 'too shaming' episode at the Customs, when Miss Runcible ('who had been mistaken for a well-known jewel smuggler') is stripped and searched, and Adam loses his autobiography (' "that's just downright dirt, and we burns that straight away, see" '). As before and after in Mr Waugh's work, a case of mistaken identity and imputed bawdiness heralds a frightening plunge into the world of unreason.

The character of Adam has been regarded as a dress rehearsal for the notorious cad of later works, Basil Seal. But this is to see him from the end of the book, the selling of Nina to Ginger, and the Great Christmas Imposture at Doubting Hall. Initially, and for most of the book, Adam, about whose first appearance 'there was nothing particularly remarkable' – certainly nothing to attract the attention of a Mr Chatterbox – is distinguished more by his innocence and passivity than by an overt caddishness. He is more a Paul Pennyfeather than a Basil Seal; and even Paul, though more inexperienced than Adam in the world of Venus, soon learnt to temper discretion with deceit at Llanabba. In spite of the fact that, if we may leap the years, the selling of Nina is as blatant a piece of sordid traffic as Basil's exploits with the Connolly kids and the selling of Doris (in *Put out more Flags*), there is about Christmas in Doubting Hall, with its nostalgic evocation of childhood and Peace on Earth and Goodwill towards those below stairs, an atmosphere of whimsical pathos which altogether cancels out the hurt to Ginger. In a book replete with impersonation, this, of Ginger by Adam, is the most affecting; only through a stealthy impersonation of childhood may happiness, in this state of society, be achieved even for a short while. Throughout Mr Waugh's works, the passive, rather melancholy and isolated central figure will lose his first love, his *Beata Beatrix*, to the coarse-grained knight-robber of worldly success. Paul relinquishes Margot to Metroland, Adam can only share Nina by trickery with Ginger, whose one thought on his honeymoon was of a 'top-hole little place near Monte with a decent nine-hole golf course'; Charles Ryder has to possess Julia after the barbarian Rex Mottram, and Guy Crouchback is cut out in Virginia's instable affections by the Guardsman Tommy Backhouse. Only William Boot, of all those who try for the crock of gold at the end of the rainbow, loses the girl but makes the grade. But he was the protégé of Mr Baldwin whereas Adam has only the elusive and red-faced drunken Major as his fairy godfather. And Nina and Adam are too much alike in their pain and their tenderness, their futile squabbling and un-premeditated snatches at love and at happiness, for the excite-ment of physical possession to open up for the hero, even tem-porarily, a new world of experience and of truth – as happened when Paul was made free of Margot, and Charles Ryder of Julia.

The book ends – and how otherwise could it end? – in whole-sale dispersion: the individual dispersion of the Bright Young People, preceded by Agatha, roaring up the black road of her delirium, and the general dispersion brought about by the great new but unnamed war, breaking in on, shattering the surrepti-tiously filched bliss of Christmas night in the family circle. The last two scenes are each accompanied by a touch of savage irony. At Doubting Hall on Christmas Night, the message of the waits, 'Oh, tidings of comfort and joy', is followed closely by the Rector bursting in with the news that war has been declared. The scene of desolation on 'the biggest battlefield in the history of the world' is entitled 'Happy Ending'.

Mr Waugh made in all three journeys to Abyssinia – the first for the Coronation in 1930, and the second and third for the war in 1935–6. 'My problem has been to distill comedy and sometimes tragedy from the knockabout farce of people's outward behaviour.' The comedy distilled from these Abyssinian experiences took shape in two novels: *Black Mischief*, which is based more or less on *Remote People*; and *Scoop*, which draws largely on the raw material of *Waugh in Abyssinia*.

Azania – 'a large, imaginary island off the East Coast of Africa, in character and history a combination of Zanzibar and Abyssinia' – is the setting for Mr Waugh's first fantasy of barbarism, a tragi-comic portrayal of a conflict of cultures, a foretaste both of the poignancy of *A Handful of Dust* and the comedy of *Scoop*. Settled in its coastal strip by the Portuguese and then, for centuries, by the Arabs, conquered by Amurath, 'a slave's son, sturdy, bow-legged, three-quarters Negro', at a time when the decaying power of the Sultan had almost led to protection by European powers, by Amurath turned into an Empire and given an inland capital, a railway, an aristocracy and a sketchy administration, Azania is just emerging from total barbarism into an era of fitful and uncertain acceptance of Western European institutions. Seth, grandson of Amurath, Chief of the Chiefs of the indigenous Sakuyu and Wanda peoples and Bachelor of Arts of Oxford University, is the symbol of this impact of sophistication on primitivism. He is a lonely and frightened young man in whom a naive belief in the Future, in Progress and the New Age, and a determination to modernize the country at all costs ('I'll hang any man I see barefooted') struggles tensely with 'the inherited terror of the jungle', and 'the acquired loneliness of civilization'.

As the book opens, an insurrection by Seyid, Seth's uncle and

77

pretender to the Imperial honours, is put down with the primitive weapons of lies from the leadership and the long spears of the warriors. In the moment of success, Seth's imagination becomes suddenly swollen like a volcanic lake receiving the irruption of unsuspected subterranean streams. 'The earnest and rather puzzled young man became suddenly capricious and volatile; ideas bubbled up within him, bearing to the surface a confused sediment of phrase and theory, scraps of learning half understood and fantastically translated.' So he orders a programme of radical and partly self-contradictory reforms – town-planning from Paris, a Museum and penal reform, clothes from Europe, Nacktkultur from Berlin. The final stages in this progressive dementation of a ruler can be summed up in three words: boots, birth-control, and banknotes. The boots, for the Army, are foisted on the unwilling General Connolly, soldier of fortune, and Commander-in-Chief. Birth-control alienates the sympathies of the established though heretical form of the Christian religion, and of its supreme head, the Nestorian patriarch. The introduction of paper-money, whose most prominent feature is 'a large medallion portrait of Seth in top hat and European tail coat', completes the collapse of public confidence in the Government. *Quem deus perdere vult, prius dementat*; so the story deals with the elevation, headlong career, and final miserable end of Seth, the Apostle of Progress to the variegated and barbaric peoples of his Azanian Empire.

In this, his One-Year Plan for national confusion, he is aided and, until the pace becomes too hot, also abetted by his Minister of Modernization. The Ministry is a mushroom growth which gradually insinuates itself into all Departments of State except those of the Nestorian patriarch and the Commander-in-Chief; the Minister is the Mayfair adventurer who, from this work onwards, makes his 'insolent, sulky, and curiously childish' way through many of Mr Waugh's novels – Basil Seal. It is worth quoting the first description ever given of this memorable character:

'He stood in the doorway, a glass of whisky in one hand, looking insolently round the room, his head back, chin forward, shoulders rounded, dark hair over his forehead, contemptuous grey eyes over grey pouches, a proud rather childish mouth, a scar on one cheek.

"My word, he is a corker," remarked one of the girls.'

One chapter gives his whole background: the Alastair Trumpington drinking set, his fond and ever-disappointed mother, Lady Seal, his late father, the eminently respectable Sir Christopher Seal, Chief Conservative Whip for twenty-five years, his peculiar relationship with his sister, Barbara Sothill, and his more straightforward one with Mrs Angela Lyne; his drinking rackets, his dissoluteness, consistent financial embarrassment relieved by loan, guile or plain thieving, his charm, great gifts, and total unreliability, the ruthlessness with which he pursues any object which at the moment seems desirable. While Seth, at his College, was 'an undergraduate of no account . . . amiably classed among Bengali babus, Siamese, and grammar school scholars as one of the remote and praiseworthy people who had come a long way to the University', Basil enjoyed a reputation in which brilliance and dissipation were almost equally balanced, and thus became, for Seth, 'the personification of all that glittering, intangible Western culture to which he aspired'. Small wonder, then, that these two joined forces to wheedle, hector, and bully their way through the knotted undergrowth of uncomprehending, primitive ways of thought.

To a ground of primitive savagery, with a superimposed veneer of rootless Western culture, is added a study in Western civilized futility – the British Envoy, Sir Samson Courteney, a diplomatic failure and ineffectual potterer, whose requirements of life are amiable and childish (knitting, party games, and false noses), while those of Basil are vicious and childish; his wife, Lady Courteney, whose incessant preoccupation with the creation of a luxurious English garden in the ground of the Legation is as pointless as Seth's schemes and as devoid of human compassion as the surrounding jungle; and their only daughter, Prudence, who fills in a life of complete boredom with unceasing erotic imaginings (fully satisfied after the arrival of Basil), and the compilation of an adolescent 'Panorama of Life' in which savagery joins with incompetence to write a grotesque and tragic last chapter. The diplomatic scene is completed, apart from some shadowy Americans, by M. Ballon, the French Envoy, a conventionalized stage Frenchman whose stock reactions ('he was keeping his last cartridge for Madame Ballon'), Masonic convictions and penchant for intrigue provide a hilarious contrast to Sir Samson ('I dare say it'll all blow over, you know'), and the support required by the faction which overthrows Seth.

The contrast and interaction of these three elements is developed in eight concise and carefully balanced chapters which lead to the dénouement with the consistency of a dramatic action. Just before this point, by an admirable technical device, Mr Waugh introduces a new major comic figure, Dame Mildred Porch (with her English companion), travelling with the humane object of preventing cruelty to animals. The intention is to bring about a pause in the dramatic conflict, but also to devise a totally new and superbly guileless spectator, through whose eyes the *coup d'état* of Chapter Six is reported.

Not that there is any genuine substance to the dramatic conflict; this is a tragi-comic fantasy on the theme of the conflict of cultures, not a fictionalized essay on colonialism, or a romance of love in a hot climate. The heavy ground swell of primitive savagery carries all the more superficial flotsam and jetsam of Western civilization, the fragments of a hurried and short-winded 'modernization' along with it, and the final descent into chaos is but the breaking through of forces which are present at the beginning. The keynotes of this state of primitive savagery are few and unmistakable: murder and rapine, feasting on raw flesh, beef or camel, if that of a human enemy is not available, and procreation, which, in the leaders and chiefs of the race, takes on heroic dimensions. The vital urges accept and swallow up all tendencies towards 'progressive' amelioration: the boots purveyed by Youkoumian to the Ministry and issued to Connolly's native levies are taken for extra rations and eaten, before an open clash with the Minister can develop; the Pageant of

Birth Control owes its nation-wide appeal to the belief that it is the Emperor's own personal magic for unlimited fecundity, long before the procession is broken up by the strong young men of Nestorian Christian Action; the feeble efforts of Dame Mildred Porch to prevent cruelty to 'dumb chums' are swallowed up in a roar of delight at the assumption that the experienced Europeans have sent emissaries to instruct the poor retarded natives in new ways of being cruel to animals. In the face of these irresistible trends towards a lower order of existence, the *coup d'état* engineered by the disgruntled elements in this ramshackle order has no proper substance, as, in the outcome, through the death of its pretender, it has no point.

The omnipresence of these vital and unregenerate instincts is indicated by subtle and consistent touches: the casual reference to hangings for small demeanours; the recurrent appearance of gangs of convicts, chained neck to neck, on road work; the constant throb of the drums, and the backward glances to where, 'in the sodden depths of the forest, the wild beasts hunted, shunning the light'; the repeated hinting at foul practices on the enemy's body. A symbol of the invincibility of degrading inertia is the wrecked motor-car which, abandoned by its Arab driver, lies rusting, stripped of parts, its tyres eaten by white ants, turned into a habitation by a Sakuyu family, blocking the new motor-road between Matodi and the terminus of the railway to Debra Dowa. Five times it is mentioned at points in the narrative, and at the end its existence and legal irremovability is confirmed by the British Administration of the Protectorate as an example of British justice. It is in this context of recurrent reminders of barbarism that one must see the grotesque climax to the affair of Prudence and Basil, when the drink-sodden old headman at Seth's funeral feast draws across his glistening pate the beret of pillar-box red which Basil had last seen in the Legation grounds, and, in answer to his frantic questions, raises his head – ' "The white woman? Why, here," he patted his distended stomach. "You and I and the big chiefs – we have just eaten her".'

In *Black Mischief* we first find fully operative that skill in subtle structural pattern which, through repetition, contrast and counterpoint, conveys almost as much of the sense, and certainly more of the atmosphere, than the explicit narrative of events. Constantly recurring themes are the Arabs, grave, impoverished but unimpressed, chewing their ghat and discussing very old errors of litigation; Youkoumian, the egregious Armenian, with his 'I don't want no bust-ups'; the fatuous comments and childish amusements of Sir Samson; the azaleas, herbaceous border and lily-pond of Lady Courtney; and the beret of pillar-box red and amorous desires ('I've got a whole lot of new ideas for us to try') of their daughter. While 'sixty miles southward in the Ukaka pass bloody bands of Sakuyu warriors played hide-and-seek among the rocks chivvying the last fugitives of the army of Seyid' – afternoon tea was afoot at the British Legation, with a hubbub of conversation laced with the opening words 'More tea, Bishop?' Basil's amorous endearments ('"You're a grand girl, Prudence, and I'd like to eat you!" "So you shall, my sweet . . . anything you want".') and Prudence's schoolgirl anticipation of life in London, at Aunt Harriet's house in Belgrave Place, are a poignant and ironic anticipation of what the sodden jungle has in store for her. The onslaught of the rains itself on the last day of life in the Legation, steeping the later events in the Wanda country in a dank and hopeless miasma, is itself an effective association of natural and human events.

The repetition of a theme at the beginning and end of a recognizable sequence can produce a circular movement expressive of changelessness and – ultimately – of futility. The Empire of Azania, founded by Amurath the Great, and subsisting fitfully till the ignoble death of his grandson Seth, is framed within recurrent motifs so as to appear but a passing and futile interlude. The last scene, on the Matodi waterfront, renews the situation of the first. Then, as now, Arab gentlemen sauntered by the sea-wall and gossiped in coffee-houses, pausing reverently at the call of the muezzin. Then groups of Wanda and Sakuyu extended their settlement and depredations to outlying estates, public order was in decay, and 'the European powers watched their opportunity to proclaim a Protectorate'; now under the aegis of French and British warships this has been done, British policemen march two abreast through the involved ways of the native quarter, and the strains of Gilbert and Sullivan are heard from the Portuguese fort. The reign of Seth itself is marked at its beginning and in its end by the death of a pretender – Seth's father Seyid and his uncle, Achon – and by the strangling of an unfaithful servant – Ali, the treacherous Indian secretary, and Boaz, poisoner of his master Seth. Both are done to death by the same Joab, officer of the Imperial Guard.

Against this background of surface change without final hope of improvement, two figures stand out as belonging to another world: Basil Seal and Youkoumian. Jointly they exploit the chaos of Seth's short and ill-fated régime. Severally they decamp and seek new pastures: Seal to precipitate further chaos in the Mayfair set of the author's imagination; Youkoumian, a figure of irrepressible vitality and another Captain Grimes, to play an indispensable part in the Anglo-Indian Society of the Azanian Protectorate:

' "Useful little fellow, Youkoumian. I use him a lot. He's getting me boots for the levy."

"Good show."

"Quite." '

Scoop depicts some of the more incredible activities of the international group of journalists planted for the war in Addis Ababa by their respective employers, set against an international backcloth of the rival ideologies of Communism and Fascism. For the reader who knows his *Waugh in Abyssinia* there is much interest in tracing the process of imaginative alchemy by which the farcical war became the wartime farce. There is the same preposterous heap of equipment acquired at the tropical outfitters (with the addition, in *Scoop*, of that martial globetrotter General Cruttwell, F.R.S.). There is the same grotesque language of cables, partly a professional jargon, partly a measure of economy. Boot, in answer to an inquiry on the defences of Aden, cables: 'Aden unwarwise'; Waugh, in answer to a groundless atrocity story, cables: 'Nurse unupblown'. The curious can also find in the travel book the models of the Hotel Liberty at Jacksonville, the Pension Dressler and its proprietress, Popotakis's Ping-pong saloon, of Pappenhacker of the *Daily Twopence*, and of the Director of the Press Bureau, and the meeting of the Foreign Press Association is almost straightforward reporting. The abortive civil war in Ishmaelia, which is the apotheosis of the reporter Boot, is an amalgam of the more improbable aspects of Addis Ababa, the oil concession negotiated by Mr Rickett, and the well-known shibboleths of Nazi and Communist political patter; a flavour of Liberia and the Baptist-educated American negro completes the air of unreality and opera buffa.

Books One and Three contrast the mutually exclusive worlds of Copper House and Boot Magna Hall, and enclose Book Two, in which William, the Knight from Boot Magna (a Stately Home with more than a hint of Miss Stella Gibbons's Cold Comfort Farm), meets and conquers the hazards of the world of Copper House. William Boot is the innocent from the country, pitchforked into a new and frightening world, stripped of his clothes (as Paul Pennyfeather is debagged) and welcomed by a page-boy 'with a face of ageless evil'. A double mistake, if we may believe the author, one of those accidents through which the world of unreason stretches out a long arm towards the innocent hero. By an error of identity, William Boot, rather than John Boot, a distant cousin, was summoned to London when Lord Copper wanted someone to cover events in Ishmaelia for *The Beast*. The unsuspecting William, who felt that his sister Priscilla, in playfully substituting 'great-crested grebe' for 'badger' throughout an MS. of a recent article on 'Lush Places', had placed him in the wrong towards his numerous readers, was inclined to accept the summons to London in an attempt to clear his good name.

But has there really been a mistake? The switch from John Boot the successful novelist to William Boot the country squire may well reflect the author's own first feeling of strangeness when summoned from a country house in Westmeath in 1930 to cover the Coronation in Abyssinia (*Remote People*, p. 13). And,

in the event, both Boots achieve the success of their dreams.
William, the amateur journalist, scoops a world-exclusive story
when all his professional rivals are out of the running ('Every
item of news became known to us all simultaneously,' reports
Mr Waugh from Dessye, 'there was no hope of a scoop; the
wireless station remained blandly obstructive') and a life contract with a wealthy Corporation. John, the novelist, through a
reverse mistake of identity, lands a title. Mr Waugh has done
himself proud in both his public roles.

But there is really no need to bring in the author to see that
William himself is not entirely without responsibility for the
summons to London. He has given a hostage to fortune in the
dimension in which fortune acts with whimsical lack of conse-
quence, in the sphere of the day-dreaming imagination. Has he
not become a journalist on taking over the newspaper column
'Lush Places' from the late Rector of Boot Magna? 'Lord
Copper expects his staff to work wherever the best interests of
the paper call them', urges the loyal Salter; and no one can
deny that it was ultimately in the best interests of *The Beast* to
send Boot to Ishmaelia. But even when Salter asks in despair:
'"Is there *nothing* you want?"' and William answers: '"D'you
know, I don't believe there is. Except to keep my job in Lush
Places and go on living at home"' – he was not being entirely
frank. He had hidden 'the remote and secret ambition of fifteen
years or more. He did, very deeply, long to go up in an aero-
plane'. Does not fortune conspire, through the name of Boot and
the hand of Priscilla, to fulfil this secret ambition?

But fortune does not remove her hand from William. His
secret wish has been heard and his unexpressed romanticism is
to be requited in appropriate coin. Arrived in Ishmaelia he is
for the moment indistinguishable from his fellow journalists in
all except his ignorance of newspaper conventions and the costly
chattiness of his cables. Three persons open for him the magic
door to success: Jack Bannister, Kätchen, and Mr Baldwin. The
concealed struggle in Ishmaelia is between three parties: the
real and mysterious owner of the mineral rights, the Germans
who attempt to filch them, and the Russians who try to forestall

the Germans. Bannister, the Vice-Consul, first puts him wise on the strength of early school association (shades of the public school man Grimes) to the existence of the Soviet agent and the non-existence of Laku, to which almost all his colleagues are decoyed by the scheming Dr Benito. His melancholy and thwarted love for Kätchen brings him 'Stones £20' and, with this, further fragmentary insight into a confused situation. And through her William joins up with the unconscious springs of mythical action: 'For twenty-three years he had remained celibate and heart-whole; landbound. Now for the first time he was far from shore, submerged among deep waters . . . where monstrous things . . . passed silently in submarine twilight. A lush place.' Everything is in the balance. A series of cables of mounting irascibility arrive from Copper House, ending with the peremptory words: CONTINUE CABLING VICTORIES UNTIL FURTHER NOTICE (truer words than was imagined when they were sent). The rains are drawing to an end and the Russian plot is ripe to burst. It is the moment of William's and Kätchen's closest association.

'Next morning William awoke in a new world.' The rains were over, the dank weeds in crimson flower, a tropical sun blazed in the sky, and a vast sunlit landscape had come into being around the town overnight. The forces of right are gathering. William sends his first 'scoop' cable, on information provided by Kätchen, in spite of having just received another from London giving him the sack. Disclosure leads to further disclosure and he returns from the Legation garden-party with a mission – 'he was going to do down Benito. Dimly at first, then in vivid detail, he foresaw a spectacular, cinematographic consummation, when his country should rise chivalrously in arms; Bengal Lancers and kilted highlanders invested the heights of Jacksonburg. . . .' Lush Places have served their purpose, but alone they are not enough. Kätchen and her German husband – suddenly arrived in flight from the interior – leave with William's boat. The Communists begin to take over, and William is left to face the music alone, at the source, but helpless and without communications. In this extremity he sends up a plaint to the great-crested grebe, cause of all his present trouble: '"maligned fowl, have I not expiated the wrong my sister did you; am I still to be an exile from the green places of my heart? Was there not even in the remorseless dooms of antiquity a god from the machine?"' In answer there appears the implored god from the flying-machine, and solves all William's problems: Mr Baldwin lands delicately with his parachute on the tin roof and requests a ladder courteously in five languages. All is now in the hands of the gods, and of their fortune-child William. From the sky, the object of his secret wish, comes his reward. The romanticism of Lush Places has yielded for the moment to the glamour of the High Places. William's good turn, in transporting him to Paris in *his* plane, is now to be requited, as Mr Baldwin foresaw with the clear vision of the magical benefactor, in a quite extravagant and disproportionate manner. The owner of the mineral rights of Ishmaelia, and thus of those 'Stones £20' which formed the first link between William and Kätchen and turned out to be gold ore, repays the young countryman who set out from Boot Magna with three golden sovereigns, with the precious metal of a unique journalistic scoop.

A word about Mr Baldwin. Mr Waugh has himself said of his characters: 'None except one or two negligible minor figures is a portrait; all the major characters are the result of numberless diverse observations fusing in the imagination into a single whole.' On this evidence Mr Baldwin qualifies more as a minor than a major character. For he is clearly, in his taste, personal fastidiousness, and outstanding gifts, an imaginative recon-struction of M. Leblanc, the French business-man in Aden, who is described in *Remote People*, a fantasy on the theme of the patriarch, man of action and gambler which Mr Waugh there describes as the three sides of M. Leblanc. In his gift of languages there is perhaps a touch of Philbrick, talking voluble Welsh in a pub in Llanabba. He is the epitome, curiously enough, of Lord Copper's advice to all special correspondents: 'Travel light and Be prepared.' One might hazard a guess, when reading the account of his elegant arrival on Frau Dressler's tin roof ('He landed delicately on the tips of his toes . . .') that the seed of his conception was in the following words with which Mr Waugh introduces his first 'scramble' over the rocks with M. Leblanc: 'M. Leblanc stood below . . . gave one little skip, and suddenly, with great rapidity and no apparent effort, proceeded to ascend the precipice. He did not climb; he rose. . . . His whole body seemed prehensile. He *stood* there like a fly on the ceiling.'

A fly on a ceiling may have magical gifts of movement – but it does not pack much of a punch. So Mr Baldwin needs to set in motion more powerful sinews than his own: these he finds in the Swede Olafsen. Bemused and humourless for most of the book, a blinded and shackled Samson, he is awakened at last to action by strong drink and the nostalgia stirred by Mr Baldwin's perfect Swedish, and becomes the avenging figure replacing the Bengal Lancers and kilted highlanders of William's vision; but the climax is no less technicolour when the sequence of events, involving the defenestration of the Young Ishmaelites, and finally of Benito himself, 'unfolded itself with the happy inconsequence of an early comedy film'. At this moment, as also in the early comedy films with the arrival of the strong man, the fundamental rightness of the world becomes gloriously alive. Trickery and that travesty of true order, force, is vanquished. Even the animal kingdom takes part. The operations leading to the downing of Benito are opened by Frau Dressler's goat, who, 'all day . . . had shared in the exhilaration of the season . . . all day . . . had dreamed gloriously', and now in the limpid evening gathered her strength, charged, and deposited Benito's minion, the welter-weight champion of the Adventist University of Alabama, on his face amid the kitchen garbage. The milch-goat was also a Romantic and a Dreamer, an inhabitant of Lush Places, and now on the side of the angels – and when Mr Baldwin arrived on the roof, and descended delicately, 'the milch-goat reverently made way for him'.

We return to England in Book Three for the last round of the contest between Copper House and Boot Magna. The brief incursion of William Boot, whose greatest ambition is to be left in peace with 'Lush Places', into the 'foreign and hostile world' of Copper House is now balanced by the even briefer excursion of Salter, who was destined to find his level with 'Clean Fun' and 'Home Knitting', into the 'alien and highly dangerous' realm of Boot Magna. William's foray had at least ended up with the equivalent of kilted highlanders and the drone of Mr Baldwin's plane, but Salter felt like a Roman legionary, weighted with the steel and cast brass of civilization, and out of touch with his base, and attended by no more effective means of transport than Bert Tylor's slag-lorry. Another contract is signed, and another substitution carried out: Salter, returning unwined from the fantastic dinner table of the Boots, is followed up by Uncle Theodore as a tipsy intruder at the pompous banquet of Lord Copper. A third Boot has counter-attacked and milked the Copper cow. Peace falls on Boot Magna, symbolized by Uncle Theodore changing his key-tune from 'Change and decay in all around I see' to 'In thy courts no more are needed, sun by day nor moon by night'. A final joint Fantasy of the Future shows the Boots blessed with all that they can desire, and Lord Copper brooding over a vista of things which no sane man seriously coveted – a vista of empty oratory over bad food, prodigious financial outgoings, and deference in all those around him – but above all with the vision of himself as the deserted leader on whom all responsibility rests, shouldering alone the great burden of Duty.

CHAPTER 4

Disintegration

IN 'FANFARE' (*Life*, 1946), Mr Waugh tells us that *A Handful of Dust* was begun at the end: 'I had written a short story about a man trapped in the jungle, ending his days reading Dickens aloud. The idea came quite naturally from the experience of visiting a lonely settler of that kind and reflecting how easily he could hold me prisoner. Then, after the short story was written and published, the idea kept working in my mind. I wanted to discover how the prisoner got there, and eventually the thing grew into a study of other sorts of savages at home and the civilized man's helpless plight among them.'

Reading *Ninety-two Days* with the novel in mind, we may detect the genesis of Chapters Five and Six of *A Handful of Dust*. There is, firstly, Mr Christie, the negroid settler with a large family by an Indian mistress, and religious visions. He greets the tired traveller with the words: ' "I was expecting you. I was warned in a vision of your approach" '; and entertains him with rum and fantastic talk. 'The sweet and splendid spirit, the exhaustion of the day, its heat, thirst, hunger, and the effects of the fall, the fantastic conversations of Mr Christie translated that evening and raised it a finger's breadth above reality.' Mr Waugh's painful ride through the savannah, with exhaustion 'seeping up from the stumbling horse, seeping down into him from me', and ending in Christie's ranch, was raised that finger's breadth above reality to become Tony Last's stumbling, exhausted, and fever-ridden progress towards the final and inescapable refuge with Mr Todd.

Then again, there is the City. The deepest point of penetration into Guiana was, for Mr Waugh, the township Boa Vista; something in the name and the country had caused him to expect a deeply romantic, Portuguese colonial setting; the reality was a cruel deception, more than a finger's breadth below the romantic expectation. 'Gone; engulfed in an earthquake, uprooted by a tornado and tossed sky-high like chaff in the wind, scorched up with brimstone like Gomorrah, toppled over with trumpets like Jericho, ploughed like Carthage, bought, demolished, and transported brick by brick to another continent as though it had taken the fancy of Mr Hearst; tall Troy was down.'

A Crank and a City then, provide the germinating seed; or rather, a gaoler and a visionary, since the fantasies of Mr Christie are transferred, as the anticipation of the City, to the white explorer. The reality is a living grave. The final fusion of the two themes may well have come about through Mr Peter Fleming's *Brazilian Adventure* (1933), and the figure, there, of Colonel Fawcett, who was also looking for a lost world, and was thought by some to have been made a prisoner of the Indians. '. . . the idea kept working in my mind. I wanted to discover how the prisoner got there.' And so the work grew into a study of other kinds of savagery at home, of Brenda Rex, married to Tony Last, betraying him and his English Gothic home Hetton Abbey with the colourless John Beaver in a London flat; of the cruel fatuity of Brenda's friends, the group round Polly Cockpurse and Jenny Abdul Akbar; of the death of John Andrew Last, the child who was the symbol of the integrity of marriage and home; of the helpless plight of the civilized man, Tony, when he had 'got into the habit of loving and trusting Brenda'.

Civilized? – we inquire. Simple, trusting, loving, innocent, and above all boring, is how at first we see the character of Tony Last. Here is, surely, another Innocent's Progress through the World of Chaos; a Paul Pennyfeather, perhaps, in the world of Margot Metroland, followed by a trip to Azania. Another Adam Fenwick-Symes trying ineffectually to make sense of the world inhabited by his Eve, the world of parties, of gossip, of affairs and constant changes of alliance, miscalled 'romance', and of the few social sharks who turn chaos to their advantage, Beaver the sponger, Mrs Beaver his mother and the Universal Provider of furniture and flats, and of crook fortune-tellers.

No, not this time; this is the real world, not a world of fantasy. Tony Last is the Innocent who, by sheer selflessness and dedication to a principle, has become the instrument of a moral judgement. The principle is Hetton and all that for which it stood: the integrity of marriage, responsibility towards the tenantry, the village, the Church, the house and its contents, poor relatives and next-of-kin, something which one can love unreservedly with that trust which comes of an undisturbed belief in its stability. The remoteness of this principle is expressed by the preposterous nature of its embodiment: Hetton Abbey, pure English nineteenth-century Gothic, where 'there was not a glazed brick or encaustic tile that was not dear to Tony's heart'; Morgan le Fay, his childhood room, with its framed picture of a warship, school photograph, and miscellaneous 'fruits of a dozen desultory hobbies'. The very quality of childish illusion, of immaturity, in the ideal, is a judgement on the grown-up, matured savagery of others.

Mr Waugh hammers home the contrast, with an economy of narrative means emotionally restrained, but steely in its implications. Tony agrees to postpone improvements at Hetton so that Brenda shall have her flat in town: ' "I don't really deserve it," she said, *clinching the matter*' (our italics). Tony, miserable but uncomprehending at Brenda's growing coldness, declines the approach of Jenny Abdul Akbar, by which Brenda thinks to salve her remnant of a conscience, capping infidelity with infidelity: ' "What *does* the old boy expect? . . . You've done far more than most wives would to cheer the old boy up?" ' Tony demurs at Reggie St Cloud's cool proposal that Brenda shall have her freedom at a stinging price – the sale of Hetton: ' "I do think that you are behaving rather vindictively in the matter . . . you seem rather to be taking the line of the injured husband". ' Tony, in accordance with the manipulation of the law practised in the best social circles, is persuaded to assume the onus of the breach of wedlock: 'It was thought convenient that Brenda should appear as the plaintiff.'

These few words, 'it was thought convenient', sum up the torment of the innocent to which Tony is subject in the first four chapters. They send Tony to Brighton in the company of the complaisant Milly and Winnie, her *enfant terrible*, and a pair of private detectives who breathe as their natural air the atmosphere of mixed farce and degradation which constitutes divorce by collusion. One of the few passages of comment by the author to break the metallic surface of the impersonal narrative is set here to mark Tony's arrival in the lowest circle of his Hell of disorder. '. . . for a month now he had lived in a world suddenly bereft of order; it was as though the whole reasonable and decent constitution of things, the sum of all he had experienced or learned to expect, were an inconspicuous, inconsiderable object mislaid somewhere on the dressing table; no outrageous circumstance in which he found himeslf, no new mad thing brought to his notice, could add a jot to the all-encompassing chaos that shrieked about his ears.' His unwilling and bemused progress from the seclusion of Hetton to the hired company of Milly, from the boyhood memories of Morgan le Fay to 'double and single communicating rooms' at a Brighton hotel, is that of Paul Pennyfeather from Scone to the world of the Latin-American Entertainment Co. Ltd, or of Basil Seal from the sheltered ritual of his mother's room to the indecent squalor of the cannibal feast. And he knows where he is, and what he is doing, while they did not. But he still does not know why.

Complete disillusion, with the full knowledge of Brenda's worthlessness, comes immediately after, when the terms of the divorce settlement are discussed. The implicit condemnation of Brenda and her world gains enormously in force by the preservation of Tony's guilelessness till the last possible moment. Clarity does not come when the forces of disorder, in the form of Mrs Beaver's workmen, invade Hetton to introduce chromium plating into the morning room, as when the Tudor Gothic of King's Thursday was violently modernized into 'something clean and square' by Professor Silenus. Even at the death of John Andrew, when Brenda thinks first of her lover, Tony's first and only thought is for others. 'It's awful for the girl' – Miss Ripon, whose horse killed his son; 'it's awful for Jock, having to tell Brenda; . . . it's going to be much worse for Brenda; . . . I

feel awful about letting her go' – to a house-party, an engagement which she refuses to break; 'it's so much worse for her
than it is for me.' The steady crescendo of the simple, repeated
phrase hammers in the complete emptiness of self which marks
his nature. The immoral act of collusive divorce brings chaos but
not final clarity. That comes with the knowledge that Brenda
expects him to sell Hetton to buy for her the wastrel Beaver.
Tony is only implicitly a moral man. His awakening to the in-
adequacy of his and Brenda's code of conduct comes only through
the shattering of his last assumption: that either Brenda is true
or Hetton is safe. He had 'got into the habit of loving and trusting Brenda.' That illusion gone, the other also goes. 'A whole
Gothic world had come to grief . . . there was now no armour
glittering through the forest glades, no embroidered feet on the
green sward; the cream and dappled unicorns had fled.' Hence
the need to make certain beyond a shadow of doubt of her
acquiescence in the plan, the insistent repetition of the question
'Did Brenda say that?' and the telephone call to her to get her
final answer. Paul Pennyfeather's prison musings on the actions
of Margot are but a weighing-up of competing clichés – doing
the right thing by a woman, owning up and facing the music.
Paul needs no certitude, since he has only to suffer six weeks
enforced inaction in Egdon Heath Penal Settlement; Tony is
facing a life-sentence. So the curt decision of his final answer to
Reggie, spokesman of the divorce-and-settlement faction, refusing the terms of ignominy, raises the scene out of the morass of
selfishness into which it has descended on to the dry and vigorous heights of personal responsibility. An avenging principle of
condign retribution strides large through these two pages,
though its passage is followed by renewed croaking in the
swamps: ' "Who on earth would have expected the old boy to
turn up like that?" asked Polly Cockpurse. . . . "It's so like
Brenda to trust everyone," said Jenny Abdul Akbar.'

The collapse of order, and the failure of precept in Tony's life
has left, for the moment, a void; he has lost Brenda, but will not
release her, has kept Hetton but cannot stay there. Into the void
steps Dr Messinger, unfolding in prosaic tones a fantastic plan

for discovering a lost city in the interior of South America, a city which all too soon takes on in Tony's mind the familiar lineaments of the house he has left. 'It was Gothic in character, all vanes and pinnacles, gargoyles, battlements, groining and tracery, pavilions and terraces, a transfigured Hetton . . .' Transpose Gothic into Baroque, and we have Boa Vista as imagined by the young Waugh. Messinger is one of those strange figures – half comic, half serious, half real, half dreamlike, part adventurer, part charlatan – who, at a crucial moment in the hero's progress, appear at the club and beckon him on to further experience. Atwater, in *Work Suspended*, is another such figure. Messinger is the 'messenger' from the nether-world of the Brazilian jungle, his task to bring Tony Last from the Greville Club to within stumbling distance of Mr Todd's remote settlement. That done, his death by drowning, accidental, unmotivated, in a mere ten feet drop in the upper waters of an unnamed tributary of the Amazon basin, is quite logical. Tony follows his guide, inactive, a passenger almost, his mind straying back along the path he has forbidden it, to the tall elm avenue at Hetton and the budding copses. Only once is there a slight conflict. The sad, half-hearted flirtation which sprang up on the boat between Tony and Thérèse de Vitré, a Catholic Creole returning to Trinidad and an arranged marriage (a marginal sketch of the right, sacramental bond), was observed by Dr Messinger with the strongest disapproval. Such a bond might mean a turning back to life by Tony, and did not suit the book of the Messenger of Death.

Their overloaded and faltering progress into the interior is a long drawn out agony for the man for whom life holds but a memory of the past and a mirage of the future. The gallant and tragic end of a lost explorer may have all the panache of romantic fiction. Not so Tony Last's – and this not just because, in this work, the end was fixed before the beginning. Tony's fate is to live out a life of suffering, vicariously, for Brenda and the disorder that rules at home. But for a time, Tony and Brenda are united in a community of pain. ' "Half past eight," thought Tony. "In London they are just beginning to collect for dinner"' Throughout the concluding scenes, recurrent flash-backs from Brazil to London link the slow physical and mental exhaustion of Tony through heat, insects, thirst, and fever with Brenda declining into a morass of despair, sinking ever lower in love, money, and courage. Dawn breaks in London, and Brenda, over kippers and tea after a night of dancing, hears Beaver's decision to go to California; the same night the Wacushi Indian porters creep away into the jungle leaving the travellers to their fate. Tony, feverish, is visited by the figure of Brenda, reduced and waif-like, as often when she came back to Hetton from London, 'huddled over her bowl of bread and milk'. Dr Messinger is drowned; at home it is August, and all Brenda's friends have gone. Tony tries to eat some food, but without success; Brenda buys a meat pie, but finds she has lost her appetite. Tony, in his delirium, upsets his last keg of kerosene; Brenda's visit to the solicitor for money is fruitless. Both are stranded, without a companion or friend, resources or comfort. 'And lying there, wrapped in his blanket, he began to cry; . . . now at last she broke down, and turning over buried her face in her pillow in an agony of resentment and self-pity.'

'In Brazil she wore a ragged cotton gown', the narrative con-tinues; and now begins the astonishing last delirium of Tony before his rescue, a fragmented jumble of the Hetton sequence of events. This feverish, distracted disorder in Tony's mind is the true reflection of events; this *is* how it all happened, not ration-alized and conventionalized as the Polly Cockpurse and Reggie St Cloud gang would have it. It repeats, on a different plane, the drunken disorder of an earlier scene when, in a supreme effort to burst through into the world dimly apprehended as that of Brenda, Tony had gone up to London and fallen in with Jock Grant-Menzies at Bratt's. Then the drunken colloquy had ended with a pathetic telephone call to Brenda's inaccessible flat. Now, as Tony lurches through thorn-scrub, roots and hanging tendrils, his ravings end with a final mirage of the City:

'. . . he pressed forward, unconscious of pain and fatigue.

At last he came into the open. The gates were before him and trumpets were sounding along the walls, saluting his arrival; from bastion to bastion the message ran to the four points of the compass; petals and almond and apple blossom were in the air; they carpeted the way, as, after a summer storm, they lay in the orchards at Hetton. Gilded cupolas and spires of alabaster shone in the sunlight.

Ambrose announced, "The City is served".'

The City thus served was Mr Todd.

No description can do justice to the dozen pages of Chapter Six, 'Du Côté de Chez Todd', with its unreality and the grim stages by which fear and suspicion gradually ripen into certainty that Tony is helpless in the hands of a madman, babbling about Dickens. The two deaths in the book, the real and the presumed, of John Andrew Last and of Anthony Last, are both heralded by hints of the coming shadows. ' "If I'm in at the death I expect Colonel Inch will blood me." – "You won't see any death," said nanny. . . . "If you come back in good time today your dad will be all the more willing to let you come out another day." – "But there mayn't *be* another day. The world may come to an end".' It did. ' "Until five years ago there was an Englishman – at least a black man, but he was well educated at Georgetown. He died. He used to read to me every day until he died. You shall read to me when you are better. . . . I think I will put up a cross – to commemorate his death and your arrival – a pretty idea".'

As the chapter ends it is still Mr Todd who is talking, quietly, levelly – and crazily: ' "Let us read *Little Dorrit* again. There are passages in that book I can never hear without the temptation to weep".'

'I will show you fear in a handful of dust'; the quotation from *The Waste Land* appears on the title page; it is fear which dominates the book, even more than pain – fear of the unknown, fear that one's nearest companion may change into a gaoler, as in Mr Waugh's experience of Christie. Signs and portents precede events, words are charged with hidden meanings, all pointing to exile, imprisonment, and death. Figures of comedy are not excused their part in this. The Vicar of Hetton, who has served in India most of his life, reads to his stolid flock sermons composed years before for delivery in the garrison chapel. 'How difficult it is for us . . . to realize that this is indeed Christmas. Instead of the glowing log fire and windows tight shuttered against the drifting snow, we have only the harsh glare of an alien sun. . . . Instead of the placid ox and ass of Bethlehem . . . we have for companions the ravening tiger and the exotic camel, the furtive jackal and the ponderous elephant.' We laugh at the incongruity, but we are wrong. The villagers 'did not find this in any way surprising', and were right. The Vicar is a portent pointing forward to Mr Todd: Christmas in India, Dickens in Brazil. Hetton and all it stands for strikes a discord in the modern world, like the endless reading of the works of the warm, impulsive, and so very English Dickens to a crazy half-caste in the Brazilian jungle. Jenny Abdul Akbar is a woman with a sad past; she escaped from her romantic Arab Prince, 'a beautiful and very bad man', when he 'showed the Other Side of his Nature'. She is brought down to Hetton to square the peculiar moral code of Brenda's friends, by adding adultery to adultery. 'I hated her like Hell,' said Tony. But her real purpose is otherwise. She accepts, crazily but rightly, the responsibility for John Andrew's death, disclaimed by all. 'Everyone agreed that it was nobody's fault. . . . "Oh yes," said Jenny, "It was! It was *my* fault. I ought never to have gone there. . . . Wherever I go I bring nothing but sorrow".' She speaks on behalf of the weak and erring Brenda.

But Brenda, is there nothing to be said for her? There is; she also is, in the last resort, blameless. Hetton, which was for Tony liberty to devote himself to a dearly loved idea, was for Brenda a living death. ' "But don't you like the house?" – "Me? I *detest it*" . . .' Christmas games in the family circle: 'These games were the hardest part for Brenda.' Reading aloud: 'He had always rather enjoyed reading aloud and in the first year of marriage had shared several books in this way with Brenda, until one day, in a moment of frankness, she remarked that it was torture to her.' So Brenda's affair had glamour for her friends; 'for five years she had been a legendary, almost ghostly name, the imprisoned princess of fairy story, and now that she had emerged there was more enchantment in the occurrence than in the mere change of habit of any other circumspect wife. Her very choice of partner gave the affair an appropriate touch of fantasy; Beaver, the joke figure they had all known and despised, suddenly caught up to her among the luminous clouds of deity'. This is the key to the peculiar colourlessness of Beaver, blamed by no one, not even by Tony. He is the messenger sent to liberate Brenda from immurement to suffering, as Dr Messinger comes to the Greville Club to lead Tony away from suffering to immurement. *Their* very choice of partners gives the affair an appropriate touch of fantasy. The slow torture of being read to is succeeded by the slow torture of reading. The punishment is as pointless as the crime was without guilt.

Ultimately, events are seen to have moved in a circular course, and all ends in futility. Brenda is liberated, Tony imprisoned. Brenda marries Jock Grant-Menzies, as all had thought she would, before Tony Last came along. Parallels with *Black Mischief*, also circular in movement, suggest themselves. Tony is torn from the ideal, timeless world of Hetton, to a living death in the jungle; Seth is brutally wakened from his dream of modernizing Azania and hurried off to be poisoned by Boaz. Successor régimes mock their precursors but offer no real hope. The bright but rootless optimism of the Anglo-French Protectorate of Azania is but a new pattern of futility. The bright and modern device of turning Hetton into a silver-fox farm only repeats the theme of imprisonment. 'The silver-fox farm was behind the stables; a long double row of wire cages; they had wire floors covered with earth and cinders to prevent the animals digging their way out.' Only Mrs Beaver survives the upheaval, stimulating wants to which she then ministers. Having provided Brenda with the flat from which it all started, she purveys to the new Lasts at Hetton a memorial to Tony, 'a plain monolith of local stone', as Youkoumian is ever prepared to oblige with tinned fruit and Army boots.

Of this book, Mr Waugh said, many years later, '*A Handful*

of Dust . . . dealt entirely with behaviour. It was humanist and contained all I had to say about humanism.' All Mr Waugh had to say about humanism in 1934 was that it was helpless in the face of modern savagery. Decency, humanity and devotion have failed, civilized life has degenerated into 'the all-encompassing chaos that shrieked about his ears'; jolliness, respectability, and a brittle modernity cannot touch the problem. Man is doomed to remain in his wire cage, reinforced against escape, unless some other principle is found to restore to him his liberty and to banish fear. Instead of the ravening tiger and the furtive jackal, the ox and ass of Bethlehem.

The Forerunner of a New Style

She did not want me, I thought; Humboldt's Gibbon and I had done our part
— JOHN PLANT

THE TWO CHAPTERS of an unfinished novel published in 1942 as *Work Suspended* have an importance out of all proportion to their length. The plot is not, as in the entertainments, primarily farcical or burlesque; the central figure neither an innocent nor a bounder, but capable of development; the story is told in the first person.

John Plant is a composed young man, with a serious professional and family background. A moderately successful writer of detective stories, he lives in a small hotel in Fez, carefully restricting his intercourse with home and society to correspondence with his publisher, a weekly bath and dinner at the Consulate, and a weekly visit to the *quartier toléré*. The guarantee of this existence lies in the sheet-anchor of the parental relationship – the intermittent formal visits to the large house in St John's Wood, where the Royal Academician, his father, paints in a style already become historical, and looks out embattled but powerless on to the encroachments of new building.

This carefully regulated routine of writing, relaxation, and erotic satisfaction is swept away in the first line of the book, by the words 'At my father's death'. Plant senior is run over by the car of a commercial traveller; Plant junior refuses, for a time, to attend to the message of this event. 'My Uncle Andrew would see to everything' is his reaction, and he does. 'A religious ceremony of an unostentatious kind', a prudent scrutiny of the undertaker's bill, and an ex-gratia payment to the domestic staff, known as the Jellabies, seem to have closed the episode.

But it is not so. Later he realizes that, 'seldom as I slept there, the house in St John's Wood had been my headquarters and my home; that earth had now been stopped, and I thought, not far away, I could hear the hounds'. The first signs are an apparently fortuitous disturbance of his routine: Plant is flushed by a police raid from his regular establishment in the Moulay Abdullah, and the Consul is called to the telephone twice in twenty minutes to vouch for him. The exiguous tie with England is subtly disturbed, two regular supports of his routine life have been dislodged. As before in these novels, the irrational has chosen the erotic sphere in which to exercise its power over the hero. The only thing which seems left to him is to leave immediately for London, his book unfinished.

Back in London, Plant pays a last visit to the house in St John's Wood before it is sold and demolished – that earth is now finally stopped – and tries, unsuccessfully, to explain to his publisher why *Murder in Mountrichard Castle* has come to a halt. The crucial moment comes at three o'clock, that dead hour of the afternoon, in his club; the younger members have gone back to their work, their elders have padded off to the library for their afternoon nap, all his friends are busy. 'I was ready for a new deal.' Into the void thus created, as the forerunner of the hounds, baying in the distance, walks the slayer of his father, Arthur Atwater.

With Atwater, a vein of fantasy breaks into the ordered fabric of the narrative. His inconsequential appearances under a variety of aliases, his seedy financial importunities and his third-rate clubman's jargon give the narrative colour and movement and reassure those who have so far missed Mr Waugh's comic touch. He derives from Dr Messinger, of *A Handful of Dust*, and Beckthorpe, in the story *On Guard*, but much developed. He is a conflicting amalgam of moods. Plant, when he knows his companion better, sees how 'Atwater the dreamer, Atwater the good scout, and Atwater the underdog seemed to appear in more or less regular sequence'. Atwater the dreamer has wild plans for a treasure hunt in Bolivia, which depend primarily on his finding Appleby, another good scout of his acquaintance. Contact with

Appleby is only possible via the Wimpole Club, that home of good scouts; but at the moment Appleby has simply disappeared. No doubt he 'lacks the ante' to pay his subscription; Atwater should know, he also lacks the ante, and the unjust distribution of this same 'ante' provides the occasion of much recrimination against society, instigated by the underdog in him.

Atwater is indeed an amalgam of moods; but we begin to wonder whether they are really conflicting. A pattern seems to emerge: a dream, a club, a subscription; an ideal worth striving for, a community through which it can be achieved, the establishing of a vital link with this community, so that one can share in its life blood. These are ideas which are no part of the conscious mind of Plant, who has constructed himself a routine based on a denial of these needs; his ideal a classical murder story, his club a foreign pension, his most vital need a regular visit to the Moulay Abdullah with prudently emptied pockets. But may they not, for this very reason, be the projection of his unconscious mind; is not Atwater the embodiment of those forces of the personality which Plant has held too long and too strongly in subjection? Weak and seedy and shallowly extraverted at the moment, he may yet be the liberator of those forces.

The very rumness of Atwater casts an odd light on the other events in the book – for instance, the death of Plant's father, with which the book opens. Is this breaking of the parental link, ultimately the only way in which John Plant is to develop, really an accident? And, bearing in mind how much turns on money in this book, was Plant just yielding to importunity, or was he admitting complicity, when he put a ten-shilling note in an envelope 'and sent it to the man who killed my father'?

The suggestion that Atwater's role in Part One is that of a shadow figure to Plant becomes more plausible when we see how Plant turns to Atwater in Part Two at the crisis of his relationship with Lucy Simmonds. 'A Death' brings his old life to an end, 'A Birth' accompanies the founding of a new one. Plant has set about the business of founding a new life: looking for a house in the country, starting an affair with the wife of a friend and fellow-writer, Roger Simmonds, activities not markedly different, though on a slightly higher plane, from finding the little hotel in Fez and visiting Fatima, of the scarred cheeks and the tattooed face. But there is one further factor, both a hindrance and a help in the development of this new love-affair: Lucy is pregnant. The author turns aside from the story for a moment to depict that paradoxical state in which the fruition of love for the moment prevents and complicates any further love relationship. So Plant finds himself both baffled and encouraged, his suit both artificially fostered and subtly post-poned, himself both loved and exploited. The resolution of the situation and the enlightenment of the hero is delayed till the end of the fragment. When Lucy surrounds herself, at the birth of the child, with the feeling atmosphere of the biologically ful-filled woman, Plant realizes that he is no longer needed. But meanwhile, while struggling confusedly for enlightenment, he has both a channel of expression, and an instrument of self-investigation in Atwater. The technique which Mr Waugh here develops is so important for his later work, that one episode may be analysed in detail.

Consider for instance the whole dialogue sequence connected with the Gibbon ape named after Humboldt, 'a sooty, devilish creature in the monkeyhouse' at the Zoo, visited first by Plant and Lucy, and then, during the time of her labour, the scene of a peculiar colloquy between Plant and Atwater. Lucy had stared at this creature in hypnotic fascination. ' "If I have a boy I'll call him Humboldt . . . before I was born . . . my mother used to sit in front of a Flaxman bas-relief so as to give me ideal beauty" . . .' Lucy had fed the creature, but Plant, on his second visit, only pretended to do so, and the ape, when it discovered the situation, snarled with contempt. Enter Atwater; the exchanges which then follow are a perfect example of that succession of moods – good-scout, dreamer, underdog – commented on by Plant. Two women pass, feeding all the animals, and bring the desultory exchange of remarks between this casually assorted pair round to the ape.

' "Feeding animals while men and women starve," he said bitterly.

It was a topic; a topic dry, scentless and colourless as a pressed flower . . . nevertheless it was something to talk about.'

And clutching at this dry, scentless topic, in his horror at being left alone to his thoughts of Lucy in her pain, Plant starts with his alter ego a ghostly short exchange which reveals, deep down, his suffering and confusion of mind:

' "The animals are paid for their entertainment value," I said. . . . "We bring the monkeys here to amuse us."

"What's amusing about that black creature there?"

"Well, he's very beautiful."

"Beautiful?" Atwater stared into the hostile little face behind the bars. "Can't see it myself." Then rather truculently, "I suppose you'd say he was more beautiful than me."

"Well, as a matter of fact, since you raise the point . . ."

"You think that thing beautiful and feed it and shelter it, while you leave me to starve."

This seemed unfair. I had just given Atwater a pound; moreover, it was not I who had fed the ape. I pointed this out.

"I see," said Atwater. "You're paying me for my entertainment value. You think I'm a kind of monkey."

This was uncomfortably near the truth. "You misunderstand me," I said.

"I hope I do." . . .'

The whole dilemma of Plant's relationship with Lucy is in these words. The underdog in him, harking back to Lucy's visits with fruit, voices his resentment at the feeding of animals – of the ape, distorted image of the unborn child, while men and women – but especially men, Plant, the would-be lover, starve. Plant's conscious mind takes Lucy's part; the ape becomes himself, brought from Africa, encaged, fed through bars, with a distorted idea of what is beautiful in a relationship. Atwater counters once more with the theme of men starving; the sentence ' "You think that thing beautiful and feed it and shelter it while you leave me here to starve" ' is a perfect description by anticipation of the feminine apotheosis of Lucy, through the midwife Kempy, and the masculine recoil from the object of this seemingly misplaced affection. Plant defends himself: 'I had just given Atwater a pound.' But money, though welcome, is also suspect to Atwater, is counterfeit affection for the underdog in Plant himself, so his mouthpiece Atwater comes back with: ' "You're paying me for my entertainment value. You think I'm a kind of monkey".'

In the light of this exchange the earlier mention of Humboldt's Gibbon which 'we would watch morosely for half an hour at a time', and from which Lucy 'could not be got to other cages', acquires an enhanced meaning. Lucy is, for the moment, the embodiment of that predatory instinct in the human female, which appears elsewhere in Mr Waugh's works. Plant's attitude to her is instable, because based on a falsehood, an imperfect compound of dependence and resentment, he is part pensioner and part rebel. And the monkey combines in one symbol what is distorted in both – her exploitation and his dependence, her condescension and his revolt, a relationship not ideal and harmonious, such as a former generation would visualize in Flaxman's drawings, but grotesque and distorted. And Atwater is the image and mouthpiece of this internal dialogue. When Lucy's baby is born John Plant admits, in his mind, the identity of his *alter ego*, the ape. 'She did not want me, I thought; Humboldt's Gibbon and I had done our part.' *Humboldt's Gibbon and I.*

Hard on the birth followed the outbreak of the second World War, and the story remained unfinished; more correctly, it was finished under other guises. Atwater, a man of many aliases, will have no difficulty in reappearing. Plant invites him to his new house in the country: 'Stay as long as you like. Die there.' Probably the intention was that the double should become an incubus, forcing Plant to murder him, and then, as the detective writer whose dream was to construct the classical murder story, be faced with the necessity of constructing the perfect murder. But, detective stories apart, the worsting of the double is also the theme of *Men at Arms*; Crouchback and Apthorne take up the contest suspended by Plant and Atwater. Again, the theme of the country house and its role in forming the hero's personality is taken over here from *A Handful of Dust*, and passed on to *Brideshead Revisited*. From being the sign and potent cause of disintegration, it should here have become an agent of integration. Brideshead will be both: it will elicit Ryder's artistic gifts and will lead him to human love, then to sorrow, then to supernatural consolation.

CHAPTER 5

The Way to Faith

Non hinc habemus manentem civitatem
Earlier motto for *Brideshead Revisited*
Come, Paris is waiting on his carved bed
HOMER, interpolated by a later hand, in *Helena*

'MY THEME IS MEMORY, that winged host that soared
about me one grey morning of war-time.' The winged
host, more explicitly, is the 'sacred and profane memories' of
Captain Charles Ryder, ranging back over the two decades between the wars and associated with the great mansion Brideshead Castle, to which the vagaries of military service have for
the moment brought him back, and the fascinating and baffling
Catholic family which lived there. They are offered – in reverse
order to the title – in the two books which are flanked by the
Prologue and Epilogue. '*Et in Arcadia Ego*' – the period of
innocence and youth, enjoyment, charm, and dispersion to
remote parts of the earth: Venice, North Africa, Central
America. Then 'The Twitch upon the Thread', the settled years
with their deeper metaphysical needs, their clearer perception of
guilt, expiation and resignation, and the working out of Chesterton's Father Brown theme. It is the age-old succession of
expansion and recollection, diastole and systole, the progres-
sion from nature to super-nature, from a pagan to a Christian
scale of values. In Mr Waugh's own summing-up, 'the general
theme is at once romantic and eschatological'.

The eschatological aspect is further enlarged on in the
author's statement that his intention was 'to trace the workings
of the divine purpose in a pagan world, in the lives of an English
Catholic family, half-paganized themselves, in the world of
1923–1939'. Even if he had not himself admitted this intention

to be ambitious to the point of presumption, the present self-
conscious attitude of both readers and critics towards the 'Catholic novel' would ensure that the eschatological theme overshadowed the important technical problem which the Catholic in
Mr Waugh has given the novelist to solve. This is a great pity,
since the 'presumption' of Mr Waugh's intention is clearly one
of literary technique, not of theological casuistry. The spiritual
theme is, indeed, simple, though the setting is splendid. The
hard spiritual facts represented by the little chapel at Brideshead
in gaudy art nouveau are for a time either deliberately and
boldly denied, as by Lord Marchmain, or despairingly ignored,
as by Julia and Sebastian, or only fitfully glimpsed, as by Charles
Ryder, while on the high icy slopes of faith the avalanche gathers
and finally sweeps all before it, beginning with the most
Byronically recalcitrant of all, the head of the family. The high
drama of Lord Marchmain's final return to Brideshead, and the
almost barbarically splendid setting of his installation in the
Queen's bed in the Chinese drawing-room, his final reconciliation to religion, and his death amidst his family, represents for
the first time in Mr Waugh's work the apotheosis of the theme
of the great country house and of its head, the answer, on a
level above that of humanism, to the enforced separation of Tony
Last from Hetton Abbey.

And what a family! The 'family group' is conspicuously
absent in Mr Waugh's writing; it is represented very commonly
only by a more loosely knit group of relations (the Boot Magna
household in *Scoop*), or by an isolated and rather eccentric
parent (Colonel Blount in *Vile Bodies*, Plant senior in *Work
Suspended* – as Ryder senior here), or by a family group more
notable for its incoherence than for its unity, as with the Seals. Here
also, the various members are remarkable more for their variegated disunity than for their sense of common purpose. They are
given mythical stature far beyond the framework of any drawing-room group: Sebastian, the doomed Arcadian, Marchmain,
the Byronic rebel, Brideshead, the chthonic survival, Cordelia,
ageless in the wisdom of her plainness and her piety, Julia, the
mysterious quattrocento beauty, but above all Lady March-

main, whose fate it is to have the love and sympathy of all the world but not of her own family. These all seem to be linked only by their common involvement in the fortunes of a house which they do not even call home, and their membership of a Church which claims their allegiance only in the final count. The subtitle of an earlier version – 'A Household of the Faith' – has an almost ironical ring. Against the pattern of so much eccentricity of observance and non-observance, the note of unproblematical Catholic piety is unobtrusively rendered in the figure of Nanny Hawkins, and visits upstairs to her room provide a kind of ground-bass to events and crises in the family apartments below.

Into this strange and frightening circle are drawn two figures, more familiar within the range of the author's works, the artist-hero and the go-getter man of the world, the innocent and the barbarian, Charles Ryder and Rex Mottram. For the disunity of Lord Marchmain's family is of quite a different quality from the general remoteness and isolation of members of society one from another. This is indeed a period in which English society is really 'just another jungle closing in' – people falling apart 'into separate worlds, little spinning planets of personal relationships'. Brideshead will, no doubt, go the way of Marchmain House and of those other houses enshrined in *Ryder's English Homes* and *Ryder's Country Seats*. But the Marchmains' remoteness is a relation both of opposition and of attraction to those with whom they come into contact. Opposition because, fundamentally, their premises are the reverse of those held by others. Attraction because, with all this, they are, as a group, 'madly charming', with that charm which comes from their very remoteness and from the intensity with which they pursue what must seem to many a doomed way of life.

The striking thing, of course, is that the Catholicism of this 'household of the faith' – the chapel, Nanny Hawkins with her beads in an upstairs room – is not indigenous to Brideshead as a great English home, but is a recent importation dating from the marriage of Lady Marchmain into the family; and it is the granite-like quality acquired by a centuries-old indigenous

Catholic squierarchy, carrying on 'the harsh traditions of a people at war with their environment', which makes Brideshead for Ryder the symbol of spiritual claims unavoidable in their harshness and ultimate inexorability. Here was 'the origin of that grim mask which, in Brideshead, overlaid the gracious features of his father's family'. Lady Marchmain might well have the beauty and the sweetness which charmed and then cloyed, but her role of catalyst in precipitating spiritual processes, of instrument in leading back her husband and her wayward children to the fold of an ancient faith, could hardly assure her of their affection. ' "Poor Mummy. She really was a *femme fatale*, wasn't she? She killed at a touch",' muses Sebastian, broken and destitute in North Africa. But if the Chapel, closed at her death, but presumably reopened after the penitent end of Marchmain, can become, in the concluding passages, the keynote of a new hope, this is due not least to her insistent, disturbing, infuriating presence, destroying all the immediate creature happiness of several of her family, but leaving them with their essential spiritual instinct intact.

No less than for Newman in nineteenth-century England, any account of conversion in contemporary English society must be one of 'loss and gain'; nor can the gain of an absolute good be set off and weighed against the loss of tenderly held relative goods – the two are strictly incommensurate. So it is with *Brideshead*; the human love and happiness of Sebastian and Julia, and that of Charles Ryder, are thwarted, broken as on the wheel by the religious principles of their house – no amount of pious banalities can affect the poignancy of the loss. The title goes with the failure of the succession, the house becomes tenantless, Sebastian is reduced to a beachcomber existence, Julia left with nothing but her private bargain with God to 'give up this one thing I want so much'; the avalanche is down, 'the hillside swept bare behind it'. But, as Ryder quickens his pace and reaches the hut which serves as an anteroom to himself and his brother officers, ' "You're looking unusually cheerful today," said the second-in-command' – and with this the book concludes.

111

Such are the lines which a simple Greenean interpretation of *Brideshead* might follow; of this nature are the sacred, 'eschatological' memories of Charles Ryder. Within this framework, setting and characters are both exactly right and highly memorable: Brideshead, combining the morals of the catechism with the hobby of matchbox collecting, Cordelia with her nuns, gym-shoes and novenas for her pig, Lord Marchmain's death and all the details of its setting – the profane memories of the dying man and the visits of the Glasgow-Irish priest, Rex Mottram and his modern barbarism – 'a tiny bit of a man pretending he was the whole', the feline, ageless grace of the Castle of Brideshead and the contrasted gaudy modern chapel representing something immensely more permanent, in general all the magnificent, planless, historical, and hierarchical clutter of a great English home. But Mr Waugh has chosen to mirror the whole of this through the only partly comprehending, lawless, artistic, intuitive, and romantic mind of an artist; a person, moreover, who recalls emotion, jubilance, and pain as a middle-aged subaltern preoccupied in his conscious mind with anti-gas drill and swill-tubs, sentry details, and Army returns of unexplained breakages. One must admire both the artistic presumption and the absolute artistic tact which dictates the selection of this figure as the countervailing influence to Lady Marchmain in this drama of natural, human loss and spiritual, supernatural gain, and of the mode of narration by which the reader is introduced to the spiritual forum of the drama. For romance and eschatology are the natural home respectively of the artist and of the Christian; the lingering and meditative backward glance at the pattern of past experience, and the intuitive, forward discerning look towards things as yet unformed, but which lie in a pocket of the mind, 'like sea-mist in a dip of the sand-dunes', are of the essence of both the poetic and the religious approach to reality. This book, which traces 'the workings of the divine purpose' in a small section of a pagan world, through the inward eye of a pagan mind awaking gradually to art and religion, to beauty and truth, has no present, properly speaking, but is suspended between past and future, no action, but is bathed in memory and anticipation. This is the 'perhaps intolerably presumptuous' intention of which the author has spoken.

It is as well to consider how another contemporary, Mr Greene, has solved a very similar problem, that of establishing outside the retrospective statement of a first-person narrator a forum of interpretation in the light of which the reader is admitted to knowledge of providential dispositions unsuspected by himself, or even intentionally banished from his conscious mind; for the triangular relationship between Bendrix, Sara, and her faith in the *End of the Affair* is similar in its general lines to that between Charles, Julia, and her religion in the closing parts of *Brideshead Revisited*. In the words of Mauriac's *La Pharisienne* so often applied to Mr Greene's work, 'God is very often the good temptation to which many human beings in the long run yield'; so the paradoxical formulation of 'the good temptation' is resolved in the *End of the Affair* into an all-pervading system of dialectical antinomies of which Bendrix embraces, with his conscious mind, the one pole, while the reader is enabled to sense the truer reality of the other – hate and love, pursuit and attraction, distrust and trust, war and peace, time and eternity, accident and miracle. 'If there is a God who uses us and makes his saints out of such material as we are, the devil too may have his ambitions; he may dream of training even such a person as myself, even poor Parkis, into being *his* saints, ready with borrowed fanaticism to destroy love wherever we find it.' But if there *is* a God and a devil, then the devil ultimately serves the purposes of God, and Bendrix's desire, through the grotesque instrument of Parkis, to find the third man, with whom Sara may be deceiving both husband and lover, and thus to destroy human love itself, is an unadmitted desire to penetrate the veil of rational hate which conceals the divine lover and to progress beyond human love to the mystical marriage. And this happens, for Parkis and his son Lance (Lancelot, seen as the Knight questing for the Grail) discover, not a human lover, but Sara's diary, with the truth of her encounter with God. Thus Mr. Greene, by paradox, irony, and symbolism, encompasses the artistic feat of unwitting self-revelation, of showing the pursuer to be in fact

H

the pursued. His whole technique, here as often elsewhere, is based on that concept of the 'hint of an explanation' first developed in the short story of that name.

Where Mr Greene employs for this purpose a subtle apparatus of existential dialectics and the symbolical overtones of the grotesque figure of Parkis, the private detective, and his son Lance, Mr Waugh uses the more overtly imaginative technique of the seeming disorder of remembered experience and the suggestive quality of poetic images. The time sequence is hardly less straight and undeviating in *Brideshead* than in the *End of the Affair*. Eights Week with Sebastian at Oxford, 1923, is followed by a retrospect of the preceding three terms, then by cousin Jasper's monitory advice on the same period, then by Charles's own personal additions to Jasper's comments. Much later the news of Rex's engagement to Julia is followed by a glance back to Julia's progress from 1923 and the age of eighteen. Charles's further meeting with Julia, nearly ten years later, is the occasion of her relating her past life since her engagement to Rex. At one point two years of the relationship between Charles and Julia are recollected, without previous warning, in a conversation between them. 'All this I learned about Julia, bit by bit, from the stories she told, from guesswork, knowing her, from what her friends said, from the odd expressions she now and then let slip, from occasional dreamy monologues of reminiscences; I learned it as one does learn the former – as it seems at the time, the preparatory – life of a woman one loves, so that one thinks of oneself as part of it, directing it by devious ways, towards oneself'. All this the reader learns in the same way. All this, at the end, the recent convert sees to have been in the disposition of Providence, directing it, by devious ways, towards Himself. ' "Something quite remote . . . has come . . . out of the fierce little human tragedy in which I played; something none of us thought about at the time . . ." '

Similarly, by the use of poetic images at important points in the narrative, Mr Waugh underlines and suggests the dreamlike mystery of half-understood relations, emotions, and events,

later to develop in all their inner significance. Julia, at the onset
of her womanhood, noting idly the existence of Charles Ryder
as one glances at the title-page of a book one may read later;
wondering, dispassionately, like a strategist hesitating over a
marked map, whom she might marry. Ryder, finding his enchanted garden through the low door in the wall he had sought
and found, in Sebastian's company, at Oxford; losing it again,
and being drawn, through the strange similarity of brother and
sister, from Sebastian to Julia, from 'the forerunner' to – perhaps another forerunner. ' "Perhaps," I thought, while her
words still hung in the air between us like a wisp of tobacco
smoke . . . "perhaps all our loves are but hints and symbols . . .
perhaps you and I are types and this sadness which sometimes
falls between us springs from disappointment in our search, each
straining through and beyond the other, snatching a glimpse
now and then of the shadow which turns the corner always a
pace or two ahead of us." ' Ryder, reflecting at night in the darkness, ' "how often, it seemed to me, I was brought up short, like
a horse in full stride suddenly refusing an obstacle, backing
against the spurs, too shy even to put his nose at it and look at
the thing." ' And this last image leads on, in the half-conscious-
ness between sleeping and waking, to the controlling image of
the latter part of the work: the arctic trapper, alone in the
ordered warmth of his log hut, with the blizzard raging outside,
and the snow piling up against the door; soon the sun will come
out on the upper, icy slopes, and an avalanche will gather and
gain speed and momentum, till the whole carefully safeguarded
refuge disappears into the ravine, till, in the final words of
Charles Ryder's sacred memories, 'The avalanche was down,
the hillside swept bare behind it; the last echoes died on the
white slopes; the new mound glittered and lay still in the silent
valley'.

But, for Ryder, the fitfully illuminated landscape of faith is
preceded by a short, bright, cloudless morning in Arcady. To
gain access even to the scene of the drama, Ryder must suffer the
brusque intrusion into his life of a messenger from a world
other than that of his cranky father and dull College friends,

awakening him to the realization that 'to know and love one other human being is the root of all wisdom', rousing in him the artist who will afterwards seek to portray what he experienced when he stepped through the little gate in the wall into the enchanted garden. Love comes, improbably enough, through the chance of Sebastian getting drunk in Ryder's College, and being sick in – or rather into – his rooms, an event of a kind known to Mr Waugh's heroes from Paul Pennyfeather onwards. Art comes to him through the personality of Anthony Blanche, lineal descendant, in the Waugh genealogy, of Ambrose Silk, burdened with the experience of the Wandering Jew, but sustained by the same ageless vitality, and the spokesman throughout the book of Ryder's artistic conscience. Thus the first part of the work develops the early conflict between Sebastian and Anthony for the artistic soul of Charles, in the setting of a long, lingering backward glance towards the vanished delights of youth and post-war Oxford. 'The languor of Youth – how unique and quintessential it is! How quickly, how irrevocably lost!' But how unfortunate if unnecessarily prolonged, warns Anthony. ' "You see, my dear Charles, you are that very rare thing, An Artist. . . . It is not an experience I would recommend for An Artist at the tenderest stage of his growth, to be strangled with charm." '

Anthony Blanche's stay at Oxford is shortened by the vagaries of his impressionable nature – as the fourth term begins we hear of a flat in Munich and an attachment to a policeman there – and the course of Charles's life is then wholly dominated by the Marchmains, by Sebastian's decline to the status of the family black sheep, and by Charles's growing artistic and social success. But the artistic conscience is not banished for good, and reappears, appropriately enough, at Ryder's first major exhibition. A voice from the past, 'an unforgettable self-taught stammer' is heard at the turnstile, and there follows the significant question: ' "Where are the pictures? Let me explain them to you." ' The explanation is final and condemning: ' "We know, you and I, that this is all t-t-terrible t-t-tripe . . . a very naughty and very successful practical joke. It reminded me of dear Sebastian when he liked so much to dress up in false whiskers. It was charm, again my dear, simple, creamy English charm, playing tigers." '

It is easy to dismiss this aspect of the work as an entertaining irrelevancy, and to hurry, with Charles Ryder, along the broad road which leads, through Sebastian, the forerunner in different ways of both Celia Ryder and Julia Marchmain, on to the Catholic setting of the final tragedy in Brideshead Castle. That way, indeed, lies Charles's ultimate conversion. And yet, are we to regard as entirely eccentric the note of reproof to which Anthony Blanche again returns: ' "I was right years ago . . . when I *warned* you. I took you out to dinner to warn you of charm. I warned you expressly and in great detail of the Flyte family" '? Can it be that Anthony Blanche was right? It was, after all, when one returns to examine once more that opening picture of Oxford, bathed in the light of memory and romance, as much Blanche's setting as that of Sebastian. Or rather, while it is Sebastian who provides the languor, the grace, the ineffable romance of memory, it is Anthony who provides the unique oddity of life when young. From the moment he enters the book, he sheds 'a vivid, false light of eccentricity upon everyone, so that the three prosaic Etonians seemed suddenly to become creatures of his fantasy'. While his spirit was still potent, we are given that magnificent figure of eccentricity, Ryder senior. When he left, 'Anthony Blanche's set broke up and became a bare dozen lethargic, adolescent Englishmen. . . . They lumbered back into the herd from which they had been so capriciously chosen. . . .' Not so Sebastian, a creature of the unconscious imagination as much as Anthony – he had no herd into which he could lumber back. So there sets in his poignant decline into seediness. ' "Oh, Charles, what has happened since last term? I feel so old." ' But to feel old is a mortal affliction for one representing 'the languor of Youth'. And so Sebastian repines, but Blanche is ageless.

But before there sets in Sebastian's slow decline into dipsomania, and his long purification through suffering in Africa, he gives Charles all that there is in his nature to give in that midsummer interlude at Brideshead to which Charles is summoned from his father's home by the over-dramatic message: *Gravely injured come at once Sebastian.* Those few days were for Charles the turning-point in his life. They gave him that essential thing for the artist, the experience of inner recollection which is the source of his inspiration: 'languor – the relaxation of yet un-wearied sinews, the mind sequestered and self-regarding, the sun standing still in the heavens and the earth throbbing to our own pulse.' They gave him the first deep aesthetic experience of that vast house – 'this was my conversion to the baroque'. They summoned him to his first essay in painting and draughtsman-ship, pressing into his ready hand a large japanned-tin box of oil-paints deriving from a past enthusiasm of Lady Marchmain. They gave him the sight of the first priest he had ever met, and the first exchanges with his friend on his religion. Opening with the shock of realization that 'to love one other human being is the root of all wisdom', and closing with the glimpse of a larger, embracing love, this interlude has given Ryder implicitly, as in a seed-kernel, all he will learn in the book.

And the return made by Charles for these inestimable and un-covenanted benefits? – A bout of steady drinking, followed up much later by the deliberate defeating of Lady Marchmain's attempts to separate the now completely rudderless drinker and the bottle. Sebastian, only partly willing his actions, and not at all their end, has served the purpose for which he was sum-moned into the life of Charles Ryder; the 'self-regarding' Nar-cissus, an aspect of the inner vision of any artist, has for a brief moment mirrored his own enchanting features in the running water of life, and has woken to the impossibility of arresting that moment. For him also, as for all men, there is an appro-priate form of holiness: it is in finding one other person – ' "only of course it has to be someone pretty hopeless to need looking after by *me*" ' – towards whom he can stand arrested, so to speak, in the hieratical gesture of loving and serving one other human being, which is the root of all wisdom. That more hope-less person he finds in Kurt, the ex-Foreign Legionary. Even the concrete setting is repetitive of the earlier incident: the ban-daged foot, the supported leg, the easy chair, all link Sebastian at Brideshead with Kurt at Fez. Deprived of this one purpose in life, after Kurt's suicide, there is nothing more for Sebastian but the bottle, the pious practices, the oddities and endless suffering.

Languor and eccentricity, romance and satire, the sensuous abandonment to mood and the critical judgement of the result have, in the figures of Sebastian and Anthony, made their claim on the artistic soul of Charles Ryder. In this encounter, the age-less principle has the vigour of constantly replenished life, and the figure of languor runs to seed. Anthony cannot properly reproach Charles for his attitude to Sebastian. Has Charles, in transferring his life, after the lapse of years, to Julia as the other half of this hermaphroditic pair, rightly incurred Anthony's displeasure?

Women play a peculiar and interesting role in the works of Mr Waugh. His male figures are not notably successful in their relations with the opposite sex – there are many love affairs and many married couples, but never a successful love affair leading to a stable marriage. His most successful women, artistically, are those who, for good or evil, carry the principle of their vitality uninvaded within themselves – Margot Metroland, Brenda Last, Julia Stitch, Barbara Sothill. Angela Lyne is a mask, Aimée Thanatogenos a symbol, Virginia Crouchback a tart – all highly desirable qualifications for a successful and sharp delineation. Celia Ryder, the sister of Boy Mulcaster, is one of these. ' "I was glad when I found Celia was unfaithful," said Charles. "I felt it was all right for me to dislike her." ' So it was, artistically, since Ryder's dislike is the key to the author's success in depicting her, one of the long line of vapid and pre-datory females descending from Brenda Last and Lucy Sim-monds. Women who are being fulfilled in their biological func-tions receive short shrift from Mr Waugh: Celia Ryder sea-sick is Lucy Simmonds in child-birth. 'I brought her the flowers from the sitting-room; they completed the atmosphere of a maternity ward which she had managed to create in the cabin.' . . . ' "Mrs Clark is being so sweet"; she was always quick to get the servants' names.'

The world of Mr Waugh's novels is essentially a male world;

women gain admittance through being boyish, gamine and intelligent, or feminine, disreputable and disliked. The romantic heroine, compelling the ideal love of the male, the 'She' of the popular novelist and the psychologists, is mercifully absent. Only in the figure of Julia has she almost gained admittance, a figure from the vasty deeps of the unconscious without benefit of critical reason or humour, without the release of tension which comes from the occasional side-step into the world of whimsy, with hardly a touch of the eccentric oddity required by Charles's aesthetic mentor Blanche. It is not her charm alone which is the source of her weakness. The treatment of Julia in the first books, with the story of her débutante year, her thoughts of marriage, and her delightful fantasy 'of the kind of man who would do', is still, in spite of the fairy story touch, wholly suitable. It is not, entirely, that she is a Marchmain – one of the family against which Anthony uttered his comprehensive warning. Sebastian is charming, and not a little odd, and his oddity increases and becomes more poignant when he is relegated to the wings and the safe aesthetic distance of Anthony's account of the present and Cordelia's fantasy of the future. He is, if not morally blameless, at least 'right' by Brideshead's mad certainty of decision. Lady Marchmain is both charming and odd, saintly and yet a *femme fatale* – ' "they never escape once she's had her teeth in them",' reports Anthony Blanche; the discrepancy between neurosis and piety is ours to welcome, not to reconcile or explain. Charming and odd, charming and infuriating, charming and beastly, charming and disgraceful, all these combinations could plausibly be saved from Blanche's condemnation – but not just ' "creamy English charm, playing tigers".'

The moment of Charles's captivation to Julia's creamy charm comes quite early. It comes with the fantasy of Julia as a 'heroine of a fairy story turning over in her hands the magic ring; she had only to stroke it with her finger-tips and whisper the charmed word, for the earth to open at her feet and belch forth her titanic servant, the fawning monster' – Rex Mottram. Now it was not unusual in Mr Waugh's earlier works for the heroine – if such a term is appropriate – to throw in her lot with the successful, coarse, extravert male; Margot Beste-Chetwynde marries Lord Metroland and Nina goes off with Ginger. But there is very good reason why the hero should relinquish her and return to his College or to his loneliness; we are not concerned with the inner history of the female psyche after its association with the shallow man of affairs. Here, however, the heroine of the fairy story, when Charles meets her after ten years on the liner from New York, has, through contact with the world of Rex Mottram, become waif-like, her beauty has acquired an added air of sadness, 'this haunting, magical sadness which spoke straight to the heart'.

To Charles' heart, in fact. Or to the author's heart? We have here the difficulty, common in first-person narratives, of assessing whether the author is writing in person or in character. The critics had no doubt that the dinner in Paris where Charles, lost in the magical world of Marchmain, indulges himself at Rex's expense in a meal which might have been taken out of a restaurant brochure, was Mr Waugh speaking in person, as an epicure, and said so caustically. There is certainly a streak of maudlin sentimentality about Charles, brought out and emphasized as, with the progress of their affair, Julia again recedes into a mysterious distance, and becomes, in her tight little gold tunic and evening gown, ever less tangible as an inhabitant of a real world. The peak of their inner estrangement, barely concealed by the accepted habit of past possession, and the summit of tension between the two, is the brutal reminder which Brideshead delivers of her irregular status, her passionate revolt against the very presence of her lover, and their momentary reconciliation. The lush passages increase and are spun out beyond the requirements of a disciplined style: 'I saw her to bed; the blue lids fell over her eyes; her pale lips moved on the pillow; but whether to wish me good-night or to murmur a prayer – a jingle of the nursery that came to her now in the twilight world between sorrow and sleep: some ancient pious rhyme that had come down to Nanny Hawkins from centuries of bedtime whispering, through all the changes of language, from the days of pack-horses on the Pilgrim's Way – I did not know.' We are back in the world of Chesterton, but without his philosophical stringency. A way into the Church for Charles, this Tudor romanticism of pack horses on the Pilgrim's Way? Perhaps, but not the way of many others, and only one part of that of Mr Waugh. A quotation from Mr Waugh's review of Mr Greene's *The Unquiet American* comes appositely to hand: 'Fowler is base. So base that it is a disagreeable experience to be forced into intimacy with him, to have to hear the story from his lips and see it through his eyes.' Substitute 'Ryder is sentimental' for 'Fowler is base', and the parallel, for passages such as this one, is exact. The review continues: 'This can hardly be called an artistic fault, for it is part of the artist's plain intention, but I think it is a lapse in taste.' Mr Waugh's artistic intention is, regrettably, not so plain.

It is not surprising that the passage considered above is followed by two full pages of the political-conversation pastiche which we have learnt to expect whenever Rex and his associates are introduced. Effective, this contrast of two worlds, but technically just out of focus, just emancipating itself from artistic tact. ' "I wonder which is the more horrible," ' says Charles to Julia, ' "Celia's Art and Fashion or Rex's Politics and Money." ' Artistically, there is no doubt; Celia is perfectly delineated, but Rex suffers by too obvious contrast with the creamy charm of Sebastian and Julia. Well sketched in the early stages, Rex handling troublesome policemen, giving Julia a tortoise studded with diamonds, Rex swallowing religious instruction like a double brandy, is excellent. But the jangling and brash conversation of his political set, though effective, gives rise by reaction to Charles's dinner at Maillard's – 'soup of *oseille*, a sole quite simply cooked in a white wine sauce, a caneton à la presse, a lemon soufflé' – and the haunting, magical charm of Julia's later moods. Julia's hysterical outburst against her burden of sin – ' "no way back; the gates barred; all the saints and angels posted along the walls" ' – is magnificent. But Charles's own sentimental reaction surely justifies Anthony's warning not to fall a victim to the Marchmains and their charm. Perhaps the warning was also valid against the author. Perhaps, even, Sebastian and Anthony represent the two contrasted sides of Mr Waugh's own writing – always balanced and at loggerheads, usually holding each other in strict check, the one tempting to indiscretions, the other leering at the lush scene through an *oeuil de boeuf*, the one erring disconsolately, banished from his Arcadian home, the other wandering insatiably, an inhabitant of all climes and of none.

It is a far cry from the England of the twentieth century to Roman Britain, Rome, and Jerusalem in the third and fourth, the place and time of *Helena*. And yet there are points of similarity. Helena – as Mr Waugh reminds us in his essay *St Helena, Empress* – is remembered for a single act, the discovery of the timber since venerated throughout Christendom as part of the true Cross. This act was both personal and historical. Personally, it was the natural and supernatural culmination of a long life about which little else is known. Historically, it was unique. Once accomplished, it could never be repeated. It was the historical turning point which gave Christianity a sure foundation in the Mediterranean world. In choosing this Saint and the act which was uniquely constitutive of her personal and historical sanctity, the author has a clear field in which to build up a rounded picture of a life and of a social and historical setting whose every line of development converges on one point. Legendary in its beginning and its end, historical in its middle course, this book – both a legend and a novel – embodies with great artistry the living and inherited historicity known as the tradition of the Church.

The finding of the Cross, is therefore, in the *Brideshead* image, the avalanche for which all else is a preparation; but the setting is otherwise quite different. For the mood of recollection, we have the intermingling of history and legend; for the middle-class artist, a central figure of the highest birth and status. Instead of aching natural loss on all sides, only just outweighed by supernatural gain, we are given Helena relinquishing with little regret home, husband, fame, and the comforts of a dignified old age, to carry out her one appointed task. Instead of resistance to the gift of faith, a quest for truth, joyfully embraced when it is revealed. Indeed it is not the moment of conversion to which the whole action leads, but a task undertaken as a result of conversion. The general aim of the novelist is the same – 'to trace the workings of the divine purpose in a pagan world' – but the specific purpose of his main figure is astonishingly concrete; it was 'to turn the eyes of the world back to the planks of wood on which their salvation hung'.

Mr Waugh's reconstruction of the historical situation in which this was necessary should be read at length in the essay. Quite simply, it was the moment when the mythical thinking of the East bid fair to defeat the central fact of the new, blunt religion for which the martyrs had died: 'that God became man and died on the Cross.' All else could be defined, interpreted away, but not this; but even this was in danger, in the absence of the one solid object which could provide incontrovertible evidence of that fact. It is therefore anything but a specious effect of frivolous modernity which Mr Waugh achieves when he makes Helena say to Pope Sylvester: 'Just at this moment when everyone is forgetting it and chattering about the hypostatic union, there's a solid chunk of wood waiting for them to have their silly heads knocked against.'

In his *Preface*, Mr Waugh gives briefly the few facts known about Helena and renders account of the liberties he has taken with history and tradition. Of the surmises concerning her origin, he chooses to accept the one which made her the daughter of a British chief, and gives her two dominant qualities of mind: an unshakable realism and a childlike questing for some half-perceived ideal. Critics who view with distaste the Gothic revivalist setting of *A Handful of Dust*, or the sacred and secular ornateness of *Brideshead*, should be happy when they see Helena in youth, hobnobbing with Roman soldiers in the stables, and with sailors over the fishmeal, and later, as the first lady in the civilized world, living with the nuns of Mount Zion, 'where she did her own housework and took her turn in waiting at table'. She does not hesitate to reject as 'bosh' the characteristic subtle-

ties of the ancient world – in Ratisbon, the intricacies of initia-
tion into Eastern cults, in Jerusalem, the speculations of scholars
concerning the probable composition of the True Cross. But she
does not leave it at that: she asks constantly what is the truth of
the matter. All who come into contact with her are subjected to
the same persistent questioning, in youth sometimes wide-eyed,
in old age often short and impatient; her tutor Marcias on Troy,
her husband Constantius on Rome, its citizenship, and on
Mithras, Marcias again on Gnosticism, Lactantius on Christianity, and finally Pope Sylvester on the whereabouts of the
Cross, in which all Christians claim to believe. Her questions
narrow down, and become more explicit, until at last she has
no more to ask; on the night of Good Friday, in Jersualem, 'she
lay quite relaxed at last, like the body in the tomb', and the
answer was vouchsafed to her in another mode: through revelation in a dream. Hers was the grace and the humility to know
what question to ask; when it is first put to Pope Sylvester, he
says: ' "I don't think anyone has ever asked before".' This
sums up the theme of the whole book.

Against this central core of inspired and questing common
sense are set, as foils and contrasts, most of the other characters
and situations. Constantius asks questions indefatigably, but
only those directed to a knowledge of men and the acquisition
of power. Marcias has his dreams; but they are poetic dreams of
the City of Troy as an invisible Republic of Letters, or gnostic
dreams of a spurious mysticism isolated from the world of reality. Pope Sylvester is pious with the piety of religious quietism.
To Helena's remonstrance that 'it stands to reason' that God
expects us to find the Cross, he answers: 'Nothing "stands to
reason" with God. If he had wanted us to have it, no doubt he
would have given it to us. But he hasn't chosen to.' Constantius
describes a Roman triumph: elephants, tigers, the plundered
resources of the known world; dinners with partridges made of
sugar, peaches of mincemeat, a debased taste which finds a sen-
sation in things which are not as they appear. Against this is set,
by anticipation, Helena's Triumph, which consisted in finding
just six baulks of timber, for which in all humility she left Rome

and sought an Eastern site, impelled by a fundamental solidity of mind which never forgot that wood was wood and nothing else.

Constantine, the first Christian Emperor, is poised between the old world and the new. In his dealings with the new-fangled sculptors over the carvings on his Triumphal Arch he shows the robust spirit of his mother: ' "spoken like a man, my son",' is her comment. But there is much of his father in him – 'Power without Grace' is Helena's summing up – and in the Labarum he creates the perfect pagan counter-symbol to the True Cross. *In hoc signo vinces*' was the divine message which Constantine received at the Milvian bridge, whereupon his soldiers fashioned themselves rough crosses and bore them through to victory – the immediate prelude to his elevation of Christianity to the dignity of officially recognized religion. But one day the half-crazed Emperor showed his mother, as a special favour, *his* Labarum, a superb and sumptuous product of the jeweller's art, with the bland assertion that this was the emblem which the vision bade him make. There follows this dialogue:

"But it must have taken months to make."

"Two or three hours, I assure you. The jewellers were inspired. Everything was miraculous that day."

"And whose are the portraits?"

"My own and my children's."

"But my dear boy, they weren't all born then."

"I tell you it was a miracle," said Constantine huffily.'

The Labarum is the epitome of that falsification of the past in the spirit of myth which is the mark of pseudo-religions; its fashioning is the true antithesis to the finding of the Cross, and both events are covered by the term 'invention'. For Constantine, enjoying power without grace, the Cross is an attractive and useful myth, to be fashioned at will. For Marcias, the slave, with neither power nor grace, Troy is another beautiful myth, a world of which 'there is nothing left but poetry'. For Helena, with both power and grace, the Cross and the City of God are realities; her task is to show their solidity by knocking silly people's heads against them.

Very well, then, said the critics; the historical construction is excellent – economical and poetically apt. But the central figure is lifeless; the vital event, her conversion, is missing, the frivolous red-head at the Court of Coel in Colchester and the pious Dowager do not add up to one character. Saints must be shown doing saintly things from their first years, not flirting in the Royal Stables with visiting junior officers, or, even worse, bursting out with ' "Oh, what sucks!" ' when the tutor Marcias reads from the classical epic the passage where Helen of Troy slipped away from her husband and her attendant women to lie on the carved and fretted bed with Paris.

A moment's pause will show that psychological analysis and the conventional requirements of hagiography are both inappropriate here. The guidance of the divine purpose is not revealed in this or that imputed human motive, nor need it supplant nature by supplying a wholly adult form of heroic virtue in one of tender years. The novelist is restricted, in his imaginative reconstruction of this unique act, only by the one terminal point of the finding of the Cross in accordance with the divine will. The unity of this mind and of this life can therefore only lie in a theme which unites nature and supernature in a seamless whole without subordinating one to the other, and this can only be a poetic theme. Mr Waugh therefore selects two poetic symbols with which to construct his bridge: the City and the bridal bed; both are united in the fantasy set up in the mind of the adolescent Helena by her tutor's reading of the story of Helen of the City of Troy, who was borne away by Aphrodite to an assignation with her lover Paris.

' "It is an incident quite inconsistent with the heroic virtues",' said Marcias after his pupil's unmaidenly outbreak of glee. The reader who expects at least a suggestion of heroic virtue in the making of a Saint, will agree with Marcias. ' "For that reason the great Longinus considered it the interpolation of a later hand".' Here also we may agree – it is an interpolation by the later hand of Mr Waugh; the passage is not to be found in Homer, it is one of the novelist's many fantasies creating a poetic symbol on which the action of the work rests.

127

Helena, daughter of the chieftain Coel, who is equally proud of his Roman citizenship and of his descent from the more remote Aeneas and Troy, spends her life questing for her true origin and searching for her true and final lover; this is the train of symbolical allusion which runs like a coloured thread throughout the work, and which can here be suggested only in the barest outline. Constantius and pagan Rome present themselves to her as the fulfilment of one and the other fantasy: the lover and the City. Both are shown to be inadequate; they are, in the language of *Brideshead*, the 'forerunners' of the all-embracing *civitas* of Christianity and of the union with the divine lover on the bed of the Cross. ' "Why don't people dig? Some of Troy's bound to be there . . . when I am educated I shall go and find the real Troy – Helen's." ' Which is just what she does, when she digs for the Cross. Marcias, of course, is convinced there is nothing to dig for: ' "The guides will show you anything you ask for – the tomb of Achilles, Paris's carved bed, the wooden leg of the great horse. But of Troy itself there is nothing left but poetry." ' But the act of heroic virtue, which neither Marcias, nor Longinus, nor Constantine could understand, was prefigured, in this improbable and human guise, in Helena's life from the beginning. It was implicit in Marcias's reading of the 'interpolated' Homeric passage: 'Aphrodite . . . sought Helen where she stood among her women . . . plucked her perfumed gown and said: "Come, Paris is waiting on his carved bed, radiantly clad as though he were resting from the dance." ' The call took a lifetime to answer; Helen tarried long, perhaps beyond the natural span of years, with no apparent major aim in life. Appropriately, she was finally led to her goal after invoking the aid of the Three Kings of Bethlehem, 'patrons of all latecomers', and by the appearance, in a dream, of that other homeless figure, the Wandering Jew. But only she, in all that historical scene, could accomplish the deed. The showmen like Constantine would assent to and exploit the myth as far as it was profitable to them; the learned men, like Marcias and the Coptic elder who assured her, 'that the Cross was compounded of every species of wood so that all the vegetable world could

128

participate in the act of redemption', could exploit and refine on its inherent poetic beauty, till it was more like the Labaram than an instrument of execution. But only Helena was prepared to take the alleged wooden leg of the great horse in its solid and repugnant reality: as an invitation to enter through the tomb of Achilles, through complete submission to a supernatural purpose, into the chamber where Christ was waiting on His carved bed of the Cross.

'The wooden leg of the great horse'; this is a third natural fantasy of the supernatural life, the mystical marriage, which accompanies Helena throughout her life: the horse and its bridle. The passage in which Helena, during the epic recital in Coel's banqueting hall, indulges in an exhilarating daydream of being a horse which is ridden, then, catching Constantius's eye, falls in love, is a magnificent symbol of erotic struggle and surrender. Constantius nicknamed Helena 'stabularia', the ostler, when he found her next day in the stables with a bit in her mouth, and the name remained with her. Towards the end, the True Cross and the Nails having been discovered, Constantine puts one of the nails to the idiosyncratic use of having it forged into a snaffle for his horse. Helena, hearing this, was at first a little taken aback, but then giggled, and was heard to utter the single, enigmatic word 'stabularia'. She had recognized, though grotesquely reversed by her son, the reaffirmation of this intimacy of association between the human and the divine which was for her the absolute submission of her aristocratic and vitally assertive nature to the beloved and divine will. In his conclusion, Mr Waugh falls back into the hunting theme. The divine huntsman has used Helena to put humanity back on to its right course. 'Hounds are checked, hunting wild. A horn calls clear through the covert. Helena casts them back on the scent.'

CHAPTER 6

Four More Entertainments, 1942–53

'. . . the new world taking shape beneath the surface of the old.'
MISS BOMBAUM, in *Scott-King's Modern Europe*

P*ut out more Flags* is Mr Waugh's record of 'that odd, dead
period before the Churchillian renaissance, which people
called at the time the Great Bore War'. He describes the
activities of that 'race of ghosts' which peopled his earlier
novels, from *Decline and Fall* to *Black Mischief*, much more the
creatures of the roaring twenties than of the political thirties,
and even more uncontemporary when, in 1939, the 'rough intrusion of current history' set them scampering confusedly this
way and that like insects once their protecting boulder has been
removed. And yet their follies are not entirely unproductive of
'food for thought', especially as the 'sagacities of the higher
command' are, during this interlude, hardly clear enough for
study. As in any momentary confusion, when the comforting
structure of old, familiar habits of life has rudely been struck
away, their headless antics are redolent of memories of the past
and big with expectations of the future, even if they have little
present sense. This little work is poised on the frontier of
memory and anticipation: memory of the bright social world of
the earlier works, from *Decline and Fall*, anticipation of the
military world of later works like *Men at Arms*.

Basically it is all about Basil Seal and Ambrose Silk, two
figures for whom the outbreak of war meant the sudden elimination of their chief means of existing: Ambrose because the ideal
of uncommitted literature had ceased to have an obvious purpose, Basil because 'the system of push, appeasement, agitation,
and blackmail', by which he had conducted his life, had become

general. ' "Here is the war, offering a new deal for everyone; I alone bear the weight of my singularity", ' complains Ambrose. ' "I want to be one of those people one heard about in 1919; the hard-faced men who did well out of the war", ' states Basil – but for the moment, 'the new, busy, secretive, chaotic world' of Whitehall is so much like the old Basil Seal that it is deaf to his blandishments.

It is deaf also because, though the ant-heap has developed immense internal activity, no new purposive design has emerged to canalize so much effort; so the community falls back on inherited ancestral memories. With fine irony, these are represented in the figure of Sir Joseph Mainwaring, prophesying in 1939–40 in the mood of totally unjustified optimism of 1914. 'Sir Joseph Mainwaring was appointed to a position of trust and dignity. He was often to be seen with Generals now and sometimes with an Admiral.' In this he is ably supported by Lady Seal, whose version of history is one of national wars undertaken 'often on quite recondite pretexts, but always justly, chivalrously, and with ultimate success.'

Lady Seal is not the only female character in whom the sudden impact of war causes a reversion to an older ancestral cult; at this moment 'three rich women thought first and mainly of Basil Seal. They were his sister, his mother and his mistress' – Barbara Sothill, Lady Seal, and Angela Lyne. The first two, in their thoughts of this brilliant and wayward person, were united by one instinctive reaction: the war was Basil's chance. ' "I believe it's what he's been waiting for all these years." ' ' "It's always been Basil's *individuality* that's been wrong." ' These two created round him, from childhood associations, their myth of Young England: T. E. Lawrence, Rupert Brooke, Wolfe at Quebec. The third, in her loneliness derived from seven years of alternate attention and abandonment, delved into deeper layers of the mind: 'Basil in the pass at Thermopylae. . . . Death the macabre paramour in whose embrace all earthly loves were forgotten; Death for Basil, that Angela might live again . . .' No wonder even Basil complains to Barbara that ' "when there really were people gunning for me, no one cared a hoot", ' while

131

now that he is living in enforced safety and idleness, the only thought of Lady Seal and of Angela is to get him killed off.

His sister's reaction to this is apparently inconsequential, but follows well-worn lines of thought in relation to Basil: ' "No new girls?" ' Yes, there are some – and another group of three females makes its appearance, following the sequence of Autumn, Winter, and Spring into which the book is divided. There is firstly Poppet Green, a peculiarly incompetent artist, then the young nameless bride of Grantley Green, and finally Susie, the A.T.S. clerk at the War Office. All three have that transcendent silliness which is the immediate guarantee of his transient affections. Failing an immediate achievement of his plans for doing well out of the war, Basil at least breaks into military circles on the distaff side, and muscles in on the rights of Bill, called up into the yeomanry, and of Colonel Plum, of the War Office. 'Rupert Brooke, Old Bill, the Unknown Soldier – thus three fond women saw him, but Basil breakfasting late in Poppet Green's studio fell short and wide of all these ideals.'

For Basil, also, reality falls short of the ideal. *His* fantasy of military glory is not that of a subaltern in a trench at zero hour, but that of receiving a top secret assignment from 'a lean, scarred man with hard grey eyes' at an obscure address in Maida Vale. 'You're a rascal, but I'm inclined to think you're the kind of rascal the country needs at this moment' . . . The reality: an invitation to lunch with Sir Joseph Mainwaring to meet the Lieutenant-Colonel of the Bombardiers, whose re-action to Basil's airy suggestion of a commission followed by 'something more interesting' on the staff, is 'a scarcely human croak and an eloquent gesture of the hand . . . that the interview was over'. Only much later does an officer in uniform, Colonel Plum of the War Office security branch, admit to having an accurate knowledge of Basil's past and a limited use for his services in the present; this is the scene so often rehearsed in his mind, *this* 'the lean, masterful man who had followed Basil's career saying "One day his country will have a use for him" . . . ' The assignment is the inglorious one of spying for Communist and Fascist suspects within his own circle; the cost, the betrayal of his old friend Ambrose Silk, tricked into flying to the West of Ireland; the reward, the installation of the delectable Susie (filched off Colonel Plum) 'with a face of transparent, aethereal silliness' in Ambrose's vacated flat.

An anticlimax? A characteristic caddish trick of Basil's in the known frivolous taste of the author? More than that, surely. The contest Seal contra Silk is a classic one. Ambrose was an Oxford contemporary of Basil's, 'with whom he had maintained a shadowy, mutually derisive acquaintance since they were under-graduates'. The cosmopolitan Jewish pansy and the English Mayfair adventurer have in common, to adapt an earlier ex-pression, 'the weight of their singularity'; this is the bond which links the artist, even if he *is* a pansy, with the man of adventurous action, even if he *is* a cad. ' "Why" – Ambrose won-dered – "do real intellectuals always prefer the company of rakes to that of their fellows?" ' So the onset of war is marked by a quick, short tussle between action and uncommitted art, be-tween the War House and the Ivory Tower. Ambrose's fantasies, though epicene in their mode of expression, are the inverse of those of which Basil is the object: the exquisitely horrible fate of the Jewish, Communist fellow-traveller at the hands of invading Fascists reflects in reverse the world of T. E. Lawrence and of Nelson; the inglorious end of Beddoes and Oscar Wilde is the obverse of the glorious fate of the Spartans at Thermopylae and of Wolfe at Quebec. The reality is, as with Basil, more mundane, an anticlimax: sudden flight in clerical disguise to the West of Ireland, there to live out the war years, inarticulate, writing nothing, restless from 'the dark, nomadic strain in his blood, the long heritage of wandering and specu-tion'. The creative artist is banished to the dark shore of the restless ocean for the duration.

The bombshell exploded by the machinations of Basil in the editorial office of The Ivory Tower claims two victims: Am-brose Silk and Old Mr Rampole, the senior partner of Rampole and Bentley. Both are utterly innocent of fascist, or even of sub-versive aims – the irruption of catastrophe, from *Decline and Fall* onwards, needs only imputed guilt in the victim – so while

Basil does the dirty on Ambrose, the plausible Bentley slips out and leaves Rampole to face the music. The two sacrificial sheep are united in one single section: 'Poor Ambrose had moved west . . .' 'Old Rampole sat in his comfortable cell . . .' Ireland and Brixton Gaol – creative frustration, and the endless reading of the cosy female novelist Ruth Mountdragon, so long published but now at last 'discovered' by Mr Rampole – these are symbols, burlesque in their association, of the explosive impact of total war on literature. Unite the two, the Jew incarcerated in the lush Irish countryside, Rampole spending the war sampling 'the delights of light literature', and you have Tony Last reading Dickens to Mr Todd in Brazil.

General dispersion is indeed the keynote of much of the book, the destruction of social and cultural pattern as when an ants' nest is disturbed. Superficially, billeting and evacuation (the ineffable Connolly kids), security arrests, the breaking of family ties by mobilization, service in the field and death in action, all reinforce the general note. But spiritually, also, there is that flight into inner isolation which may have either a positive or a negative note. It is positive for Alastair Trumpington, who volunteers as a private, and refuses a commission, allegedly so as not to have to meet the wartime officers on social terms, more deeply, however, in the halting words of Sonia, ' "as a kind of penance or whatever it's called that religious people are always supposed to do"'. It is negative in the wealthy Angela Lyne, and in her dilettante architect of a husband, Cedric Lyne, who have had years of experience of the state before even the book opens. The daughter of the Glasgow millionaire of humble origins, 'aloof . . . and living in a cool and mysterious solitude of her own creation', had accepted the young officer with artist leanings, 'as being like herself a stranger in these parts'; but the arrival of Basil, two years later, had banished them both to the more cruel isolation of a marriage broken but not dissolved. 'For seven years she had been on a desert island; her appearance had become a hobby and a distraction'; the war brings even deeper isolation, with solitary drinking bouts in a service flat high up above Grosvenor Square. Cedric's hobby and distraction had been the furbishing of his country estate with caves and grottoes. 'The lonely and humiliating years . . . each had its monument.' This pathetic series of grottoes is a symbol, both of marital union and of isolation, of birth and rebirth, but also of the hermit's contemplation. It is varied only by one other poignant comment on their relationship. The year in which Angela had refused a divorce, Cedric 'had spanned the stream with a bridge in the Chinese Taste, taken directly from Batty Langley'.

Symbol of the hermit's contemplation. Ambrose had a word for this – as indeed often in Mr Waugh's books the homosexuals are the most conscious and articulate in matters of the aesthetic conscience. In his disquisition on the superiority of Chinese over European scholarship, he declares: 'European culture has become conventual; we must make it cenobitic.' The accumulation of facts in monasteries is inferior to the exercise of true taste and wisdom. 'Their scholars were lonely men of few books and fewer pupils, content with a single concubine, a pine tree and the prospect of a stream.' Little did he know that he was on the verge of being betrayed and deserted by his audience of two, Bentley and Seal, and condemned to practising the cenobitic life on the Atlantic shore of Ireland, in a little fishing town with the great waves pounding on the rocks below his windows. But his words spring to life again in the minds of those he has left. Both Cedric and Basil echo them. Cedric, on his lonely way between the cave which housed Bn. HQ ('It was curious, he thought, that he should have devoted so much of his life to caves') and flanking Companies, strode happily towards the enemy, 'shaking from his boots all the frustration of corporate life. He did not know it, but he was thinking exactly what Ambrose had thought when he announced that culture must cease to be conventual and become cenobitic.' The end, for him, was a German bullet and death, for Angela and Basil the possibility of a new life. ' "I knew we needed a death," she said, "I never thought it was his."' Basil impossible as a husband? Angela is in no doubt about this. ' "But you see one can't expect anything to be perfect now. In the old days if there was one thing wrong it spoiled everything; from now on for all our lives, if there's one thing right the day is made".' '"That sounds like poor Ambrose in his Chinese mood",' answers Basil. In the concluding words of the author on Basil's pompous counterpart, Sir Joseph Mainwaring, 'he was bang right'.

But the reader is not to be left on a note of Ambrosian whimsicality; the insects momentarily dispersed rearrange themselves in a new pattern: Special Service units are being formed. Peter Pastmaster, Alastair Trumpington – now reconciled to a commission – and even Basil Seal find a place in the new force whose officer complement is being listed in Bratt's Club. '"Most of the war seems to consist of hanging about,"' says the absurdly youthful colonel. '"Let's at least hang about with our own friends."' The world of the author's own war service, and of his post-war chronicles of the military life, comes into view.

Scott-King's Modern Europe is a sad little story, finely wrought and economical in its effects, but sad. Superficially it owed its origin to a visit to Spain, where Mr Waugh joined in the celebrations in the summer of 1945 for the tercentenary of Vittoria, at Salamanca, and had his first experience of the machinery of official hospitality in the post-war world. But it contains his first reflections on the wider scene of mid-twentieth century Europe. Even without the footnote that 'The Republic of Neutralia is imaginary and composite and represents no existing state', we should recognize overtones of Jugoslavia and the Dalmatian coast, and the wider echoes of decay in European historical values everywhere. Combined with this is the radical uncertainty whether anything positive can ultimately have been achieved by a war which, appearing first through the medium of common-room wirelesses under a heroic and chivalrous disguise, became later 'a sweaty tug-of-war between teams of indistinguishable louts'. Uncertainty of the achievement, certainty of the losses incurred, these are the sad strains of the music which is here played.

The musician selected to perform is himself the reverse of distinguished. After failing to achieve a College Fellowship Scott-

King has been classical master at Granchester for twenty-one years; Paul Pennyfeather, if he had stayed at Llanabba, would have been his contemporary. He has become a school institution, lamenting in a slightly nasal voice over modern decadence, and rejoicing in his reduced station through the defection of classical specialists to the Modern Side, fascinated by obscurity and failure, his own first and foremost. And his strange adventures during that summer of 1946 strike a note of dimness all along the line. Neutralia, through remaining out of the second World War physically, as did Scott-King spiritually, 'became remote, unconsidered, dim'. Dim also was Whitemaid, his sole English academic counterpart at the celebrations at Bellacita. Care and the fear of failure dogged and finally overcame Arturo Fe, Doctor of Bellacita University and official in the Ministry of Rest and Culture, Bogdan Antonic, the International Secretary, 'whose face was lined with settled distress and weariness', and Garcia the Engineer. Even with Lockwood, a former prize pupil and Scott-King's rescuer from No. 64 Jewish Illegal Immigrants Camp, the same mournful note is struck. 'Sad case, he was a sitter for the Balliol scholarship. Then he had to go into the army.'

But all these scattered notes of failure, of promise run to seed, of high hopes dashed, are gathered together in the name of Bellorius, 'The Last Latinist', the poet whose 1,500 lines of tedious Latin hexameters gained for him from an ungrateful Hapsburg nothing more than the cancellation of his court pension. Bellorius died poor and in some discredit in 1646; he is the patron-saint of dimness in this work, and it is this 'blood-brotherhood in dimness' which first drew Scott-King to study his work. The new-old and degenerate state of Neutralia could not have made a better choice when it put its first International Secretary on to searching the records for some suitable anniversary to commemorate, some occasion out of which to make political capital. And what irony in the subject to which this unknown early Neutralian humanist chose to devote his Latinity: 'a visit to an imaginary island of the New World where in primitive simplicity, untainted by tyranny or dogma, there subsisted a virtuous, chaste and reasonable community.' Such was the humanist dream which held Scott-King enthralled for fifteen years. The temptation represented by the engraved and embossed card on his breakfast table fell on fruitful soil in a man who for years had been secretly wedded to the warm Southern seas – 'all that travel agent ever sought to put in a folder, fumed in Scott-King's mind that drab morning' – and he went. The awakening could hardly have been ruder.

It was a world of unreason into which he thus stepped, with the one fundamental nightmare characteristic of unreason: nothing is as it seems, all is facade, covering an ugly reality. The air stewardess seems an amalgam of midwife, governess, and shopwalker; Miss Bombaum might be an actress or harlot or lady-novelist, but is in fact a topliner in modern journalism; Arturo Fe might be a slightly ageing film-actor, but is scholar, lawyer, and civil servant. The Hotel 22nd March, known through its political past under a score of aliases, but always referred to as the Ritz; the National Memorial at Simona, which turns out to commemorate a piece of political thuggery; Bellorius himself, confused by Miss Bombaum with the totally different Byzantine General Belisaurus, and finally commemorated by an appalling statue commissioned years before by a fraudulent commercial magnate, representing no one, show that even institutions have but an uncertain hold on reality and stability. It is perhaps but a belated recognition of the power of the genius loci when Scott-King departs by the 'underground railway' as an Ursuline nun, and arrives in Palestine as an illegal Jewish immigrant. All appearances are deceptive in this modern masquerade – a stage-set indeed, but an ominous one.

Appearances are deceptive since in this constant process of scene-shifting which calls itself modern European history the features of the new dispensation are constantly becoming apparent beneath the fading outlines of the old; and in this general dissolution the new is ugly and brash and the dispossessed old is tired and uncomprehending: too wise to be chagrined, too cultured to protest. Those few remaining Neutralian aristocrats, descendants of the Crusaders and Knights of

Malta, who haunt the Ritz like lingering shades, gazing with 'inky, simian eyes' at that portent of the new Europe, the statuesque Miss Sveningen, are blood-brothers of the Arabs of East Africa whom Mr Waugh met in the clubs of the seaboard towns; dispossessed by protectorates in Somalia, Aden, Tanganyika, and Zanzibar (*Black Mischief, Remote People*), and by more ruthless methods of penetration in Harar (*Waugh in Abyssinia*).

It is to this aristocracy of the dispossessed that Scott-King finally and defiantly commits himself in his last words to the headmaster: ' "I think it would be very wicked indeed to do anything to fit a boy for the modern world. . . . I think it is the most long-sighted view that it is possible to take." ' Long-sighted, since Scott-King has finally seen the fallacy of moving with the times: taking up economic history because of the decrease in classical specialists. For change, like revolution, has the saturnine propensity of eating its own children. The more international politics become, the more men reach across the barriers of communities to link up with their ideological brethren, the more of their fellow-men find themselves displaced, dispossessed, outcast. ' "It is extraordinary how many people without the requisite facilities seem anxious to cross frontiers today." ' Thus the Neutralian Major of Police, who significantly doubles his official functions with running the underground escaping organization. ' "That is where my position in the police is a help. . . . I also have a valued connexion with the Neutralian government. Troublesome fellows whom they want to disappear pass through my hands in large numbers." ' The machinery of the modern state is Janus-headed, facing both ways, creating both tyranny and graft, 'supporting a vast ill-paid bureaucracy whose work is tempered and humanized by corruption'. Miss Bombaum was more right than she knew when, quoting from one of her recent articles, she described the underground as 'an alternative map of Europe . . . the new world taking shape beneath the surface of the old . . . the new ultra-national citizenship'. And the new world is the caricature of the old. The 'Republic' of Neutralia is itself a travesty of that more ancient form of state which reaches back to the Greek polis. The Underground, the symbol of the new fraternity of the displaced person, as it takes shape below the surface of old citizenships, is appropriately enough expressed in the symbols of the French Revolution. At the little seaport of Santa Maria, itself a palimpsest of Mediterranean history, from Athenian colony to Napoleonic conquest, there lies on the cobbled water-front a large warehouse, now Underground dispersal centre, a birthplace of the new ultra-national citizenship. Here, ensconced in a bed by the door, whose coverlet was littered with food, weapons, and tobacco, lay the female guardian, sometimes making lace like a tricoteuse of the Terror, while her husband, as supervising officer, made a brief appearance at the door in the hour before dawn, and called the roll of those who were to be 'despatched' on that day.

This was Scott-King's last visual impression of modern Europe when he embarked on the final stage of his adventure – that sea-journey in the battened-down hold of a ship over whose horrors the narrator draws a veil, and from which he emerges, first fully conscious, 'sitting stark naked while a man in khaki drill taps his knee with a ruler'. And at this point a memory from an earlier work of Waugh comes back, a parallel to this total loss of personality insistently demands entry to the mind. Is not the spiritual odyssey of Scott-King which takes him from Granchester to Granchester via Bellacita, the Underground and a Palestinian camp, this escape from the innocence of academic life into the seaminess of modern existence, and a return in-cognito across the waters – is not this all strangely reminiscent of the progress of Paul Pennyfeather from Scone to Scone via Llanabba, King's Thursday, the Latin-American Entertainment Co. Ltd (another underground railway), and Blackstone Gaol? And if this is so, has nothing been achieved in the twenty-one years in which Scott-King has dreamed his dream of the Mediter-ranean? Paul, when restored to Scone and reflecting how right the Church had been to put down early Christian heresy, has at least laid the ghost of religious doubt. What ghost has been laid by Scott-King's excursion into the world of unreason? Can it be

Bellorius? In the staff-room on his return to Granchester he admits:

> ' "To tell you the truth I feel a little *désoeuvré*. I must look for a new subject."
> "You've come to the end of old Bellorius at last?"
> "Quite to the end." '

But why, we may ask, must Bellorius go? Or rather why, in the years which lie ahead of Scott-King, may we be certain that no other Bellorius will absorb his devoted powers? Had there been still some mark of imperfection, one small blemish on the otherwise perfectly dim mental outlook of Scott-King? Even this suggestion seems strange in a man so abstracted from the realities of the moment as Scott-King, who finished the work of translating Bellorius's Latin hexameters into Spenserian stanzas 'at the time of the Normandy landings', and who composed his threnody on 'The Last Latinist' at the time of the peace celebrations; or for a man who 'positively rejoiced in his reduced station'. Far from harbouring a baffled sense of having missed all the compensations of life, he was definitely blasé; and a passage of concealed quotation from Pater's famous description of La Gioconda gives him, in this freedom of the mind, the mysterious agelessness of one who was 'jaded with accumulated experience of his imagination'. And his description of himself as 'an adult, an intellectual, a classical scholar, almost a poet', becomes his leitmotif in the undignified situations into which he is plunged.

And yet, when the story opens, Scott-King is still one small, one minute stage removed from genuine detachment: though superficially content with, nay fascinated by his reduced station, he compensates with the life of the dreamer. After years of labour on his translation, his opus, his 'monument to dimness', the shade of Bellorius still stood at his elbow demanding placation – that shade which was perhaps the temptation to glory in the distinction of being 'The Last Latinist', to create a mental Utopia in the form of an imaginary island governed by reason and free from tyranny and dogma, the temptation to escape and to dramatize the conditions of escape, to invert the pattern of one's own dimness by erecting a model to dimness elsewhere. So, to discharge his last obligation to Bellorius, Scott-King distilled his learning, wrote his last little essay and thereby gave a hostage to the outside world of noisy Neutralians – and the embossed and engraved invitation on the breakfast-table was the sign that the challenge had been accepted. There he was to learn the total irrelevance of the mental landscape of his mind to the modern age, to be finally disabused of the expectation of ever finding a 'virtuous, chaste and reasonable community', be these qualities never so diluted.

More than that, the man who has raised one monument to Bellorius is brought to make a speech before another monument, and, having done so, and the cord having released the enveloping cloth, is confronted with a likeness, in the eyes of the world, of his hero: 'It was not Bellorius . . .; it was not even unambiguously male; it was scarcely human.' That unveiling was the last lesson which Scott-King has to learn, to be reconciled finally to his own dimness, and to the dimness, seen in the light of the world, of the subject and outlook which he represents. In the state of mind in which he returns, even the erection of monuments to a forgotten world is a senseless gesture, even the consciousness of being 'an adult, an intellectual' is excessive, even to be blasé is hybris. The only thing is to accept one's own obscurity, to be content to administer a wasting patrimony, without even the consolation of being a martyr, an outpost, a forlorn cause. The intellectual and classical scholar was, in the academic life, as was Bellorius at the court of the Hapsburgs, a pensioner of such figures of the new order as Griggs, the civics master, dilating on the sufferings of the Tolpuddle Martyrs. Now even the pension has been cancelled, and no voice will be raised to extol the humanist and regret his passing. A sad story – delicately wrought, but still sad.

The Loved One is a traveller's tale. At Hollywood, on the edge of the great Californian Desert, Mr Waugh came upon an almost unknown settlement of poor whites living at cultural subsistence level on a low diet of beliefs and attitudes inherited from their European ancestors, and calling themselves, to the exclusion of poor blacks, Caucasians. Being themselves expatriates, 'uprooted, transplanted and doomed to sterility', the Southern Californians compensate for the spiritual poverty of their living conditions by an elaborate cult of Death. Their lives, homes, and reputations are precarious, insubstantial, like stage sets, a man's name is forgotten after a week. Suicide is often the concomitant of failure. Life is a hurried pursuit of material goods; pain, deprivation is feared and shunned. In Whispering Glades the Southern Californian has created a necropolis devoted to the service of Death, in the image of which he escapes from the shallowness of life. Change is trumped by permanence – 'their name liveth for evermore who record it in Whispering Glades'; unhappiness, pain, and failure are banished by the conjuration of happiness and success. At Whispering Glades the bodies of the dead are last seen as in buoyant life, 'transfigured with peace and happiness', from there the soul starts 'on the greatest success story of all time'. The services of the necropolis are available to all Caucasians on a non-sectarian basis, but the adherents of certain sects, such as Jews and Catholics, prefer to conduct an obscure cult of failure and bodily dissolution elsewhere. The practices of the dominant caste, associated together in Megalopolitan Pictures Inc., determine the architecture and liturgy of the Cult. 'Liturgy in Hollywood is the concern of the Stage rather than of the Clergy'; the Churches and administrative buildings of Whispering Glades look like stage sets, but are in fact the only buildings in the settlement of permanent structure, being proof against fire, earthquake, and nuclear fission. The liturgical language in which the mysteries are expressed avoids all overt mention of Death in its physical guise, and the division between life and death is resolved, in the interests of abundant life, by terms such as 'to pass over' (*to die*), 'the loved one' (*the dead man*), 'the waiting ones' (*the living*). Like its remote ancestor, Christianity, the cult practised at the necropolis of Whispering Glades is particular to guarantee the ultimate success of those whom material life has rejected. Suicide is the supreme sign of failure, so embalmers and cosmeticians devote their highest art to preparing the disfigured remains of loved ones who passed over by their own hand, so as to look as they did on their wedding day. This service is available even to those Caucasians forming a small group of more recent immigrants, who congregate at the Cricket Club, whose speech, dress, and habits seem to the traveller to preserve in degenerate form an earlier cultural stratum of his own country, from which they have been brought. This vestigial culture is indeed the reason for their importation. Their articles of subservience to the older poor whites, their masters, are recorded in their 'contract'. Escape from bondage is rare, manumission not unheard of, but strangely enough condemned by the group loyalties of the new poor whites themselves, who refer to any attempt to emigrate to the dominant group as 'going native'. Caught by this conflict of ethnic loyalties, their only safety is in their contract; their racial memory preserves a lively horror of the expression 'his contract wasn't renewed'. When this happens, the only logical way out, as for Sir Francis Hinsley when the tale opens, may appear to be suicide.

Into this setting Mr Waugh introduces his hero, Dennis Barlow, one of the subjected minority for whom the lapsing of a contract with Megalopolitan Studios is not attended by ethnic compulsions, for he is an artist. Without indulging in the grosser gestures of going native, he sought a post in a humble station and found it with Mr Schultz, of the Happier Hunting Ground. Here a mortuary service was offered for the animal pets of Los Angeles deriving from the authentic tradition of Whispering Glades; here Dennis settled down to work on his poem, which, through constant spasms of composition and excision, continued just perceptibly to grow. 'There at the quiet limit of the world he experienced a tranquil joy such as he had known only once before, one glorious early Eastertide when, honorably lamed in a house-match, he had lain in bed and heard below the sanatorium windows the school marching out for a field-day.' Mr Waugh has established his hero in a place of reflective withdrawal, suffused with childhood memory, and patterned on the model of the larger scenes of life to which he is to be called.

The call comes through the suicide of Sir Francis Hinsley, Dennis's friend and landlord. Faced with the impossible task of providing Juanita del Pablos ('Maenad of the Bilbao waterfront') formerly the Jewess Baby Aaronsen, with a new identity as an Irish colleen, he crumbles. So the one-time chief scriptwriter to Megalopolitan Pictures Inc. finds himself replaced by a Mr Medici ('only he says it "Medissy"'), someone's wife's cousin, and Dennis finds his host strung to the rafters, the suspended body, mottled face, and protruding tongue spelling 'Failure'. Saddled with the arrangements for the funeral, he pays his first visit to the parent establishment of Whispering Glades. 'As a missionary priest making his first pilgrimage to the Vatican, as a paramount chief of equatorial Africa mounting the Eiffel Tower, Dennis Barlow, poet and pet's mortician, drove through the Golden Gates.' Life – or in this case Death – will soon have him in its thrall.

There is no need to tell in detail the story of Whispering Glades – the gardens and garden statuary, the Churches in Grade A steel and concrete, replicas of older structures in Europe, the zoning of resting places, the arrangements for preparing, embalming, and exhibiting (by chaise-longue or half-exposure) the person of the Loved One for leave-taking in the Slumber Room, all this Mr Waugh has taken in great loads from the *Illustrated Guide* which he brought home, and shaped it into his narrative. We are concerned with the hero. Two things happen to Dennis Barlow. Among the numerous Mortuary Hostesses, standard products of a continental American culture, one stands out as unique. This is what Dennis has vainly sought during a lonely year of exile, 'sole Eve in a bustling hygienic Eden, this girl was a decadent . . . her eyes greenish and remote, with a rich glint of lunacy'. Among the many outdoor settings, he is drawn, by some obscure, mounting inspiration within him, to seek out the peaceful inner sanctuary of the cult and the most expensive plot in the grounds, the Lake

Isle of Innisfree. Ferried by a slightly ribald Charon across the waters of forgetfulness, he lands and finds what his ferryman calls 'the poeticest place in the whole darn park'. There is a constant murmur as of innumerable bees; but the murmur is from empty beehives, equipped with electrical motors. No stray dogs or cats can invade the trimly kept paths and glades – only young people come, in pairs, 'lapped in an almost visible miasma of adolescent love'. On the island is the burial plot of the Kaiser family; a name known throughout the land from Kaiser's Stoneless Peaches, which taste like a 'ball of damp, sweet cotton-wool'. Peace comes to Dennis; not now can he work on his poem, or produce the valedictory verses promised for Frank Hinsley's funeral. 'The voice of inspiration was silent', the voice of duty muffled. Now was the time to watch the flamingoes and meditate on the life of Mr Kaiser.'

And then, as if in answer to this threefold evocation of poetry without pain, the flesh without the kernel, hives without bees, peaches without a stone, and adolescent love, there appears again his 'sole Eve in a bustling hygienic Eden', his decadent, Aimée Thanatogenos, communing with herself on the twin themes of Art and Death. As junior cosmetician in Whispering Glades, her role is to demonstrate the triumph of Art *over* Death, as the hives and the peaches and the whole settled desert of Southern California demonstrate the triumph of Art over Nature. Dennis recognizes in her the living embodiment of Whispering Glades. For him she is 'Aimée', the beloved and the loved one; she is 'Thanatogenos', born of death and born to die. Approaching the island, Dennis is no longer the Innocent, observing with unstated, shocked surprise the travesty of an older culture; he is the artist scenting a theme. 'His interest was no longer purely technical nor purely satiric. Whispering Glades held him in thrall.' Now, on the island, he realizes that 'this hot, high afternoon was given for reminiscence rather than for composition'; the rhythms which begin to move in his mind are reminiscences of the anthologies: '. . . For many a time I have been half in love with easeful death . . .' Both sense and poetry of these lines are, for Aimée, beautiful; Dennis may send his next poem to her, but not to her home. '. . . send it here, to Whispering Glades. This is my true home.'

Then begins the contest between Dennis and Mr Joyboy, chief embalmer and leading mortuary technician of Whispering Glades, High Priest of the cult of the dead, for the possession of Aimée. Mr Joyboy is also, in his chosen medium, an artist. 'Before he came there had been rumours in the embalming-room that Mr Joyboy was a mere theorist. These were dispelled on the first morning. He had only to be seen with a corpse to be respected.' In this contest each wooer speaks the language of conventional poetic diction best known to him, each ransacks his thesaurus and selects of its best. Dennis, in the idiom of the Old World, searches the Oxford Book of English Verse for suitable offerings; Joyboy, in the idiom of Southern California, woos with corpses. 'When I send a Loved One in to you, Miss Thana-togenos, I feel as though I were speaking to you through him'; so the expressions of the Loved Ones, when they arrive in her cubicle, tell the story of Joyboy's heart, waxing from serenity to jubilance, reverting to an expression of bottomless woe, re-placed after Dennis's discomfiture by a grin of triumph. None who saw Mr Joyboy making his daily rounds among the staff, 'sometimes laying his gentle hand on a living shoulder or on a dead haunch', would expect otherwise. In what more fitting coin could Joyboy and Barlow pay their tribute to Death personified than in the mortal integument of men's existence or in the in-herited products of their minds?

In Aimée, the decadence of the Old World has entered an instable alliance with the derivative and standardized jargon of the New. 'As she grew up the only language she knew ex-pressed fewer and fewer of her ripening needs.' To express those needs it offers her only a debased pidgin; for the mystery of romance and religion only the 'poetical', non-sectarian patter of the Glades. Her nature responds to Barlow's suit, disturbingly 'unethical' and un-American though it is. But her New World personality brands him as a liar and a cheat for his plagiarism of the Oxford Book and the implied parody of his job at the Happier Hunting Ground. What irony that Aimée should feel

147

her confidence abused when Dennis woos her in the poems of others, some 'by people who passed on hundreds of years ago', and yet should feel 'kinda holy' when Joyboy conveys his emotions through the corpses of those who passed on yesterday. What irony that she who works and has her being – and even proposed to marry the revered Joyboy – in Whispering Glades, an institutionalized parody of love, poetry, and religion, should object to Dennis because 'the language he daily spoke in his new trade was a patois derived from that high pure source' – a patois of a patois. Both are decadents, but only Dennis knows it; 'in the dying world I come from quotation is a national vice'. What Aimée does not realize is that Whispering Glades is one entire quotation – not indeed even from the classics, but from something akin to the slim volumes in Victorian lambskin, or the Edwardian frivolities of Frank Hinsley.

Poor Joyboy is hardly more acceptable. Though wholly American, undoubtedly ethical and an artist at his trade, he has a background which brings disillusion, a drab bungalow in a down-town building estate, a coarse and insulting Mom drooling over Sambo, an obscenely naked parrot in a cage. This is native Amercanism, the vigorous hedge-plant which supports the noble florist's bloom of a Senior Mortician. '"When Mom takes a fancy to people she treats them natural same as she treats me." "She certainly treated me natural."'

As the conflict mounts in intensity, masks are stripped off; each contestant throws *haute école* to the winds and takes to sweaty lunge and parry; Dennis becomes more cynical, Joyboy more 'natural'. Sambo's funeral at the Happier Hunting Ground, which is Aimée's lowest ebb of disappointment, sees the duellists meeting first on the mutually agreed ground which is to witness their final contest. Blown away like gossamer in the wind are the fine phrases of equality which led Joyboy to contemplate making Aimée an embalmer. Each suitor speaks to her in tones of native proprietorship. ' "Aimée, as your future husband and spiritual director, I must tell you that this is no way to speak of the man you love."' ' "Now, honey-babe, I'm going to be firm with you. Just you do what Poppa says this minute or Poppa will be real mad with you."' In her extremity, Aimée's spirit cannot do other than revert also to native stock, to 'the eagle-haunted passes of Hellas' and to 'the high places of her race . . .; Aimée withdrew herself into a lofty and hieratic habitation'. So she consults the Guru Brahmin, who dispenses his wisdom in the guise of a bearded and almost naked sage, in a daily column of a local newspaper. But, true to the parodistic nature of the civilization whose air she breathes, this is no mythical Greek maiden approaching at dawn, bare-footed through the dewy grass, the mystery of some local Delphic oracle. Aimée is the daughter of a religious crank and an alcoholic; the Guru Brahmin is Mr. Slump, a drunken and totally unethical journalist. As the exchange of letters and advice works up to a peak, Mr. Slump also reverts to native tradition. Pursued to Mooney's Saloon on the evening of his discharge from the newspaper, he hands Aimée, in the last stages of despair, the mystic message and brutal advice which solves all her problems: ' "Do? I'll tell you what to do. Just take the elevator to the top floor. Find a nice window and jump out. That's what you can do."' Aimée's acquired desire not to present the embalmers with any 'special little difficulties' caused her to vary the manner in which she started out on the greatest success story of all time, from that oracularly enjoined on her, to an injection of cyanide, for which she chose, quite without design, Mr Joyboy's workroom. But her mind was at rest. Truly, the Guru Brahmin, alias Mr Slump, had been moved by the spirit when giving his advice. ' "Wasn't I right?" – "You know best, brother." – "Well, for Christ's sake, with a name like that?"'

There remains the problem of the disposal of the body. The manner chosen by Mr Waugh – incineration by the resourceful Dennis at the pet's cemetery – though appearing to be entirely unethical is, in fact, deeply poetic. What irony that Joyboy, called to the art of preserving dead bodies, should be unnerved by actual death, and be forced to escape an ugly situation by concealing the death and disposing of the body! What satisfaction for Barlow to pound up the remains of the parodistic Aimée as a meet return for the destruction of his old friend

149

Frank Hinsley through the agency of the fraudulent Juanita del Pablos! Where else could the last 'natural' meeting of this trio, each of which had reverted to its own vigorous stock, take place but in the Happier Hunting Ground? As a parody of Whispering Glades it is a meet setting for the satirical finale; as a derivative from that high tradition, the pet's cemetery experiences a moment of glory when coming to the rescue of its nobler relation.

Thanks to the emergence, during the closing scenes, of some of the more incisive qualities of Basil Seal, Dennis comes away from this experience with the tickets for an affluent return home – a further settling of accounts on behalf of poor Frank Hinsley, whose contract did not even include any provision for repatriation. As for Joyboy, we need not worry on his account. The disappearance of Aimée and Dennis at the same moment, with its suggestion of unethical conduct, may mean for him some slightly unwelcome commiseration, but the alibi is a good one.

As for Mr Waugh, he is most to be congratulated. He, like Dennis Barlow, carried home from California, to an 'ancient and comfortless shore', his chunk of experience, 'to work on it hard and long, for God knew how long'. He has worked off the immediate excitement of the scene in this totally unsentimental exposure of a great travesty of art and of death; the pounding of Aimée is a satisfying reversion to a natural, primeval mode of dispensing justice. He has also carried out, in his own person, a salutary cleansing rite which had been for some time impending. Mr Waugh was in Hollywood for the filming of *Brideshead Revisited*. But, on his own admission, he spent almost more time in the cemetery of Whispering Glades than in the studios of Los Angeles, '. . . all the while his literary sense was alert, like a hunting hound'. Perhaps the Muse was there trying to convey to him, as she was to Dennis Barlow, 'a very long, complicated and important message'. Perhaps she was trying to tell Mr Waugh that, like Dennis Barlow, he was a man 'of sensibility rather than of sentiment'; not a satirist, or a romantic novelist, but something quite different. *The Loved One* is a satire; it is also, in its chosen allegorical mode, a work of great poetic tact and sensibility. There were, for Dennis Barlow, 'certain trite passages of poetry which from a diverse multitude of associations never failed to yield the sensations he craved; . . . these were the branded drug, the sure specific, big magic'. Parody can also be big magic. Mr Waugh has left his card, his memento mori, with the American public in the annual reminder that 'Your Aimée is wagging her tail in heaven tonight, thinking of you', and in the valedictory words pronounced over an Alsatian's grave by the Reverend Errol Bartholomew, non-sectarian clergyman: ' "Dog that is born of bitch hath but a short time to live, and is full of misery. He cometh up, and is cut down like a flower; he fleeth as it were a shadow, and never continueth in one stay . . ." '

But no, the Muse is not yet quite content; her message is 'very long, complicated and important'; it is about 'sentiment' and 'sensibility', and it concerns Mr Waugh. Since 1939 he had been nagged by the memory of *Work Suspended*, the murder of Atwater by John Plant, which was never written. All Mr Waugh's heroes are addicted to fantasy; all of them are forced out into the open and made to face the consequences of their fantasy being taken seriously. John Plant, a writer of thrillers, who had dreamed of the perfect murder plot, would have been hustled into constructing in the real world the perfect plot of his fantasy when he found the corpse of Atwater on his hands. That theme is taken up here: Joyboy is an artist in death who finds himself, for the first and only time, with a corpse on his hands. The Muse becomes importunate – *But Joyboy broke down. Who disposed of Aimée?* Barlow and the Happier Hunting Ground. A cynical, parodistic agent in a 'natural', primitive setting. Basil Seal and Azania are resuscitated to help Plant out of the mess. The killing over, the shade of Frank Hinsley placated, Barlow could leave California unravished but enriched, sloughing off 'something that had long irked him, his young heart'. Mr Waugh also left behind something which had long irked him, the romantic world of *Brideshead Revisited*, the product of a youthful fantasy which the world had taken seriously, and which he then found, an unexplained corpse, on his hands. He acted

151

like a man, not of sentiment, but of sensibility. A book which was, as some thought, on the verge of self-parody, written in a style too much like the rhythms from the anthologies, was at least denied to the grossly sentimentalized and parasitical idiom of the film studio. Aimée should at least be denied to Joyboy. There remained his own private rite of expiation. In Aimée, a creature of religious mania out of alcoholism, he consigned the world of Julia Marchmain and Sebastian Flyte to the furnaces of the Happier Hunting Ground. From now on, happier hunting!

In a lecture given in 1953, Professor Romano Guardini commented on the loss by modern man of the primeval images of human existence: the road, the spring of water, the flame of fire. The road was no longer a thing to be walked, stumbled, toiled along, an image of man's earthly way, but the geometrically shortest route between map reference A and B; flowing water was no longer a reminder of time, an occasion of reflection on the whence and the whither of human life, but a jet of liquid from a tap; fire was no longer both comfort and retribution, the living, leaping flame of inspiration, but a tamed demon in a lighter, flicked on, flicked off, to accompany the inevitable cigarette.

In the last sentence of *Love among the Ruins*, written during work on the Crouchback novels to provide an hour's amusement for the still civilized, Mr Waugh strikes just this same note: 'Miles felt ill at ease during the ceremony and fidgeted with something small and hard which he found in his pocket. It proved to be his cigarette-lighter, a most uncertain apparatus. He pressed the catch and instantly, surprisingly, there burst out a tiny flame – gemlike, hymeneal, auspicious.'

Hymeneal, auspicious? An augury for the success of his nuptials with the State-provided Miss Flower? Or a comforting reminder that there was always a way out? Did he feel that 'something small and hard' with the comfort of a groom fingering the ring in his waistcoat pocket, or of a cornered criminal fingering his knuckle-duster? Probably the latter. Faced with the hideous mess the State had made of his lover's, Clara's face, he had walked out at random and anguished, and arrived at

Mountjoy Castle, the scene of his imperfect rehabilitation by a beneficent if not beneficial State policy. 'He knew what he wanted. He carried in his pocket a cigarette lighter which often worked. It worked for him now. . . .' After the great holocaust, his mind was calm and empty. 'The scorched earth policy had succeeded. He had made a desert in his imagination which he might call peace . . . the enchantments that surrounded Clara were one with the splendours of Mountjoy.' All the paraphernalia of the State, the Ministers of Rest, Culture and Welfare, the Mountjoys Old and New, the Dome of Security, and Service of Euthanasia, the Method of Reform, Remedial Repose and Rehabilitation, even the Result, Miles Plastic, as shown to the world, are one and all no more than stage properties of this Grand Guignol of the future. The genuine symbol, the touch of mania in the whole scene, that rich glint of lunacy in the eye which distinguished Aimée from her fellow receptionists, the note of a primeval urge distorted and diverted from its proper channel, is seen in that small and hard object which enables man to burn his past without however being able to rise, Phoenix-like, from the ashes. No liberating action, this, as when Dennis Barlow burnt his immediate past in the furnaces of the pet's cemetery, no sloughing off of a young heart before returning enriched to the roots of one's culture. Miles, the Modern Man, is the conditioned personality who recognizes his own image when confronted with a simple, rough packing case, model of the new Mountjoy Castle to rise on the ruins of the old. For him, there is no ticket back home; the gutted prison and the rehabilitated prisoner means no more than the destruction of a richer past for the benefit of a poorer future; the Revolution, as in *Scott-King*, eats its own children. The Common Man is an inverted myth, a counter-Prometheus, not one who steals fire from the Gods, but one who fondles a small hard presence in his pocket as a guarantee of the power of unlimited destruction.

The story is a 'romance' of the not so distant future. Mr Waugh is pleased to imagine, for our entertainment, the condition of a State-made desert in which the boredom of prison is the general condition of society, and a certain tranquil melan-

choly, conducive to some degree of culture and individuality, is
only to be found in prison. Social life in the Welfare State is a
fate worse than death, the Euthanasia Centre – a kind of Whispering Glades in reverse – the most popular service. Short of
Euthanasia, residence in places like Mountjoy Castle under a
new Penology, whose fundamental principle is that 'no man
could be held responsible for the consequences of his own acts',
is the most desirable thing.

Here lies a rich quarry of material for flashes of paradoxical
humour: the law-court, which all but acquits Miles for incendiarism, and all but commits the bystanders, bereaved relatives
of the airmen he has incinerated, for contempt of court; the
Euthanasia Service, slack when a strike or anything of human
interest is afoot, but normally so popular that foreigners with
one-way tickets are turned back at Channel ports; the infinite
advantages of being an Orphan rather than the product of a Full
Family Life; and the minor diverting possibilities of the State
newspeak – *State be with you, State help me.* The new Penology
descends ultimately from Sir Wilfred Lucas-Dockery, Governor
of Blackstone Gaol, as the old lags of Mountjoy, Sweat and
Soapy, with their melancholy regret that 'there's no security in
crime these days', echo the sturdy individualism of the aged
burglar at Egdon Heath, who urged Paul to stand up for his
rights when given caviar for cold bacon.

The planned dilapidation of Satellite City and of its main permanent State building, the Dome of Security, is the contemporary note: an ironic comment on communal lack of enterprise by
one who saw only too keenly the shadow side of the *panem et
circenses* provided by the 1951 Festival buildings, and by their
most prominent feature, the Dome of Discovery. The Dome of
Security itself is an epitome of the whole self-defeating nature of
social security schemes in this story: 'The eponymous dome had
looked well enough in the architect's model' – say, for instance,
the Beveridge Report – 'shallow certainly but amply making up
in girth what it lacked in height. . . . But to the surprise of all,
when the building arose and was seen from the ground, the
dome blandly vanished'. Security for all is planned, but blandly

evades the planners, just as 'great sheets of glass planned to "trap" the sun, admitted a few gleams from scratches in their coat of tar'. A prime urge of the human race vanishes into thin air at the touch of a blueprint; the sun cannot be trapped, and fire is reduced to the incendiary possibilities of a cigarette-lighter.

The pointlessness of the plan at large is paralleled by the desultory progress of Miles Plastic's last, melancholy attempt to achieve love among the ruins; his affair with Clara, on whom two State-enforced operations end by foisting a facial mask as unnatural and obscene as the smirking travesty of a face given to Frank Hinsley at Whispering Glades; and his final resort to the last ecstasy of wholesale conflagration. And it is in a desultory and whimsical manner that Mr Waugh has chosen to point his reflections on the decline of our culture by the allusive employment of fragments from three artists of a banished age: Tennyson, Browning, and the neo-classical sculptor Canova. Tennyson's 'Now sleeps the crimson petal, now the white', and 'Come into the garden, Maud', provide the setting and the concealed quotations for that 'rich, old-fashioned Tennysonian night' at Mountjoy Castle, which is Miles's last night in Arcadia before an inscrutable State decrees his rehabilitation and thrusts him out into the world for which he has been conditioned. Browning's poem 'Love among the Ruins' takes over the setting: 'the site once of a city great and gay', treeless slopes where once

> . . . the domed and daring palace shot its spires
> Up like fires . . .

Here there remains of past glory but a single turret, but the poet knows

> That a girl with eager eyes and yellow hair
> Waits me there . . .

as Clara waits for Miles in her cubicle in a Nissen hut, filled with the bric-a-brac of a vanished civilization. And Henry Moses's reproductions of Canova's marbles – so reminiscent, in its 1876 binding, of the Victorian drawing-room with perhaps a Venus de Milo in the corner – provides the starting point for the illustrations. By means of a homely paste book technique which must have given Mr Waugh much innocent amusement, he constructed the figures for the ironic juxtapositions of life in the Greek Polis and in Satellite City: the drawings 'Exiles from Welfare', 'Experimental Surgery', and others, bearing such inscriptions as 'Canova fec., Moses delin., Waugh perfec.'

To Tennyson's mysterious Maud and to Browning's girl with the yellow hair, to Canova's groups of Cupid and Psyche and of the Three Graces, Mr Waugh has added one further, delightful fancy, that 'long, silken, corn-gold beard', which was the only feature that broke the canon of pure beauty in Clara's face when Miles first beheld it, complemented as it was by the voice, with its 'deep, sweet tone, all unlike the flat, conventional accent of the age'. But for Miles, this crowning feature, whether seen in the clear light of Satellite day, or 'silvered like a patriarch's in the midnight radiance' of another Tennysonian night, *is* the canon of beauty. ' "On such a night as this," said Miles, supine, gazing into the face of the moon' – and echoing all unknowingly the *Merchant of Venice*– ' "on such a night as this I burnt an Air Force station and half its occupants." ' That was the only moment of ecstasy he had then known. The beard brought, for Miles, the dawning of the proscribed emotion of love, 'a word seldom used by politicians and by them only in moments of pure fatuity', which singles out two persons from the herd and gives them an indelible, rubber-stamp obliterating impress. But what State has given, as an unexpected result of the Jungmann operation, State may take away. The removal of the beard by experimental surgery, and its replacement by a synthetic rubber skin, 'a tight, slippery mask, salmon pink', is the end. Miles retches unobtrusively, walks off and burns down Mountjoy; revolt is exorcized in a moment of ecstasy. '. . . his brief adult life lay in ashes; the enchantments that surrounded Clara were one with the splendours of Mountjoy; her great golden beard, one with the tongues of flame that had leaped and expired among the stars . . .'

The theme of the lovers brought together, and parted, the one disfigured by act of State, is common to this work and to George Orwell's *1984*. But here we must at least say, *thank State for the beard*; for it is that which discharges harmlessly, like a lightning conductor, the more sultry implications of this sad little love story. Orwell develops the theme with the full attendant resources of brutality which seem now inevitable in any sombre view of the future. Mr Waugh's short story never loses its astringent humour and freedom from sentiment. Both qualities are guaranteed, not only by his own style and outlook, but also, in this particular case, by the beard.

CHAPTER 7

Faith and the War

*The algebra of fiction must reduce its problems to symbols if they are
to be soluble at all –* JOHN PLANT in *Work Suspended*
'. . . all gentlemen are now very old.'
CORPORAL-MAJOR LUDOVIC in *Officers and Gentlemen*

A COMIC WAR-NOVEL is something of a contradiction in
terms. 'The organized dispossession, capture and killing
of his own species' may be, in Mr Waugh's own words, 'among
the activities which, like husbandry, distinguish civilized man
from brute creation'. But the killing can only be heroic, grim,
tragic, or senseless; it is the organization which has its comedy.
'Army life, with its humour, surprises and loyalties . . . comprises the very essence of human intercourse,' Mr Waugh continues in the same essay. So *Men at Arms* is a comic novel of
army life, rather than of war.

Guy Crouchback, when this book opens, is a maimed romantic. Romantic by nature, he has been maimed by ill-fortune. For
eight years, since his wife, Virginia, left him, he has lived in a
spiritual desert; deprived of love, not *simpatico* with his fellow-
men at Santa Dulcina delle Rocce, politically isolated by the
omnipresence of Fascism, possessed of only a few dry grains of
faith. Such an existence has fostered to an excessive degree the
substitute life of the dreamer. As a romantic, he has a special
affection for the English Knight and would-be Crusader, Sir
Roger de Waybroke, whose tomb in the town has stolen the
honours from the more official sanctuary of Santa Dulcina. As a
maimed romantic, he has an especial dislike for the crudities of
the Modern Age. The outbreak of war provides this modern
romantic crusader with a goal and an incentive, but no more;
the goal is the defeat of the enemy, 'the Modern Age in arms'.

The opposition of the romantic visionary and the modern age is, of course, a staple of Mr Waugh's writing: Tony Last in Mayfair, William Boot and Copper House, Scott-King and Neutralia, come to mind. Nor is it difficult to bring them together; a chance meeting at the club is enough, a mistaken identity, an embossed invitation card on the breakfast table will do. The irrational is always breaking in, seeking out the hero's secret, unadmitted ambitions: Boot's desire to fly, Scott-King's wish to visit the Mediterranean. Fantasies have a habit of coming true, or at least one's dream-life may take real, perhaps unwelcome shape. John Plant, who as a writer of thrillers deals professionally in murder and sudden death, is suddenly made to sort out what remains of his life when his father is run over in the street. The outbreak of war is, for Crouchback, the challenge of the irrational, the apparent coincidence of a real and a dream world.

But *Men at Arms* continues the line of straight novels, not of entertainments, it follows *Work Suspended*, not *Scott-King*; and this presents Mr Waugh with a problem. The theme is the comedy of Army life; a bitterly tragic ending to the life of an innocent man deeply wronged, as in *A Handful of Dust*, is therefore out of question. Nor may the Innocent return to his Limbo, as do Boot, guileless but successful, and Scott-King, wise and resigned; the setting of the Second World War is too real for this. Guy's return by plane from overseas at the end of *Men at Arms* is purely episodic, not final like Boot's from Ishmaelia and Scott-King's from Neutralia. Nor do the hero's fantasies determine properly the course of events. The scenes devoutly desired by William Boot, the spectacular, cinematographic consummation, with Bengal Lancers, kilted highlanders, and the like, precipitate the technicolour ending. Crouchback's fantasies also have a 'last-minute' quality, religious or military – 'serving the last Mass for the last Pope in a catacomb at the end of the world', saving the Captain Truslove of his schoolboy reading at the eleventh hour from an awful death at the hands of the Pathans. But world events do not allow themselves to be treated in this way; there is no Mr Baldwin to act as *deus ex machina*.

Clearly such a man as Crouchback is in no position to become the immediate bearer of the external action of a novel about Army life; a process of acclimatization is necessary. In the meantime, while the hero remains apparently passive, both friend and foe will behave in the exaggerated manner of shadows thrown more than life-size on the retina of the inward eye. So, as we are warned on the dust-cover, the plot is chiefly concerned with 'two highly peculiar officers, his brigadier and a junior officer of his own batch', Ritchie-Hook and Apthorpe. Ritchie-Hook receives the projection of all Crouchback's compensatory romanticism; he is the adventurer and figure of irrepressible vital force, a distant descendant of Captain Grimes in *Decline and Fall* – and like him, always in the soup. He assumes the role of the Captain Truslove of Guy's youthful reading. Apthorpe receives the projection of all the lamed Crouchback's desired contacts with his fellow men at arms, he is the inner compensation of a person who has always known himself to be non-*simpatico*. So these two are contrasted embodiments of the ideal of the 'man at arms', and the dispossession of Apthorpe by Ritchie-Hook in Crouchback's loyalties is the main theme of the book. Here is action enough proceeding deep below the numbed surface of the hero's soul.

A word on the ancestry of Apthorpe. He is basically the personification of the 'Good Scout'; by name and by nature he descends from Appleby (*Work Suspended*), Beckthorpe (*On Guard*), and Atwater (*Work Suspended*), with perhaps just a dash of Mr Wodehouse's Ukridge. Not that Apthorpe is just another Atwater, any more than Crouchback is another John Plant. Atwater was a man, if man is the proper word, of many conflicting moods. 'Atwater the dreamer, Atwater the good scout and Atwater the underdog seemed to appear in more or less regular sequence.' But Crouchback has spent eight years in the spiritual desert which Plant was perhaps only just entering. So Crouchback assumes the role of the dreamer, while the underdog is played by the Trimmers, Leonards, and Sarum-Smiths of *Men at Arms*. And Atwater, stripped of some of his many conflicting moods, and in whom – as we are told in the postscript to *Work*

160

Suspended – in the course of the war 'the Good-scout predominated', Atwater is reborn as Apthorpe, fortified to bestride
the action of *Men at Arms*, a Colossus though with feet of clay,
while Crouchback treads the longer and stonier way of self-
integration.

The feet of clay are of course not immediately obvious. The
rise and fall of this grotesque figure whose centre of gravity is
not in itself, but in Crouchback, provides the successive themes
of the three books of the novel: *Apthorpe Gloriosus*, *Apthorpe
Furibundus*, *Apthorpe Immolatus*, the Triumph, the Lunacy, the
Slaying of Apthorpe. Of the batch of young officers who joined
the Halberdiers with Crouchback, 'Apthorpe alone looked like a
soldier'; predestined by similarity of age and foreign background to be thrown into his company, Crouchback is at first
absorbed into this figure of the modern Miles Gloriosus,
'haunted by Apthorpe in the role of doppelgänger'. But as he
has lent his more flashy counterpart the vitality not immediately
accessible to himself, so from the first moment he begins to
withdraw it; significantly, it is the appearance of Ritchie-Hook –
in the words of *Helena* Crouchback's 'second heroic myth' –
which gives him the strength to do so. At his first meeting with
the truculent Brigadier, Guy is mistakenly assumed to be
Apthorpe; Apthorpe may well bluster – ' "taking advantage of
another chap's illness to impersonate him" ' – but the damage
is done: the supplanter has this once been supplanted. But Guy's
main weapon in the silent struggle is the one available to the
rational man over his more naive brother, irony and detachment; this is the mood in which he draws refreshment from the
epic struggle between Apthorpe and Ritchie-Hook over possession of the 'thunder-box'.

As is common in such cases, a resounding fiasco precedes and
overshadows the beginning of recovery: Guy's attempt to
resolve his one civilian problem, by establishing marital relations with his former wife Virginia, separated from him by civil
divorce only. This misconceived operation is undertaken under
the influence of Mr Goodall, a fellow-Catholic and pious crank,
and in the spirit of Apthorpe. These two caricatures of Crouch-

back's motives in joining the Army, the desire for a religious crusade and the need for fellowship in arms, preside jointly over the attempted seduction, undertaken – again very suitably – on St Valentine's Day, that 'patron to killers and facetious lovers'. Perhaps the failure happened because the lover set out as a 'killer'. Not only do Apthorpian elements (a monocle and a sprouting moustache) bulk large in the motivation of Crouchback's new-found confidence, but Apthorpe's constant telephonic interruptions of what was planned as a tender scene are a determining factor in the ultimate fiasco. When the bell rings for the last time, after the rift between Guy and Virginia is painfully manifest, the following conversation takes place:

'"I say, Crouchback, old man, I'm in something of a quandary. I've just put a man under close arrest."
"That's a rash thing to do."
"He's a civilian."
"Then you can't."
"That, Crouchback, is what the prisoner maintains. I hope you aren't going to take his part."
"Virginia don't go."
"What's that? I don't get you, old man. Apthorpe here. Did you say it was 'No go?'"
Virginia went. Apthorpe continued . . .'

If this interchange between Crouchback and his grotesque double is read as a colloquy between two parts of Crouchback's own mind on his ill-advised attempt to place *the civilian Virginia* under bodily restraint, the extent of the domination of Crouchback by his double is patent. Apthorpe appeals to Crouchback 'as an officer of His Majesty's Forces', because 'I don't happen to have my King's Regulations with me'. But King's Regulations do not cover such problems as the relation between Guy and Virginia, and cannot be solved along the lines of moustache and swagger. It is the peak of the external domination of Crouchback by Apthorpe. It is also a close parallel to Plant's grotesque exchange with Atwater in front of the caged Gibbon ape at the London Zoo, a veiled commentary on his

unsatisfactory relationship with Lucy Simmonds. But the interrupted tête-à-tête, burlesque or tragic, is clearly a type situation
with Mr Waugh. Years before Lottie Crump had disturbed the
attempted seduction of Baroness Yoshiwara by Walter Outrage,
and Tony Last had tried, despairing and drunk, to get through
to Brenda, in the arms of Beaver.

The Battle of the Thunder-Box is a complex engagement. It
is, firstly, a straightforward situation: the Brigadier seeks to
deny a junior officer, Apthorpe, the consolations of the private
possession and use of a chemical closet, one of the more cumber-
some articles of his extensive kit. But it is also a 'tense personal
drama', played out against a military and a liturgical background, and resulting in the transference of Guy's allegiance
from Apthorpe to Ritchie-Hook. As a military operation, it is a
supreme illustration of the tactics of 'biffing' the enemy, by one
who 'saw war itself as a prodigious booby trap'. As a time of
purgation it began with the Brigadier's first avenging descent
on the officers' training course on Ash-Wednesday, and rose to
a climax in Holy Week at the very end of the course. Even the
object for whose possession, and denial to the enemy, the battle
is fought, is complex. It is a defence against infection, a piece of
property, a reminder of the past and a promise for the future, a
sign of all that desire for fastidious withdrawal felt by the
civilian turned soldier, symbol of the private personality, still
resisting the dedication and the promiscuity of the soldier's life.
'Thunder-box' is indeed, as Guy reflects at its passing, 'the
mot-juste'. For it is 'something rare and mysterious', a throne,
a source of power, and the Brigadier, in shattering it, has broken
its owner's hold on Crouchback; he has *stolen Apthorpe's thunder*.

Having cleared the ground for operation, the Brigadier can
now dispense his own brand of bush magic. If the spell of Apthorpe was a blatant extraverted one, and to that extent false
for the maimed and introverted Romantic, Ritchie-Hook speaks
to him with a potent spell which bridges the gulf between
reality and dream, fact and fiction, and reaches back into his
childhood imaginings. ' "Gentlemen," he began, "to-morrow
you meet the men you will lead in battle." ' With these and later

pronouncements by Ritchie-Hook ringing in his ears, Guy is back in his preparatory school listening spellbound to a boyhood romance on a summer Sunday evening. ' "I've chosen your squadron for the task, Truslove. . . . And I can tell you this, my boy, I'd give all my seniority and all these bits of ribbon on my chest to be with you." ' The chimes then set swinging in Guy's mind do not fall silent in this volume, and the further development of the Truslove fantasy acts as an inward commentary on later external events.

The spirit of Ritchie-Hook-Truslove is strong in the two further incidents in the book: Guy's reconnaissance patrol against Beach A at Dakar, and Apthorpe's death in hospital at a British port in West Africa. The operation at Dakar was strictly against orders – 'a little bit of very unofficial fun' – but very much in accordance with the higher doctrine of 'biffing'. Ritchie-Hook, chafing for action, smuggles himself ashore as a supernumerary passenger among Guy's patrol, and runs into trouble; he brings back as a trophy the head of a negro sentry, but is himself wounded. This, as Guy reflected, was all 'true Truslove-style'; later, he privately referred to it as 'Operation Truslove'. But such private escapades do not for the moment fit the book of the Force Commander, still less of the War House, with whom the 'true Truslove-style' and the 'old, potent spell' of the gallant Brigadier is at a discount. So Operation Truslove has a double face. Guy rescuing his wounded Brigadier from the results of his own boldness is, in Truslove terms, Captain Congreve, the dark horse, turning up at the last minute to rescue Truslove from the Pathan fortress where he awaits death by torture. But the War House is a more difficult place to storm than a Pathan fortress. So the negro head, which Ritchie-Hook hands to Guy, symbol and trophy of the tactics of 'biffing', turns into a booby-trap directed against the author of these tactics. Ritchie-Hook has come very near to blowing himself up, and Guy with him. At the end of the book, the two perpetrators of the escapade are flying home to appear before a court of inquiry.

And yet, as with the thunder-box, booby traps, besides being dangerous to the enemy – and even to their own wielders – are elements of purgation. So the Dakar incident does not end in unrelieved loss. 'The flying-boat made another turn over White Man's Grave and set its course across the ocean, bearing away the two men who had destroyed Apthorpe.' One, Ritchie-Hook, operated with 'a bomb in the rears', the other, Crouchback, if one may continue in the spirit of Mr Waugh's language, with 'a bottle of whisky in the guts' (Agatha Runcible's last party, once more). The whisky bottle which Crouchback smuggles in to Apthorpe, lying fever-sick in hospital, continues the theme of both the booby trap and the severed head. Objects to which power, and thus responsibility attach, have a habit, like booby traps and severed heads, of blowing a hole in an officer or his reputation. But Apthorpe is a different matter, being himself less offensively minded than a challenge to offensive tactics in others. And so the passage of the whisky-bottle, from the Brigade Major to Crouchback and then to Apthorpe, becomes a cleansing and purging act of the first order. Crouchback has graduated, by his action at Dakar, and his symbolical slaying of the impostor here, from being – in Truslove terms – Congreve the tarnisher of the regiment's honour to the Congreve who has proved his worth in action. '"It takes some time to kill an old bush hand",' said Apthorpe, '"But they'll do it. They wear one down".' The last phrase becomes almost a leit-motif in the final scene between Crouchback and his double.

Many critics regretted the demise of this 'richly comic personality'. But Apthorpe cannot other than die; and it is better that he should. For he is not genuinely comic. This strange embodiment of a false attitude to things military is grotesque, poised, as the grotesque always is, between comedy and tragedy, and limited, unless it is to become altogether more daemonic, to a short and disturbing course. As a doppelgänger, he must either die, to the lasting benefit of his counterpart, or live and draw the life-force from the hero. Did those critics desire for Crouchback the same fate that befell Dostoevsky's Golyadkin or Stevenson's Dr Jekyll, when faced with and worsened by *their* doubles? And did those critics, who in the same breath commended the comic richness of Apthorpe and condemned the lifelessness of Crouchback, realize that they could not have their bread buttered on both sides? Fortunately, from the moment when Crouchback first impersonates the impersonator, there is no doubt which one the author intends to emerge the victor; but both Crouchback and Mr Waugh only got away from the spell of Apthorpe just in time.

But there is a further reason why the impostor must go. The saga of Apthorpe, as it unfolds in training and then in Scotland, is placed against a background of wider perspectives: the tactical policy of the Brigadier, of which it provoked a supreme demonstration, the season of Lent, in that for Guy at least it strengthened his sense of dedication, and lastly the march of public events and the operations of the enemy. It is not just a touch of burlesque when Ritchie-Hook is stated to have launched the first attack, by invading Apthorpe's undisturbed possession of the thunder-box, 'two days after the fall of Finland'. The steady crescendo of events abroad puts flaps and wrangles about seniority at home at a discount and biffing at premium. The phoney war and the official mind, with its facile optimism before a reverse and its glib explanations after, is replete with the spirit of Apthorpomania. Apthorpe is the phoney double, both of Crouchback and of Crouchback-England. The spirit of the thunder-box is exploded in the military life of the hero by Ritchie-Hook, in the political life of the nation by Churchill.

An important element in the disease of Apthorpomania was the spy-craze and the secret weapon craze – witness Apthorpe's flaps about enemy parachutists and arsenical smoke. This is the theme of a small chapter of four pages in Book Two, in which two brief contrasted scenes take place in the dark early hours of Good Friday, an anonymous colloquy in a Most Secret headquarters in London, and Crouchback senior, with Guy, praying before the Altar of Repose at Matchet. The first is, on the surface, a further hilarious variation on the theme of the thunderbox; a fragment of information, transmuted by the alchemy of official stupidity, lands Guy and his brother-in-law Tony Box-Bender on a Most Secret Index. A file is opened on each of them as possible spies associated with a secret weapon of the enemy.

But the scene in Matchet, what of that? May we not surmise that Guy, and with him Tony, now on active service, is being recommended to another Most Secret Authority; that Divine Providence is being asked to open a file on both of them, and take them under its especial care? May we say that the pathological susceptibility to the omnipresence of the enemy, a genuine trait of Apthorpomania, is here trumped by the elder Crouchback's simple, unshakable faith in the omnipresence of the Divine hand?

Many readers will regard such a construction as fantastic. It is, of course, fantastic; but then all Mr Waugh's fantasies have a close bearing on the inner workings of his plots. Readers to whom doubts occur may consider an even more innocent fragment of dialogue in this inconspicuous scene. ' "You're wearing that medal?" – "Yes, indeed." ' The medal is one of Our Lady of Lourdes, worn by Guy's brother Gervase on his one and last day in the trenches, and intended by the father for Tony Box-Bender, but given, after Tony's hurried departure, to Guy. ' "If you get hit and taken to hospital, they know you're a Catholic and send for a priest." ' There is nothing memorable about this, but the circumstances are interesting. All Guy's attempts to pull wires and get accepted into the Army have come to precisely nothing; he visits his father at Matchet, and is presented, as on a plate, with a holy medal – and a commission, ' "It's remarkable," said Guy. "I spend weeks badgering generals and Cabinet Ministers and getting nowhere. Then I come here and in an hour everything is fixed up for me by a strange major." ' The strange major is Major Tickeridge, of the Halberdiers, who immediately recognizes, in Crouchback senior, with none of the soldierly externals, an *anima naturaliter halberdiana*.

A special aura always attaches, in Mr Waugh's novels, to those figures – Mr Baldwin, in *Scoop*, is one – who facilitate the hero's movement in a strange world, and enable him to achieve his ambition. It looks as if Mr Crouchback has some secret reserves of power.

His power is, of course, his simple sanctity, which is the

fountain-head and inspiration of all that his sons, Gervase, Ivo, and Guy, possess of religious dedication. The function of the father, Mr Waugh said to the present writer, was 'to keep audible a steady undertone of the decencies and true purpose of life behind the chaos of events and fantastic characters. Also to show him as a typical victim (parallel to the trainloads going to concentration camps) in the war against the Modern Age.' The contrasting scenes on Good Friday were one way in which the steady undertone was kept audible. The thunder-box and the medal are contrapuntally associated as secret weapons, both sources of power, of *mana*, the one spurious, giving Guy and Tony a place in that crazy collection of suspects on the files of the Most Secret headquarters in London, the other genuine, ensuring his entry into the Army, and marking his status in a wider spiritual brotherhood.

A fuller development of this contrast between the Communion of Saints and the Brotherhood of Suspects is reserved for the second volume. But it is touched on once more in two small incidents in the Dakar sequence. Guy finds Halbardier Glass, his stolid batman, chasing a Goanese servant out of his cabin. ' "Caught this black bastard in the very act, sir. Mucking about with your kit, sir." ' The Goanese protests that he is the cabin-boy, and no native, but a Christian Portuguese, and in proof produces a gold medal from his blouse. Guy is confused, tips the Goanese and reprimands his own servant, losing face with both. Better men than he, he reflects, would have brought out his own medal, 'would perhaps have said "Snap" and drawn a true laugh from the sullen Halberdier and so have made true peace between them.' The sequel to this occurs on Beach A at Dakar where Guy, in completely unmotivated manner, sends Glass back to the boat with – of all things – a coconut. ' "What me, sir? This here nut, sir? Back to the boat?" – "Yes, don't talk. Get on with it." ' This is the counterpart, at the Sancho Panza level, of the tragicomedy of the slaying of Apthorpe. Guy's failure to find a common denominator between Glass and the Goanese, which is his own incomplete poise between the active and the contemplative life, has been partly retrieved. 'He knew

168

then that he had lost all interest in whether he held or forfeited Glass's esteem.' Guy has just failed to ignite the fuse of the medal, his secret weapon; he has fallen short of true brotherhood with the Goanese. But at least he has extinguished the false brotherhood with the 'black bastard' outlook of Halberdier Glass, as later he will cut himself free from Apthorpe with the aid of the whisky bottle. The spirit of Captain Congreve, who let the side down, is being exorcized on Beach A at Dakar.

'*Men at Arms* began with its hero inspired by an illusion. *Officers and Gentlemen* ends with its deflation.' An aspect of this illusion was Apthorpe, so the book begins with the placation of his spirit – entitled, in an earlier draft, *Apthorpe Placatus* – 'a ritual preparation for the descent into the nether world of Crete'. The act of *pietas* required of Guy is to find that odd character Chatty Corner, to whom Apthorpe has bequeathed his voluminous kit. This, and Guy's attachment, pending his return to active service, to Tommy Backhouse's Commando in the Isle of Mugg, provides the external action until the hero leaves for the Middle East. Chatty is found, curiously enough, on Mugg, and reveals to Guy the secret of Apthorpe: his unheroic African past, a civilian post with a tobacco company, the emptiness of all his pretensions to toughness and bushcraft. When Chatty had signed, in his large and irregular writing, the fateful words: *Received November 7th, 1940 Apthorpe's gear. J. P. Corner*, the wind dropped, the sky was clear, and the spirit for ever silent.

The quest for Chatty, with nearly two tons of kit in the conditions of war-time, beleaguered England, resolves itself into a problem of movement; at this moment there appears, out of the blue, 'Jumbo', otherwise Colonel Trotter of the Halberdiers. Like Mr Baldwin he grants the hero the fulfilment of his desires; like Major Tickeridge he establishes complete understanding with the elder Crouchback, who is thereby relieved of the unwelcome attentions of Grigshawe, ex-Halberdier drill-sergeant, now Major and Quartering Commandant. Crouchback senior is again effortlessly in touch with the charmed circle of those in command.

As the volume progresses, the deflation of Guy's illusions on the war and the military life, which has begun in the first book, goes on in clearly marked stages: the home front under the Blitz with its proliferation of staff bodies and useless formations, of Air Marshals and Public Relations Officers, and the mockery of the Regimental Depot, with all the elements of the traditional life of a fighting unit removed for the duration, and, as the climax, the disastrous operations in Crete and their aftermath. As Guy acquires a deeper understanding of 'the classic pattern of army life . . ., the vacuum, the spasm, the precipitation, and with it the peculiar impersonal, barely human geniality', he gradually turns away from this parody of the dedicated task as he had fondly imagined it, at first, at Santa Dulcina.

Against the declining world of real soldiering is set the rise of Trimmer, the figure of the people in arms, a development of Hooper in *Brideshead Revisited.* He is the new and ugly reality which supplants the old illusion which was Apthorpe, he is the denial of all form, tradition, honour. A fraud himself, he is quick to recognize the fraud in others – in head-waiters, for instance, with their phoney French; he is free of the under-world of the spurious, and succeeds, at a long remove, Guy and Tommy Backhouse in the favours of Virginia. His very meta-morphoses, from Trimmer the Cockney to Gustave the hair-dresser, then to McTavish the Major of the Argylls, parody the varied roles of a Grimes or a Philbrick, and the spasmic changes of military life. Parody, in fact, varying from the comic to the blasphemous, is his life element, as the grotesque was that of Apthorpe. Heroes are in strong demand, but not such as Guy, the 'Upper Class', and the 'Fine Flower of the Nation'. ' "This is a People's War," ' says Ian Kilbannock, with the cynical flair of the publicity man. ' "We want heroes of the people, to or for the people, by, with and from the people." ' In short, they want Trimmer. Operation Popgun is his apotheosis, laid on as a publicity stunt by a mushroom Headquarters, and written up in complete disregard of the unheroic behaviour of Trimmer and his sappers; a spurious burlesque of Guy's raid at Dakar, which was undertaken against authority, in a spirit of offensive initiative. Ian comes off the island, drunk, with a whisky bottle, as Guy came away with the head of a Negro sentry; his last words to Trimmer, before they leave, parody the famous last words of Cranmer to Ridley; planned on Holy Saturday, 1941, the operation is an infamous counterpart, in the resurrection of popular feeling that it stimulates, of the one true Resurrection. And it is wholly effective. The Minister who minutes his desire for 'an assurance that McTavish has been found employment suitable to his merits', travesties all unknowingly a similar Churchillian message concerning Ritchie-Hook. Ian Kilbannock finds the right answer to this: sex-appeal for factory hands. Trimmer is sent to travel the industrial towns with the unwilling Virginia, to provide a fillip to arms production through the exploitation of his only genuine attributes, his vulgarity and his sex-appeal. He is another Miles Plastic, sent to lecture the country with Miss Flower and an up-ended packing-case, the pattern of things to come. He is the hero of a false religion, that of the People, the Sir Roger de Waybroke of the publicity men, a crusader, and even, in his unwilling peregrinations, something of a martyr to the cause.

In *Scott-King* Mr Waugh describes the new fraternity of the displaced person, itself the corollary of the modern police-state, the 'new world taking shape beneath the surface of the old . . . the new ultra-national citizenship.' Here also, the forces of disorder are progressively taking over. Two aspects of these forces may be summed up in the words: sex and military security. In *Men at Arms* spy-mania was contrasted, to its disadvantage, with the piety of Mr Crouchback; here it is opposed, as a distinction without a difference, to sexual promiscuity. In the leave hotel in Glasgow, the place of promiscuity and rootlessness, on the lower floors scenes reminiscent of the tortured restlessness of the underworld of Hell are being enacted; and in an upper room, Trimmer and Virginia pursue their sordid liaison, a travesty of the Villa Hermione and of the sacramental union of marriage. Meanwhile, in London, Colonel Grace-Groundling-Marchpole, 'lately promoted head of his most secret department', is filing the latest item of crazy intelligence on the suspect Crouchback, linking 'the Box Case' with the Scottish Nationalists, 'a direct connexion from Salzburg to Mugg'. In Glasgow the new cameraderie of the promiscuous, in London the new ultra-national citizenship conferred by suspicion; the one knowing no frontiers, the other no reserves. Both are powerful dissolvents of illusions based on the belief that the war is being fought by men of principles, by *Officers and Gentlemen*.

Through all this Guy Crouchback pursues his lonely way, in and out of various webs of military organization which compete, in spasms, for his person. His strong emotional link with the Halberdiers, except for a brief, chance meeting in Crete, is broken. Deprived of this bond, he is reduced to making half-hearted, uncertain personal contacts, as that with Ivor Claire, show-jumper and aesthete in peacetime, now an officer in Tommy Backhouse's Commando. The bond with Apthorpe had been a link with conformity, with the 'soldierly type'; that with Ivor is the instinctive fellowship of the unclubbable, 'a common aloofness, differently manifested – a common melancholy sense of humour; each in his own way saw life *sub specie aeternitatis.*'

Guy's increasing inner distance from his country's cause is hinted at again by an incident in Alexandria. He makes his Easter duties at a civilian church; the priest, of enemy origin, tries to draw him out on troop movements; Guy's attempt to investigate the matter leads to a report that he is consorting with spies, and a further black mark in the delighting Colonel Marchpole's files. ' "It all ties in," he said gently, sweetly rejoicing at the underlying harmony of a world in which duller minds discerned mere chaos.' It does indeed. Guy's religious allegiance is a sphere of ultra-national citizenship; a rift is opening between this and the simple issues propagated by those who will see in the Russian Alliance an accession of strength, merely, to the foes of Nazism. Guy's new hearkening to this allegiance is promptly registered by the counter-organization, pursuing *its* ultra-national aim with that distorted single-mindedness which comes of being the obverse of the truth. The union of sacred and secular ideals in the person of Sir Roger de Waybroke, English Crusader and Saint by local acclaim, is about to break down.

The end of the illusion is Crete; this signal defeat of British arms, in which a military machine dissolves into near chaos, is related in Book Two under the finely ironic title 'In the Picture'. Guy's personal drama is played out with the assistance of three other characters: Major Hound ('Fido' to his friends), Corporal-Major Ludovic, and Ivor Claire, three names which may be pondered for their appropriateness of sound and sense. The character given to Hound is the epitome of all the most savage views of the regimental officer on 'the staff'; in his combination of the externals of soldiering with inner weakness, he is the counterpart of Apthorpe. Like Apthorpe, also, he is reduced by a combination of irony and direct attack. Guy supplies the irony; his active opponent, the Ritchie-Hook of this episode, is the remarkable figure of Corporal-Major Ludovic.

Ludovic is one of those peculiar natures known to all serving soldiers, the aesthete – other ranks might say 'pansy' – whose hold on life and on the realities of a situation remain tough and sure, when more rigid though seemingly more manly types break down under stress. His aestheticism and basic contempt for military convention he shares with Ivor Claire, and these two sustain the note of sceptical observation with which Crouchback is too withdrawn, too inarticulate, to be charged. He is also, however, intensely active. He pricks the pretensions of Hound, and senses the disillusioned withdrawal of Crouchback, acting as a chorus to the drama of conflict between the two men. To him it is given to draw the whole moral of the book, by noting Crouchback's pleasure that the veteran Greek General Miltiades is a gentleman. 'He would like to believe that the war is being fought by such people. But all gentlemen are now very old.' He observes and encompasses the final downfall of Hound. He carries out, finally, the most heroic single action of the reported events of the Cretan campaign – significantly an action of escape; 'godless at the helm' he steers the escape boat to safety, and then, with superb resilience, carries Guy ashore at Sidi Barani, and recovers after only two days in hospital. With his detachment and his toughness, he is a principle of vitality, a mythical figure of the life force, the antithesis of the trumped-up People's hero, Trimmer. He continues the line of figures in the novels which combine sensitiveness and tenacity, elegance and strength, especially Mr Baldwin. Like him, and like Philbrick, in *Decline and Fall*, and Ian Kilbannock in this book, he has the gift of tongues, speaking now in strong plebeian tones, now in the fruity and plummy mode of his assumed self.

The life-force in Ludovic, impelling him to leave Crete and bear Guy with him, raises no ethical problems; escapers are not deserters. At the officer level, principles are involved. Claire is a man of simple and irregular solutions, directly counter to all principles of honour and military duty. His unorthodox answer to the problem of placing his troop on their objective in the tactical exercise in Mugg is a foretaste of his action in leaving Crete against the explicit order to Hookforce scribbled in Guy's pocket-book. Having defied the code, he is also saved by it; to avoid the scandal of court-martial, Tommy Backhouse, effectively supported backstairs by Julia Stitch, packs him off to India. Guy, who thought he was 'the fine flower of them all . . . quintessential England, the man Hitler had not taken into account', is left at the end with a handful of broken fragments. The implied unity of the title of the work, *Officers and Gentlemen*, is ironically dissolved. Ludovic, who alone senses the gentleman in Crouchback and Miltiades, and their isolation, is no officer. Claire, who alone recognizes Trimmer's exploit as spurious, is no gentleman. In a wider sense honour has been lost through the bungling muddle and confusion of the Cretan affair; in the widest sense by the news of 22 June 1941, 'a day of apocalypse for all the world', when the Germans invaded Russia, and the Allies gained an Ally with the features of the Beast. For Guy, the issues which had seemed so plain at Santa Dulcina are confused again, 'and he was back after two years' pilgrimage in a Holy Land of illusion in the old ambiguous world, where priests were spies and gallant friends proved traitors and his country was led blundering into dishonour'.

Honour murdered is the meaning of the dead but apparently

uninjured body of a young English soldier, which Guy finds in a deserted Cretan village. Shown by his identity disk to be 'R.C.', he lay 'like an effigy on a tomb – like Sir Roger in his shadowy shrine at Santa Dulcina. . . . Guy saluted and passed on', and with that gesture left behind him his first fine enthusiasm, his crusading ideal. But his military training prompted him to carry away, for the record, the red portion of the identity disk; higher formation must be told of the passing of an illusion, must have notice that henceforth his allegiance is limited to the strict bounds of military discipline and obedience.

And now follows the most ironical touch of all. Guy has brought two things out of Crete: his notebook, the only remaining evidence of his friend's desertion, and the identity-disc, the sign of general dishonour. Mrs Stitch knows of and fears the evidence of the notebook, and is stimulated to action by the imminent arrival of Ritchie-Hook, notorious for his ruthlessness in hounding down officers who have disgraced themselves. To prevent the spark from reaching the charge, she encompasses the immediate and peremptory dispatch of Guy by the longest route home, round the Cape. Unknown to her, Guy has burnt the pocket-book, a symbolic act; but before leaving he attempts to communicate to GHQME the more subtle message of the identity disk, with an accompanying message: 'Taken from the body of a British soldier killed in Crete. Exact position of grave unknown.' Entrusted to Mrs Stitch for delivery, it is dropped by her without more ado into the wastepaper basket, in the belief that it contains the evidence against Claire. For Guy the general message is important, individual dishonour only symptomatic; for Mrs Stitch it is the reverse. Where gallant friends prove traitors, the country cannot preserve the justice of the cause. The simple message from Lieutenant Crouchback of the Halberdiers of the death of an ideal, 'exact position of grave unknown', cannot be delivered, for there is no one worthy to receive it. The world has reasserted its old ambiguity against the illusion that war and an ideal can be run in double harness; crusades are over when principles are sacrificed to expediency. As we learn, in the 'Epilogue', from the list of books asked for by Tony Box-Bender, vocations are now only possible in prison camps.

As with *Men at Arms*, personal issues are projected on to a backcloth of public events, and this is supported by echoes of Greek mythology and Christian, especially the Easter liturgy. An air-raid in London reminds Guy of Holy Saturday at Downside, 'paradoxically blessing fire with water', and the blast of a bomb is 'a pentecostal wind'. Where Good Friday was something of a keynote in the first book, Easter Saturday takes its place in the second; on that day we are given cross-sections of events at Sidi Bishr, at the War Office, and at Matchet. The isle of Mugg is the halcyonic prelude to events in the nether world of Crete. Ludovic, 'godless at the helm', is a Charon making the reverse journey with a handful of incorporeal souls plucked from the realm of shades. Some of the overtones are apocalyptic: the Russian Alliance, gas drill at the Halberdier depot. Guy's first sight of soldiers marching in gas-masks – 'ten pig-faces, visions of Jerome Bosch, swung towards him' – is a prelude to his discovery of the havoc wrought by total war in the beloved traditions of the Depot Mess. Events on the main stage of the action are parodied by creatures in the wings, like grotesqueries in the margin of a medieval manuscript of unimpeachable piety. Guy's mixed religious and patriotic motives in joining up are given distorted reflection in the views of Mr Goodall, of Southsands, and his belief in an imminent rising of Catholic Europe, 'led by the priests and squires, with blessed banners, and the relics of the saints borne ahead'; and in the mad figure of Katie Campbell with her outspoken Nazi sympathies – 'England's peril is Scotland's hope'. The Commando activities of demolition, covering ground, and living off the country are reflected in the mad, blue eyes of Campbell of Mugg, and the precise and academic, but not less demented tones of Dr Glendening-Rees, protagonist of the seaweed diet. Indeed, madness is rife, in this as in other works; and it is usually in the eyes. Katie's eyes are 'wide and splendid and mad', while in another mode, Ludovic's eyes, at a moment of crisis, are 'the colour of oysters', and Mrs Stitch has 'true blue, portable and compendious oceans'.

176

It is tempting to linger over the eyes of Julia Stitch. As Guy drove away at the end, leaving her with the vital message of the identity disk, 'she waved the envelope; then turned indoors and dropped it into a waste-paper basket. Her eyes were one immense blue sea, full of flying galleys.' The allusion is to Hérédia's sonnet on Cleopatra, whose eyes were '*toute une mer immense où fuyaient des galères.*' Like her greater precursor, Julia is the undisputed queen of the mixed civilian and military society of war-time Alexandria; she is protectress of X Commando and the *dea ex machina* who restores to Guy his power of speech, then condemns him to a weary return to England and to spiritual silence. She sails with supreme charm and confidence through the final episodes of the work, as the presiding deity of the world of ambiguity and unreason which Guy has come to recognize. In the manner of Margot Beste-Chetwynde, who lured Paul Pennyfeather into the ambiguous world of King's Thursday and the white slave traffic, Julia Stitch, with fine disregard of traditional moral principles, traffics in the persons of dishonoured officers. Her creature, General Headquarters Middle East, combines the features of Latin-American Entertainment Co. Ltd with those of Fagan's Private Sanatorium. Guy's return to England by the long sea-route from Julia's house is Paul's return to Scone via Margot's Albanian coastal villa. Her destruction of the identity disk is once more the deception played by Mr Todd on the rescuing expedition; Crouchback, like Tony Last, is condemned to indefinite silence. Scott-King is spirited away across the water from Neutralia, the world of unreason, to Palestine, and ultimately back to the dim but comforting obscurity of his post at Granchester, relinquishing his long-cherished Mediterranean ideal, after the experience of its reality. So also Guy Crouchback; the return from the world of chaos leads to the acceptance of the dimness of service in an obscure station. Pennyfeather returns to Scone and theology, Scott-King to Granchester and the Classics, Crouchback to the Halberdier Barracks and the drill square. Guy's Odyssey in the world of ambiguity started with drill on the square under Halberdier Colour-Sergeant Cook, and the detail for piling arms; it

M　　　　　　177

ends with Halberdier Colour-Sergeant Oldenshaw and precisely the same drill: ' "I'll just run through the detail. The odd numbers of the front rank . . . – all right?"

'All right, Halberdier Colour-Sergeant Oldenshaw. All right.'

Part Three

THE ARTIST

CHAPTER 8

Comedy from Chaos

*My problem has been to distill comedy and sometimes tragedy from the
knockabout farce of people's outward behaviour*
                                    — EVELYN WAUGH

EVELYN WAUGH, AS Dame Rose Macaulay has said, is the
most amusing and perhaps the most gifted world-creator of
our time. 'Brilliantly equipped to direct the radiant and fantastic
circus he has called into being, he can stand within it cracking
his whip while his creatures leap through his paper hoops with
the most engaging levity, the gravest fantastic capers.' The
critic who seeks to display the inner mechanism of this world
may well be seized with trepidation. Not only does the author
refuse to be drawn by those who seek 'to detect cosmic significance' in his work, 'to relate it to fashions in philosophy,
social predicaments or psychological tensions'. His self-con-
fessed positive aims are just as non-committal. They may be
reduced to two: he writes to delight an audience, and he produces books as would a craftsman. 'Writing should be like clockmaking.' Unfortunately, no plans of the finished product are
preserved, and there is always the risk that analysis will leave us
with a heap of parts, but no clock.

His silence, in his own person, on his intentions, is paralleled
by his avoidance of comment, as narrator, on the processes in the
mind of his creatures. There is an almost complete absence of
introspective analysis and of that ironic comment so much
affected by writers of our century. Take, for instance, the opening sentences of *A Handful of Dust*: ' "Was anyone hurt?" –
"No one, I am thankful to say," said Mrs Beaver, "except two
housemaids who lost their heads and jumped through a glass
roof into the paved court." ' The inward eye of intuition is

operative throughout, but its perceptions are extra-projected into dialogue, action, and terse narrative comment, interspersed with numerous images which take on a life of their own. The main figures and their behaviour being so much the product of an intense inner vision, the author's conscious intention is largely freed and directed towards matters of style and construction. The characters push their way on to the stage of the inner eye, while the novelist pursues them to make some adjustment of make-up or costume, and to arrange the lighting. This skilful disposition of effect by grouping, contrast, and lighting, is done with a care not commonly recognized, and is the only key to the author's intentions. Only in *Brideshead*, perhaps, have the actors taken both play and setting out of the hands of the producer.

Authenticity and composed contrast are the twin pillars of Mr Waugh's narrative style; costume and lighting are always uncannily effective. Authenticity is conferred largely by an extensive use of dialogue; speech, not gesture or scenic effect or psychological atmosphere, is Mr Waugh's preferred medium. Group languages are his especial forte; it is astonishing what a wide range of specialized and professional jargon he has at his command: criminals, drunks, Bright Young People, newspaper men, undergraduates, officers and other ranks, schoolgirls. His dialogue is almost certainly not naturalistic, like the sloppy and formless idiom of unscripted radio conversations; nor is it impressionist. A process of heightening – of selection, restriction and stylization – operates together with the recollection of things heard. He makes but sparing use of pseudo-phonetic transcription to confer authenticity on dialogue. Youkoumian dropped his aitches, but not Mr Sweat. *His* idiom is in the diction: ' "What price the old strings tonight, chum?" ' We shall never know, since Mr Waugh does not tell us, how he pronounced 'Debussy pizzicato'.

As much of our life is spent in the herd, dialogue confers authenticity on whole periods and series of events: the party language of the Bright Young People, the newspaper jargon of *Scoop*, the wartime language of the ranks or of the Mess, liberally besprinkled with Army technicalities. Reminiscences of sight, smell, and taste come far behind the rhythmical pattern of conversation and phrase, and are far less commonly stimulated in later life. The shock of imaginative recollection comes mainly through the inner ear.

Mr Waugh once said: 'I like the spectacle of a strange crowd, not the contact of a familiar one.' A group may be characterized by group dialogue overheard, thus housewives in a train to Aylesbury (*Vile Bodies*), or financial tycoons (Rex and his associates, in *Brideshead*). Or representatives may be summoned out for brief characterization, after which, like Anthony Blanche's set at Oxford, they lumber back into the herd from which they have been so capriciously chosen. Numerous side-line charac- ters – journalists, drunks, soldiers, Irish priests and Teutonic foreigners – stray in and out of his pages. The shorter their appearance, the more authentic they must be, the more imme- diate the shock of recognition; for this, absolute precision is needed, a sparse and austere characterization, pared down to essentials. To this they owe their 'oddity', not to the more leisurely process of whimsical tracery in which an earlier genera- tion – Oscar Wilde, Ronald Firbank – delighted. They are not dressed for their part but are rather like the member of the public who has stumbled by accident, in day-clothes, before the glare of the footlights, blinking, his suit suddenly as soiled and baggy as Chaplin's.

Drunks lend themselves especially to this inconsequential treatment. The remote ancestor of Apthorpe makes his unsteady bow in less than a page of *Vile Bodies*, accosting Adam with the words: ' "You don't know me. I'm Gilmour. I don't want to start a row in front of the ladies, but when I see a howling cad I like to tell him so." ' At another party a drunk gets up from his corner and challenges the company to bet on a coin trick: ' "Bet- you-can't-do-this" . . . "Chap-in-a-train showed me" . . . "Toss- you-double-or-quits." ' Here again, there are none of the hiccups or droolings of a spurious naturalism, but instead perhaps the only example of characterization by hyphenation in literature. Other characters, though playing a more extended role, are remembered for a characteristic besetting phrase. Grimes:

' "That's been my trouble, temperament and sex." ' Youkoumian: ' "There ain't no sense in 'aving bust-ups." ' Mr Salter: ' "Definitely, Lord Copper" . . . "Up to a point, Lord Copper." '

A slight extension of speech and authentic specialized jargon provides those fragments of literary and journalistic pastiche which reflect the development of the story. The hectic events of *Vile Bodies* are mirrored in sections of the gossip columns, written by various of the characters; Crouchback's wartime experiences are accompanied by marginal comment in the form of a recurrent evocation of his boyhood adventure stories. In this manner, Mr Waugh compères his own show, creating a second level of reality which replaces introspective analysis of the minds of the characters: the Bright Young People know they are acting in a gossip-column charade, Crouchback is seen to be acting out a childhood myth. So the scene acquires depth, and the setting itself is the author's ironical or compassionate comment. In *Black Mischief*, Seth's periodical Proclamations to his People are a kind of *leit-motif* to the action, and are opposed to the telegraphese of the newspaper men. Both are types of barbaric-progressive utterance; ironically, the black man uses the curial mode of civilized pronouncement, the white men a debased newspaper pidgin. In *A Handful of Dust*, a cross-relationship is established, by flashback, between Tony, destitute in Brazil, and Brenda, destitute in London, and is the vehicle of the author's compassion at their common suffering. Elsewhere, a simple technique of the travelling camera is used; in *Vile Bodies* composite scenes are presented by what Mr O'Faolain has called the 'quickie technique of disconnected snapshots' – travellers on a cross-Channel steamer, knots of people talking at a party.

There are, in fact, at least two men at work on one Waugh novel. One turns out authenticated sequences of dialogue or literary pastiche linked with narrative comment, the other is in charge of cutting and continuity. The first Mr Waugh, who delivers the film, has a sensitive ear for tone and modulation of speech, and a penchant for caricature; the second Mr Waugh, who is responsible for the *montage*, has an eye for a contrast, and a tendency to burlesque. It is worth looking more closely at this second man's activity, before examining their joint product.

The most fruitful field for anyone with 'an eye for a contrast' is, in our century, that of the conflict of cultures. The small change of modern journalism abounds in what may be called the 'montage cliché' (*land of contrasts where camels and Cadillacs jostle in crowded alleyways*), and it is not improbable that it was Mr Waugh and his fellow travellers of the thirties who brought home the gold of their first, fresh impressions to be broken up by others into the tired small change now in circulation. Mr Waugh's entertainments, especially *Black Mischief* and *Scoop*, are full of this kind of confrontation; but the accent is different, the observation both fresher and deeper. Mr Waugh is interested in what happens to the camelman who acquires a Cadillac – and what happens to the Cadillac. The savage acquires the trappings of civilized life; shirts black and red, waterclosets and post-offices, but converts them to his own uses. With his goats, he makes his home in a broken-down motor lorry. His reaction to boots and birth-control is the *reductio ad absurdum* of the 'civilized' purpose of these things. Dame Mildred Porch is fêted – as the harbinger of an era of new and better cruelties to animals. 'Ladies and Gentlemen, we must be Modern, we must be refined in our Cruelty to Animals.' Both sides are reduced to futility: civilized gentility no less than the rank chaos of the jungle.

For Mr Waugh, as for Mr Pinfold, most of the myths and events of recorded history are centred in the Mediterranean. By contrast to this, the forests of the North, and all those countries in which no historical, classical, or Christian tradition is preserved, or where it only survives in primitive fragments are, by definition, a savage and unordered chaos. But chaos is ambivalent, and primitivism may have its positive note. Charles Ryder 'sought inspiration among the gutted palaces and cloisters embowered in weed . . . the wild lands where man had deserted his post and the jungle was creeping back to its old strongholds.'

So, presumably, did Mr Waugh in Guiana; certainly he did

not go there to make a patient study of tribal tradition, to trace the archaeological and anthropological remains of indigenous cultures, least of all to 'go native'. An early reviewer of *Ninety-two Days* wondered why he went at all: 'the reader may be puzzled to understand why Mr Waugh, whose spiritual home is, he infers, Bath, should have betaken himself to Guiana'. But this is just the point. Mr Waugh's spiritual home is neither Bath nor Guiana, but Bath *in* Guiana, or Guiana encroaching upon Bath. Foreign Office failures such as Sir Samson Courteney would go unnoticed in Bath, but in Azania they spread comic confusion. 'It's just another jungle closing in', said Charles Ryder of England; not hookworm established in Mayfair, but Anchorage House and its fellows subjected to the indignity of conversion into 'shops underneath and two-roomed flats above' – the natives in the broken-down motor lorry, in reverse. 'For myself,' Mr Waugh confesses in *Ninety-two Days*, '. . . there is a fascination in distant and barbarous places, and particularly in the borderlands of conflicting cultures and states of development, where ideas' – here is the crux of the matter – 'become oddly changed in transplantation'. Not Guiana, or Abyssinia, or India, but Mr Todd reading Dickens in Brazil, Seth, Bachelor of Arts of Oxford University and Sir Samson Courteney in Azania, Gilbert and Sullivan echoing over the old port of Matodi, Goa the outpost of Europe in India; England in California, Sir Ambrose Abercrombie flaunting at the Cricket Club his deer-stalker cap and Inverness cape, while uptown sandals and grass-green open-necked silk shirts are formal dress for dinner – a comic, non-introspective taste for the spectacle of the expatriate. The subject has provided absorbing interest for other writers of our time – Norman Douglas, Aldous Huxley, D. H. Lawrence. Such a spectacle, in which the strange and the familiar mingle, never fails to excite Mr Waugh's imagination; it is this which drew him constantly to *Remote People*, the title of the travel-book from which the following quotation is drawn: 'It is to *Alice in Wonderland* that my thoughts recur in seeking some historical parallel for life in Addis Ababa . . . it is in *Alice* only that one finds the peculiar flavour of galvanised and translated reality'.

The two Mr Waughs, the one who delivers the film, and the one who cuts it, work excellently together. Consider how often a single word shifts the focus of a phrase and causes it to leap into comic life. Aimée Thanatogenos, slightly short-sighted, recognizes Dennis Barlow with a start: ' "Oh . . . Pardon me. . . . My memory's very bad for live faces"', for Aimée is a mortician of Whispering Glades. Dame Mildred Porch notes in her diary: ' "Fed doggies in market place. . . . Road to station blocked broken motor lorry. Natives living in it. Also two goats. Seemed well but cannot be healthy for them so near natives"' – for Dame Mildred travels on behalf of the League of Dumb Chums. The context is behaviourist; the reader accepts the familiar touch of the idiom, but the shock arrives at the end, in the one unexpected word. The statements are in character, and have strict internal logic, but the ordered system they represent is revealed as disorder when applied imperialistically to the whole of life. Order in human affairs is, in fact, a civilized disorder, at the highest a hierarchy of values (men before beasts, the living rather than the dead), at the lowest a homely anarchy of common sense. It is the inhabitants of private worlds who are quite logical, and, in the extreme case, quite mad. The method is one of the utmost economy, the author, in his own person, has not said a word.

This is caricature; the author prolongs ever so slightly the line of the attitude – as boys prolong noses on public hoardings – and the speaker finds herself in the pillory of her own statement. But there is also burlesque, the special joy of the second Mr Waugh, who mixes the film sequences with an eye to a grotesque contrast. On the first page of *Decline and Fall*, the Bollinger Club is meeting: 'from all over Europe old members had rallied for the occasion . . .' (and so on for seven lines) '. . . all that was most sonorous of name and title was there for the beano'. Although the reader is prepared by the mention of 'epileptic royalty', 'uncouth peers', and 'illiterate lairds', the unexpected slump to rock bottom with the last, slang word 'beano' – a technique often used by Mr Wodehouse – destroys the sonority of the opening and reveals the true nature of the occasion. Burlesque is the wanton destruction of a formal aesthetic quality, as caricature is the wanton exaggeration of a feature. Max Beerbohm distinguishes the two effects thus: 'Burlesque consists in application of incongruity. Caricature consists merely in exaggeration. To burlesque a statue of Hermes, you need but put a top hat on his head. To caricature it, you must exaggerate its every limb and feature.' The word 'beano' was the top hat on the Hermes statue, the battered bowler where a coronet was expected.

The earlier works of Mr Waugh are full of the burlesque image. Take, for instance, two types from *Scoop*. In Lord Copper's monstrous Megalopolitan building, the hall-porter 'sat in a plate-glass enclosure, like a fish in an aquarium, and gazed at the agitated multitude with fishy, supercilious eyes. . . . William discovered a small vent in his tank and addressed him diffidently . . .' The comic effect explodes at the word 'vent', as with Dame Mildred's use of 'natives'. And again, there is the incongruous ecclesiastical image of the Wodehousian type: 'a valet picked up William's clothes, inclined gracefully towards the bed in a High Anglican compromise between nod and genuflection and disappeared . . . the typewriters were of a special kind; their keys made no more sound than the drumming of a bishop's fingertips on an upholstered prie-dieu.'

The incongruous image is part of the ebullience of the 1930's, but caricature and burlesque are staple elements in his writing. ' "What price the old strings tonight, chum?" ' says Mr Sweat – the old sweat translated by Act of State to Mountjoy – to Miles Plastic; for Sweat and his chum Soapy are, in this reformed prison, addicts of 'crime, calvinism and classical music'. '. . . to see him fumbling with our rich and delicate language,' says Mr Waugh of a fellow-writer, 'is to experience the horror of seeing a Sèvres vase in the hands of a chimpanzee.' Horror, no doubt, predominated when Mr Waugh read the book under review, but mitigated by the delight of expressing it in burlesque idiom. Our reactions to formal perfection are ambivalent, and a certain zest may be felt in the imagination at its destruction. There may be a deep satisfaction in contemplating a chimpanzee breaking a Sèvres vase, or in observing the drunken antics of members of the Bollinger club bearing sonorous names and titles. There is in most of us a touch of the *sans-culotte*. In the terms of Sir Max's definition of burlesque, who is it that puts the top hat on the statue of Hermes? Certainly not a West End hatter. An enemy of classical art, some would say. Why not a classical archaeologist after a party, liberating deep instincts held professionally in subjection?

There is no doubt, many of Mr Waugh's burlesque effects are achieved by the destruction of those Victorian settings he loves so much. In *Love among the Ruins*, Mr Waugh's wry comment on the suborning of the individual by the Modern Welfare State, the new cultural penitentiary of Mountjoy is introduced by a set piece in the style of the late Victorians. 'This was a rich old-fashioned Tennysonian night. Strains of a string quartet floated out of the drawing-room windows and were lost amid the splash and murmur of the gardens. In the basin the folded lilies had left a brooding sweetness over the water.' The reader is lulled, but the forces of destruction are gathering. 'No golden fin winked in the porphyry font and any peacock which seemed to be milkily drooping in the moon-shadows was indeed a ghost, for the whole flock of them had been found mysteriously and rudely slaughtered a day or two ago . . .' We are back in the penitentiary, the world of Tennyson's sonnets has dissolved before the brute features of the Welfare State. Then again, look at the illustrations to the same work, fashioned by Mr Waugh with scissors and paste from Moses's engravings of Canova's classical reliefs. It was the second Mr Waugh, he who is responsible for *montage*, who did this. But if he can cut up the engravings, perhaps it was he who put Mr Sweat up to slaughtering the peacocks? Is he, in fact, on the side of the peacocks or of the penitentiary? And did not the first Mr Waugh, as in the case of the Bollinger Club, rather play into his hands? After all, they are a classical pair, like a pair of stage comedians playing Don Quixote and Sancho Panza.

The slaughtering of the peacocks may be seen as both satire and burlesque farce. Satire, because it reveals the pointlessness of the New Penology of reclamation by culture (a theme as old as *Decline and Fall*). Human nature is unregenerate at this level; Sweat slaughtering the peacocks is Connolly's native levies eating the boots. Farce, because the destruction of an over-ripe aesthetic perfection is pleasurable in itself. But satire is caricature and burlesque when informed by moral indignation; and the besetting weakness of many critics of Mr Waugh is to infer satire when it is not uniformly present, but only the mixed ingredients of farce, satire, and the comedy of manners.

For one thing, it is preposterous to assume that Mr Waugh's entertainments, especially the earlier ones, are, quite simply, satirical, since we would then have to infer that he was inspired by moral indignation against a variety of social phenomena too varied even to be adequately listed: against private schools, against parties ('those vile bodies'), Jesuits and members of Parliament, negroes, whether Democrats, Fascists or graduates of the Adventist University of Alabama, against newspapermen and especially newspaper kings, against most foreigners, drunks, and retired Colonels, Americans and all makers of films. We might – indeed we must – assume that he held His Majesty's Government to have been lamentably ill-represented in the thirties in important regions of Africa like Azania.

There is something missing in the argument, the element of moral indignation. Mr Waugh is not animated by any consistent animus against any of these numerous groups of persons. It is simply that, from the heap of pieces constituting the jig-saw puzzle of modern attitudes – mainly, of course, Anglo-Saxon attitudes – he has gathered a handful of attractively coloured fragments of suitable shape and fitted them, with the aid of a simple plot and the technical principle of montage, into a fresh and entertaining pattern. He is no more speaking from the point of view of stable and settled conviction in these works than he was addicted to philately when, on first setting up home, he varnished coal scuttles with foreign stamps. Nor would he claim, for most of these works, that his arrangement of the jig-saw pieces was that intended by the maker. A comic extravaganza assembles, with economy of medium and audacity of purpose, a cross-section of the strange fauna which inhabit the social scene, and the author is amused to see them blinking in the glare of the footlights. If the selection allows us any inference to the furniture of the mind which assembled them, the inference is not to deeply held convictions, but to the opinions, tastes, and prejudices, the fads and fancies of one creative temperament.

It remains, of course, true that another person's prejudices, when they conflict with one's own, may be unlovely and uncomic; so there are physical limits to Mr Waugh's possible audience. One critic thought that the African scenes in *Black Mischief* 'very often fall through because they rely for their comic value on snob appeal and racial prejudice'. Another states, rather disparagingly, that Mr. Waugh excels when he is dealing, for example, 'with the proletariat, Americans, or other beings beyond the range of human sympathy'. A third, rather similarly, considers him to be at his best when treating subjects which are of themselves ludicrous, such as the Bright Young People, but at his weakest with problems of which he has an inadequate grasp, such as the modern State (as in *Scott-King*). Some, therefore, would restrict him to ready-made farcical themes, some would take offence when, in treating these, he evinces characteristic Anglo-Saxon attitudes. Many critics, however, tend to take farce for satire, fooling for serious comment, and make up for some deficiency in fantasy by a touch of didacticism.

It is true that there is a facility and zest about the earlier novels, *Vile Bodies*, *Black Mischief*, and *Scoop*, which is lacking in later works like *Scott-King*, or *Love among the Ruins*. It is not, however, that Mr Waugh's grasp of the problems of the modern state – as Mr Spender has asserted – is inadequate; this might equally well be said of his treatment of Azania and Ishmaelia. It is, quite simply, that his imagination is not sufficiently stirred. The prospect of Satellite City and the Dome of Discovery arouses in Mr Waugh neither the shock of delight of the African scene nor the shock of horror and delight caused by the spectacle of Californian burial customs. The modern state is just boring, and the mode of its rejection varies between distaste and

191

petulance. But in one work of his maturity, *The Loved One*, Mr Waugh has written a genuine work of biting satire. The modern age is too vast a target, so that his fire is dispersed; but the object here, Californian burial customs, is one and clear, 'plain in view, huge and hateful, all disguise cast off', as was for Crouchback the Age of the Beast. The general moral fibre of our contemporaries is still so permeated by a traditional outlook on death, that he is certain of an audience. The grimness of the issue both challenges and justifies the audacity of the treatment.

For some the treatment was too audacious; it conflicted with the common and widespread prejudice against the macabre in art. There have always been those who have felt repulsion at some incident in the novels which seemed to them to speak of a childish and perverse delight in crudeness and cruelty for its own sake. It is interesting to collect opinions on this matter. Tony Last's end is grim, but not crude; that of little Lord Tangent is crude but briefly indicated, a light and youthful touch of the macabre. Of this kind also was the purpose which Mr Loveday set before himself when taking his famous *Little Outing*. But Basil Seal's eating of Prudence is almost universally abhorred, commonly also Dennis Barlow pounding up his Loved One's pelvis, and Constantine roasting the intriguer Fausta in her bath. Mr O'Faolain finds Youkoumian's treatment of his wife revolting, but defends Basil Seal against Mr O'Donnell. Seal in *Put out more Flags* is, he says, like Attila, the Flail of God, who arrives with the Connolly kids as his Mongolian cavalry to persecute the soft-living bourgeoisie. Mr O'Donnell's explanation of the killing of Prudence, Aimée, Fausta and the living death of Tony Last and Charles Ryder, as a pattern of crucifixion of the woman and of self-crucifixion, to be found in the imaginative life of a whole group of Catholic writers, is interesting. But as a defence – if it is so intended – it is too remote; the shock of revulsion requires a more immediate aesthetic discharge for the ordinary reader to feel relieved. In a lower key, Basil Seal's rejoicing 'in the spectacle of women at a disadvantage' causes discomfort to many. Mr Mikes can take all Mr Waugh can give, with the sole exception of Mr Joyboy preening himself over children's smiles – grinning childish corpses, that is – in *The Loved One*: ' "there is something in the innocent appeal of a child that brings out a little more than the best in me." '

One must tread gently here. The world of Mr Waugh's novels is a fantasy world, but with moral implications. One can neither argue that it is all really harmless, nor that it is all morally justified. It is not just a fantasy world of *Ruthless Rhymes*, or of events at *St. Trinian's*, a valuable occasion for the 'abreacting' of the instincts for savagery in us. Still less can it be defended as the innocent world of childhood, since childhood is unconscious rather than innocent, its cruelty no less cruel for being instinctive. The adolescent, immature cruelty of Mr Waugh is one of the main items on the charge sheet; many critics would agree with the savagery of Mr Savage on the innocence of Mr Waugh. Least of all is it a world of consistent adult moral standards, since whatever justice there is is seldom tempered by compassion.

The simplest defence is to say that while the general implications are moral, the specific fates meted out to the characters are governed by the element of fantasy. The rejection of society in general comes from the horrified perception of the romantic idealist that it is a jungle in which murder and rapine proceed as if by a law of nature, in no sense mitigated by being committed with the conventions of civilized good manners. The ravening tiger of the parson's sermon in *A Handful of Dust*, and the silver foxes, caged and finally skinned, set the tone. The fantasy of eating and of being eaten is indulged in by Angela Lyne as well as being realized in the fate of Prudence. 'No one is to blame', neither killer nor victim, neither Brenda nor John Andrew, Basil nor Prudence, neither the Guru Brahmin nor Aimée.

But where guilt is general, fates are poetically just. Prendergast had committed spiritual suicide; his crazed murderer was acting under proper instructions from the All High. Brenda and Tony had killed their marriage, by incapacity to meet and become one flesh, spiritually as well as phsyically; after the death of the child, the sign of their union, comes their slow extinction in settings symbolically appropriate. Prudence, when she left Azania by air, was expecting further material for her vicious little *Panorama of Life*; she got it. Fausta sought to encompass the elimination of Helena; she encompassed her own. Aimée was dedicated to death; Death took her. Always the punishment fits the crime. In extreme cases even innocence – the innocence of Agatha Runcible and Prudence Courteney, of Tony Last and Aimée Thanatogenos – is a crime. Innocence acts as a magnet to a fate which shows us fear in a handful of dust. It is not a Wordsworthian innocence. Nor is it subject to Aristotelian laws, by which the spectacle of a good man in misfortune evokes, not pity and fear, but repulsion. The fates of Mr Waugh's victims are, indeed, shocking; but the author is also shocked. 'Several writers whose opinion I respect . . . have told me that they regard this as a disagreeable incident. It was meant to be.' In the world of the imagination, caricature may be a true and just likeness. As Sir Max Beerbohm has said in the essay already quoted, those in whom the capacity for fantasy is weak will reject caricature and rationalize their rejection by two arguments: that the picture given is no likeness, and that it is cruel. In Mr Waugh's view of society, distortion is general; within this setting, individual fates are imaginatively just, and even, in the final analysis, self-inflicted.

Single events, then, in Mr Waugh's novels are symbolically appropriate but not literally just; any expectation which conflicts with this is usually moral in nature, and proceeds from the assumption that the satirist, in his function of *ridendo dicere verum*, must apply throughout a consistent and rational principle of judgment. As Mr Waugh wrote in 1946, 'Satire . . is aimed at inconsistency and hypocrisy. It exposes polite cruelty and folly by exaggerating them. It seeks to produce shame.' How well this seems to fit his own works: the exposure of polite cruelty and folly in *A Handful of Dust*, of inconsistency and hypocrisy in *Black Mischief*, the production of shame in *The Loved One*. But he goes on to disclaim, for himself and for his age, the privilege and the possibility of producing satire. 'Satire is a matter of period. It flourishes in a stable society and presupposes homogenous moral standards – the early Roman Empire and 18th-century Europe. . . . (It) has no place in the Century of the Common Man where vice no longer pays lip service to virtue.' It is tempting to whittle away this assertion; to say that here is the later Waugh who has lost touch with his earlier intentions; that satire has flourished in disintegrating societies – such as the later Middle Ages – as well as in stable ones; that the satirist always pretends his own society to be disintegrating. In short, a satirist's disclaimer of satirical intent may be taken no more seriously than the claim of a speaker using all the arts of rhetorical device to speak the plain, unvarnished truth. Both satire and rhetoric thrive by denying their own existence.

All this is to the point; but there is some truth in the writer's disclaimer. Traditional satire does indeed castigate vices and abuses according to an ordered system – either of morals or of polite manners – known to all, taking one clear point, or one point clearly after another. From the didacticism of Brant's *Ship of Fools* to the irony of Swift's *Modest Proposal*, satire has been primarily a rational, consciously directed, and corrective exercise; farce and mimic satire were secondary elements. Mr Waugh's earlier comic extravaganzas are to traditional, objective satire as existentialism is to academic philosophy – the bottom has dropped out of the world picture. There is no correction, but only rejection. As Mr Spender has said, the underlying seriousness, even of the most uproarious of the earlier novels, lies in their narration of a search. It is a search for a solution to society's ills, and a rejection of those which experience offers; what Mr McCormick so well calls 'a metaphysic of loathing for society'. It is a search in which the author is engaged, but not – or only indirectly – his characters.

The earlier novels all bear the imprint of this. There is, firstly, their ambivalence: *Vile Bodies* is an account of young people who are disillusioned; but the author is disillusioned of their disillusion. *A Handful of Dust* relates the doings of civilized barbarians, but the author has compassion with their heartlessness, and partly agrees in their treatment of the victim. Almost all start brightly, cynically, audaciously, and end in despondence, reflection, withdrawal. As in the type novel, *Vile Bodies*, there is commonly a certain initial gusto for experience, followed by the hangover. *Black Mischief* shows Basil Seal at the height of his caddishness, and yet at the end he has almost learnt the lesson of ten years later, when he turns serious in *Put out more Flags*. Decline and general dispersion is inevitable, whether or not the book strikes this note in its external structure. *Vile Bodies* ends on a battlefield. Tony Last and Seth are swallowed up by the forces of savagery in a jungle clearing. The cenobitic ideal dimly present in the minds of Cedric Lyne and Ambrose Silk, violently dispersed at the end of *Put out more Flags*, the one to a cave in Norway, the other to the West Coast of Ireland, repeats this pattern in another key. It is the inevitability of decline which makes possible the co-existence, in these works, of knockabout farce and tragedy in a low key. The fool is a melancholy fool. *Black Mischief* is a tragi-comedy of love and chaos in a hot climate; it contains, as if in suspended solution, the tragedy of *A Handful of Dust* and the comedy of *Scoop*. Seth and Basil are complementary figures of disorder which then separate out into the contrasted figures of Tony Last and William Boot. Both the farce and the tragedy must be seen; to emphasize the audacity too much, as does Mr Edmund Wilson, is to credit Mr Waugh with a much brighter breastplate than he in fact has.

Nor is there an essential difference when the novels have a tripartite structure. Pennyfeather and Boot return in the end to Scone and Boot Magna, and there is an implicit condemnation of the régime of chaos which is thus sandwiched between two zones of relative stability. But the haven of innocence which the hero regains, somewhat out of breath, is neither idyllic nor philosophic, but simply a limbo. The return to limbo is properly neither a way back nor a road forward, but a withdrawal, a momentary suspension of action. It hides no stable norm of conduct, or implicit scheme of order waiting, so to speak, in the wings, to take the stage as soon as the author forsakes comedy and satire. No hero, except William Boot, is allowed to return to his refuge having made a clear profit out of his encounter with reality; and even William Boot is only allowed to do so at the cost of leaving it all behind, of leaving two hostages with the newspaper world – his relative John Boot, who gets the kudos, and his uncle Theodore Boot, who gets the commemorative dinner.

The highest gain that can be registered is the loss of an illusion – a theme that is with Mr Waugh right through to *Officers and Gentlemen* – symbolized often by the decay of a noble house. King's Thursday is subject to destructive rebuilding from the time when it first appeared to Paul in his imagination, set dreamingly in the English spring countryside. But this is not properly an experience at all, only the prelude to experience. For this reason one cannot accept the view of those critics who consider the alternative ending of *A Handful of Dust* – cynical and conciliatory, Tony goes for a cruise, returns and takes over Brenda's flat to deceive her – to be a more fitting ending than immurement in Brazil. Quite apart from the symbols scattered through the earlier narrative which prefigure the encaged prisoner, Tony is destined to be a victim. This bright, brittle ending is merely a variant of the ending already tried out in the short story *Love in the Slump*. Tony's exploitation of Brenda's infidelity would be as improbable as the metamorphosis of the dumb, romantic William into the rakish Uncle Theodore.

Just as the author is the implicit mainspring of his world – in Dame Rose Macaulay's terms, the circus-master cracking his whip – so the innocent hero is the concealed fulcrum of the action. Not only is the action precipitated by his contact with the world, but many of the other characters derive their role from the fantasy which lies behind the external events, a fantasy having its origin in the hero's mind. They may be tempters or doubles of the hero, as Beckthorpe, the clubman, Atwater, the good scout, and Apthorpe, the *miles gloriosus* are of Hector, Plant, and Crouchback. They may be shadow figures, as Potts and Prendergast in *Decline and Fall*; in the last analysis, it was for Paul's moral instruction that Prendergast lost his head. They may further his progress, as embodiments of the Life Force (Grimes and Youkoumian), as magicians and agents of transformation (Philbrick and Mr Baldwin), or comment on life for his benefit, as aesthetes and manifestations of the Life Force at the higher, non-material level (Ambrose Silk, Anthony Blanche, Corporal-Major Ludovic). Even Mr Waugh's delightful gallery of eccentric fathers adapt themselves to the theme or ground-bass of the book, as enunciated by the hero. Colonel Blount, like Adam, is concerned with schemes for making money. Plant senior has solved, in his own eccentric way, the problem of the relationship of art and life which his son will be called upon to face. Ryder senior, the whimsical and crafty recluse, defends his home and manner of life against the womenfolk with a tenacity which anticipates that of Lord Marchmain. Mr Goodall, with Apthorpe, provides a grotesque commentary on the motives of Crouchback in joining the Army.

Even the female figures are, in some subtle way, related to the hero. Those embodying the Life Force, characteristic *anima* figures, are both ruthless and glamorous: Margot Metroland, Julia Stitch. Their real-life sisters would so much like to be both of these things, but only succeed in being either shameless, or pathetic. Celia Ryder, Fausta, and Virginia Troy are of the one type; Kätchen, in *Scoop*, and perhaps Aimée Thanatogenos, are of the other; Brenda Last has something of both. They fluctuate between these types somewhat in deference to the mood of the hero: Kätchen takes colour from dumb, romantic William Boot, as Nina Blount from Adam; Charles Ryder is placed between Celia and Julia as his art is a field of contention between Anthony Blanche and Sebastian Marchmain. All three female types are perhaps developed, by a process of differentiation, from a social type which Mr Waugh professed to have known from the twenties. In a review of a novel in 1937, he describes the heroine as 'straight from the 1920's – elusive, irresponsible, promiscuous, a little wistful, avaricious, delectable, ruthless – how often we have all read and written about such people!'

The Innocent is thus deprived of the sharp outline of the episodic figures, the genuine oddities, and of the reflected vitality of those in whom the Life Force runs strong; he is frozen into apparent immobility by the intensity of the projected action, of

which he is the true centre. Paul Pennyfeather admits Professor
Silenus's view that 'instead of this absurd division into sexes
they ought to classify people as static and dynamic', and readily
agrees that he himself is intensely static. But this, of course, he
admits in his innocence; the true picture is quite otherwise. An
image rises to the mind, of Mrs Stitch, that demon of bright
activity, when first she is introduced to the reader of *Scoop*, in
bed, though it was past eleven, signing cheques, dictating, tele-
phoning, talking to a young man who was painting the ceiling,
hearing her daughter's daily Latin construe, and solving the
morning's crossword puzzle. But she was also receiving her
beauty treatment, so that 'her normally mobile face encased in
clay was rigid and menacing as an Aztec mask'. Something of
the Aztec mask is worn by many of Mr Waugh's central figures,
to the discomfort of many readers who do not notice that the
figure on the bed is the life and soul of the animated scene.

In a sense, all Mr Waugh's heroes, from Paul Pennyfeather to
Guy Crouchback, are Innocents; and yet, closer examination
shows the Innocent to be, not a stable figure, but a congeries of
types, ready to separate out. Perhaps only Paul, the raw young
seeker for Truth, whose mind and habits are as yet untroubled
by the duplicities of civilized life, is a genuine Innocent. He does
not acquire experience, except of an entirely amoral nature, or
depth, except of a mythical kind. But the jungle of the world
forces the innocent hero to become either an exploiter or a victim of surrounding chaos, a cad, or a dullard, though still not
properly a moral agent. To put it simply, Paul Pennyfeather has
the choice of graduating through the intermediate stage of John
Beaver to the fully developed bounder in Basil Seal; or through
the stage of Adam Fenwick-Symes to the matured victim in Tony
Last. Each type has a late version, in a minor key: the part-
bounder Dennis Barlow, and the part-victims, the characteristic
'dim' men, Scott-King and Guy Crouchback.

In the same way, Mr Waugh's heroine of the twenties, in the
undifferentiated chrysalis stage of innocence which united so
many contradictory qualities, became, in time, a cool, intriguing
creature, or a waif, with just the chance that the dominant sister

of the two might step into the mythical sphere and become a Margot or a Julia Stitch. To some extent it depends on the man she meets. Julia Marchmain starts like Margot and Julia Stitch, but her mettle is not strong enough to withstand the assault of Rex Mottram, as they were able to deal with Metroland and Algernon Stitch, and she ends up as a waif. The recipe for the female victim prescribes a little wistfulness, just enough to temper justice with compassion in Brenda Last – Kätchen is quite episodic – but too much allows a maudlin note to enter. In Mr Waugh's gallery of female portraits, there is always a waif in the shadows; it is better that she remain there.

Creatures which are so much the product of an inner vision do not wear well when increasing maturity or changed intention causes the writer to abandon his earlier plots for serious writing. Basil Seal is here instructive. He is, in the psychologist's jargon, the *animus* figure, corresponding to the *anima* figures of Margot and Julia, with the classical combination of qualities: toughness, caddishness, ruthlessness, and attraction for the opposite sex. His fate is that of the anti-hero of the early picaresque novel, a character incapable of development, and to whose career therefore no fitting end could be devised. The picaresque writers commonly threw in their hand and permitted him to escape from his seamy innocence by way of moral conversion. The Spaniards and *Simplicissimus* took this way out; Moll Flanders is simply removed to another continent. So Basil, in *Put out more Flags*, took the last corner and became serious; his sisters, Margot and Julia, retained their robustness, only becoming slightly madder. But, debarred from continued literary existence, the cad, like Eulenspiegel, has entered the popular imagination, becoming a literary folk-myth. *Basil Seal Rides Again* was the title of a recent review by *Strix* of the *Spectator*. When we have read *Black Mischief* or *Put out more Flags*, as Mr Spender has said, we constantly find ourselves wondering what Basil Seal is doing now – as did those three rich women, his sister, his mother, and his mistress at the outbreak of the Second World War.

CHAPTER 9

Fantasy and Myth

'Somehow his mind seems to work different than yours and mine.'
MRS CUTHBERT, in *Officers and Gentlemen*

O NE THING SATIRE, as a form, is incapable of doing: it
cannot provide the plot for a novel. Traditionally, satire
has always borrowed its ground-plan, parasitically and by ironic
inversion, from other forms of ordered exposition in art or in
life: misericords bear parodies of the liturgy, ironical encomia
are laudatory speeches in reverse. *Punch* prints annually a
satirical almanac for the events of the coming year. So a comic
entertainment can have, of itself, no mounting plot, no catharsis,
no terminal goal. The link binding together the elements of
comedy of manners, farce, and satire, must be borrowed from
some simple setting of the mythical imagination. Mr Waugh has
for many years rung the changes on a simple plot combining two
elements: one, the loss of innocence and expulsion from a haven
of refuge, the other, the hero going forth to win a kingdom. The
association of these two, basically disparate elements, the
one pessimist, the other optimist, provides him with that strik-
ingly consistent line of poetic fantasy which, in Part Two,
has been seen to run through all his plots; his private world
is one of constantly changing light and shade, but of stable
outlines. Even the more serious novels do not abandon the
pattern.

The innocent hero is, as was seen, the mainspring of the
action. In the setting of satire the Innocent is a Candide, but in
the setting of myth he is something more: a visionary. The
Innocent has a capacity for shocked surprise which admirably
serves the purpose of the satirical observer of life. But he has his

limitations. He cannot as much as enter the scene of his adventures except by the merest accident; he cannot properly animate the scene, or supply the mainspring of the action; he can neither develop, nor achieve the fruition of his desires, since he has none. The wide-eyed savage is brought into Society, comments with wonder and, perhaps, growing cynicism on what he sees, loses his innocence and is withdrawn.

In *Decline and Fall* and *Vile Bodies* the speed and intensity of the action relieves the hero of much of the onus of providing the initial impetus. He is precipitated into the world of chaos by the simplest fall from grace: the imputation of indecent behaviour. Perhaps Paul Pennyfeather tempted fortune by reading 'a rather daring paper' on drunkenness to the Thomas More Society; Adam Fenwick-Symes, perhaps, by writing his autobiography, a dangerous proceeding. The erotic theme is not used again till *Work Suspended*, and again much later, when it has its apotheosis in *Helena*. But from *A Handful of Dust* onwards, all Mr Waugh's heroes are visionaries. From Tony Last to Guy Crouchback their mind's eye is turned inwards, though their steps are directed outwards. Their inward vision takes always one of two forms: a fantasy of adventure, or one of allegiance, a desire for action (Seal, Boot, Crouchback), or a desire for a home, a City, a club, a *civitas* (Last, Plant, Scott-King, Helena). In all cases, fortune takes the hero by the word of his unuttered wishes, and the arm of coincidence reaches out to offer him the substance of his desires: Last a home, Plant, the expert in fictional murder, a real death, a birth, and the chance of himself being reborn, Scott-King an experience of Mediterranean realities, Crouchback a cause. In two cases, the especial remoteness of the fantasy is underlined by its being given a 'last-minute' quality: Boot, with his Bengal Lancers, Crouchback, with his Truslove and other fantasies. Helena's fantasy, also, has a last-minute quality, in that consummation is delayed till the end of her recorded life; she is, as a 'late comer', a type of several Waugh heroes. In one case, that of Miles Plastic, the vision, when it appears, is totally regressive: incendiarism and the bearded lady are the extent of his revealed secret desires, a fairground craving rather than a visionary revelation. But then his name is *Plastic*, he is the creature of a new age.

It is the quality of the hero's fantasy and of its relation to the outside world which predisposes him to develop from the innocent to the cad or to the victim. Basil Seal's visions relate to the extent to which he can precipitate disorder and profit from it, as the eater of women, the lone agent, the hard-faced war profiteer. He is a creature of chaos rather than of order; so, like his later half-brother Dennis Barlow, he finds little difficulty in achieving the fruition of his desires, as long as a disintegrating society is the setting. But in the earlier novels and the later entertainments, the answer is normally a dusty one, and the hero – Adam, Seth, Tony, or Scott-King – is delivered back to his limbo, having understood in varying degrees the nature of his experience, or is utterly dispersed. After the fall from grace, the loss of innocence, there is, in the earlier setting, no way back. Only William Boot both retains his innocence and makes the grade. Boot's two desires, fused in the figure of the great-crested grebe, are to wander among lush places, and to fly. This, the typical twofold urge of the romantic soul, is the staple of magical desires throughout the ages; the myth of Alexander and the legend of Dr Faust both take their respective magical adepts up into the sky and down to the deepest regions. His wish, therefore, being almost without realistic content, can the more easily be gratified, and for him stones become gold – another Romantic theme – and he returns with the scoop.

But from 1939, Mr Waugh began to develop a new style of writing; henceforth, it was clear, the mixed elements of farce and tragedy were to be but a subordinate ingredient in the mixture. The earlier works, as satire, had involved no statement of the norm by which the social scene had been judged and found wanting; as myth they had provided the innocent with no way forward from loss of innocence. no way back from dispersion, The disintegration of *A Handful of Dust* had to be answered by some process of re-integration, whether by flux and transformation in the hero's own character, or by the transfiguration of a world of chaos into a vision of order.

Work Suspended was to have been the first essay in the new mode. Instead of a haven to be succeeded by chaos, the hero was given a false haven, a pension in Fez, bearing in it already the pattern of a new life to which he was to be called by the incursion of the irrational. Death passed over the head of John Plant, and took the father, and the agent of death – Dr Messinger translated into Arthur Atwater – provided the first clear double in Mr Waugh's novels, in conflict with whom the transformation of the hero's character became possible. Not that fantasy was to give place to an unrelieved realism, still less to introspective analysis of mental contents. The hero's progress was still – and will always be – projected into outer figures and situations. But the discordant elements of farce and tragedy were to be fused into a uniform thread of poetic symbolism.

Indeed, the symbols of allegiance to a group, the second element of fantasy in the inner life of all Mr Waugh's heroes, now take an even more prominent place than before. From King's Thursday to Apthorpe's Thunder-box, his characters have always sought to preserve or to create a local habitation in their own likeness. Each stage in the spiritual or material odyssey of men or groups towards the country of their desire is symbolized by some architectural structure, some sign of human occupancy. Among the major symbols of this kind are the great country houses, King's Thursday and Malfrey, Brideshead and Broome. Scone College and Granchester are limbos for heroes, but also regressive symbols of academic seclusion and limitation. Blackstone Gaol and Brenda Last's flat are scenes of isolation and perverse restrictions of human liberty. The Megalopolitan building known as Copper House, neo-Byzantine and neo-Sassinian, together with the Megalopolitan Studios, its fellows in Whispering Glades, and Constantine's grandiose church, are pure frauds.

The contrast, change, and vandalistic rebuilding of these structures reflects the theme of each story, and its tone, whether comic, tragic, or burlesque. As, in the earlier works, the melancholy decline proceeds, the symbol of the City descends from the sublime to the tragic or the ridiculous. King's Thursday is perfect domestic Tudor, then a creation in chromium and glass, as Mountjoy is transmuted from its dream of a rich, old-fashioned Tennysonian night to the daylight glare of the penitentiary and the slaughtered peacocks. The setting in *A Handful of Dust* degenerates from Hetton Abbey and Morgan le Fay – English Gothic crammed with memories of childhood – to a clearing in a jungle inhabited by a lunatic, and a cage for a silver fox kept for its pelt. *Put out more Flags* progresses from Malfrey, 'a Cleopatra among houses', through images of cenobitic isolation – Ambrose's Ivory Tower, Angela's top-floor flat, Cedric's grottoes – to a command post in a cave on a Norwegian hillside. *Work Suspended* was the first novel to fuse the architectural image with a promise of integration in the hero's character. But the part completed related only the opening interchanges with his double, and the movement, so far, is regressive. John Plant comes of a generation of landless men who talk about landscape gardening. He loses, by his father's death, a Victorian house in St John's Wood, is offered by Roger Simmonds *A Composed Hermitage in the Chinese Taste*, by Atwater membership of a bogus West End club, and by Lucy occupancy of a cage at the Zoo.

It is, however, by his straight writing in the three major works of the post-war period, *Brideshead*, *Helena*, and the war novels, *Men at Arms* and *Officers and Gentlemen*, that Mr Waugh's work is now commonly judged. It is here that a consideration of the progress of the visionary hero will reveal the resources which he has been able to summon up to replace those forces which are now called on only for occasional service, in the entertainments. His achievement leads through *Brideshead* to a peak in *Helena*, followed by a – perhaps temporary – decline in the novels of Army life.

It is clear that the character of Charles Ryder cannot be measured solely by the categories derived from Paul Pennyfeather and his immediate successors. He starts off, at Oxford, as the innocent, plays the bounder fitfully in relation to Rex Mottram and his own legal wife, then twice over repeats the pattern of the victim, once when escaping to Central America, and again in the final dénouement of the book. As Julia sinks into despondent waifhood, he tries again for a moment to play the cynic, but without success. His conversion from unwilling resignation to positive acceptance of the gift of faith is not related, and receives as little formal motivation as the death-bed conversion of Lord Marchmain.

But to look for precise and realistic delineation of character in *Brideshead* is to miss half the life of the book. Mr Waugh's 'realism' has always been restricted to his secondary figures – the innocent visionary is a mythical, not a realistic figure – and here the secondary characters, from Brideshead and Rex Mottram downwards, are perfectly outlined. But the major characters draw their life-blood from the central theme, which is suggested, rather than described, in the dominant images of the work; the happy Polynesian and the Wandering Jew, the Arctic trapper, the fawning monster and the burrowing mole, these are the intuitions of Charles Ryder's inner vision, the controlling images of the remembered and recorded action. Even Charles's relationship with his father, and the leisurely and unadmitted chicanery by which Ryder senior endeavours to make his son's stay in his house as short and as uncomfortable as possible, is depicted through images of a contested territory. Each dominant image is the centre of a group of related metaphors. Charles's relationship with Sebastian is carried along by suggestions of underground luxuriance – of riches and of anarchy, the sunless coral palaces and waving forests of the ocean bed, the hot spring of anarchy, the dangerous fire below decks, the crock of gold. All these derive from the romantic nature of the theme and the mood of recollection; they are decorative and do not determine events. Not one – not even the Arctic trapper – is specifically religious in nature. The 'embroidered folds of ecclesiasticism', criticized by Mr O'Faolain, are not those of liturgical garments, but the chosen robe of the poet, who meditates on a sequence of past events. The colours are luxuriant; but the garment is his own. The dominant tone of the whole is set irremediably by the first and earliest memory on the first page of the first chapter: 'It was Eights Week. Oxford – submerged now and obliterated, irrecoverable as Lyonnesse, so quickly have the waters come flooding in . . .' All else is development.

Mr Waugh has been accused of depicting religion in *Brideshead* through excessively restrictive spectacles; for godliness, says Mr O'Faolain, we are offered obedience. If this is so, at least one must recognize that Mr Waugh has here sacrificed his one loyalty, noble tradition, to his other loyalty, religious obedience. But it is only the Army officer of the title, revisiting Brideshead in *Prologue* and *Epilogue*, who offers anything which may be described so simply as obedience. The memories proper, which these enclose, are those of Charles Ryder, the artist, and have been given by Mr Waugh a twofold structure. There is, firstly, the unforgettable youthful experience of Oxford, and of Brideshead with Sebastian, followed by the loss of innocence and dispersal to North Africa and Central America, the pattern of the earlier works. There is then a general return to Brideshead, brought about, unknown to the main actors, by the 'twitch upon the thread', followed by an even more desperate and final dispersal. The natural happiness of the family, and of Charles with them – Brideshead and Cordelia excepted, who never stray – is laid waste. The house and history of Brideshead, and the title of Marchmain, is sacrificed to the chapel in gaudy art nouveau. *Brideshead* is, artistically speaking, an elegy; it is also a lament. The *leit-motif* is the passage from the Lamentations of Jeremias in the Maundy Thursday liturgy: '*Quomodo sedet sola civitas plena populo* . . .', how doth the city sit solitary, that was full of people! Mr Waugh has not again attempted to unite the mansion and the faith. Brideshead has gone the way of Lyonnesse; Brideshead is Hetton at another level.

Helena is the first-fruit of Mr Waugh's liberation from an imagined union implicit in the term 'household of the faith', from a desire to realize a world of the spirit in allegiance to a great home. Helena scoops her prize for the simple reason that the initial fantasy – erotic and civic, Helen of Troy and the carved bed – is projected back, by way of poetic analogy, from its preordained end; submission to the Cross is the final consummation of both parts of the fantasy. The forerunner theme (Constantius leading to Christ) is taken over from *Brideshead* and becomes one of the numerous antinomies, reflecting the transition from vision to reality, on which the work is based: failure becomes success, the poetry of Troy is revealed as the fact of Golgotha, the private myth merges into the mystical vision. The pattern of dispersion and concentration, attempted in earlier works from *Work Suspended*, is finely achieved. As in *Brideshead*, the process by which the action is refocussed on to the spiritual plane is twofold. Helena leaves her British castle for palaces in Nish, Dalmatia, and Rome, and ends by penetrating into the underground structure of the cistern to find the balks of timber of the True Cross. In this final uniting, in the symbol of the spiritual marriage, of the marital chamber and the tomb, the regressive symbols of the caves and grottoes last met in *Put out more Flags* are transcended: physical restriction becomes spiritual liberation. At the same time, however, Colchester and Rome are seen as progressively more inadequate symbols of allegiance to a universal Church, the ideal of a *civitas* that should burst out beyond the *limes*.

Consider how *Helena* so completely provides the answer to the most resounding and grim failure of the Innocent in the earlier work, *A Handful of Dust*. Both central figures seek in marriage some new and better allegiance to a home: Hetton Abbey, the City of Rome; both are betrayed. Each then continues the quest for the City in another mode, Tony in his despairing archaeological expedition to the jungles of Brazil, Helena in the pursuance of her first-expressed desire to excavate the City of Troy. Tony is the 'Last' to try to find Avalon in an English county, Helena the first to find 'Troy' in the Holy Land. Both are sought out by a messenger, Tony by Dr Messinger, Helena by the Wandering Jew. The one is taken to a living death in a grotesque parody of the Eden from which he has been expelled. The other finds the True Cross in a cistern on Good Friday. Mr Waugh's sacred and profane memories are so consistent and interwoven that the profane imaginative pattern is succeeded, after fifteen years, by its sacred counterpart in the way in which type answers to anti-type in the Christian,

typological view of the continuity of history. Tony Last's expulsion from Hetton and his end in Brazil is the fall of the old
Adam – *o felix culpa!* – redeemed, in time, by the action of
Helena. The early novel shows the greatest possible dissonance
between the romanticism of English Gothic and the social novel
of present-day manners; the later one the happiest association of
poetic symbol and Christian legend.

For the general public, and the critics, Mr Waugh is still the
author of *Brideshead*, a work in which the forced and one-sided
extraversion of the war years caused a rank luxuriation of fantasy images. But *Helena*, where poetic fantasy was disciplined by
a more astringent technique to the requirements of a perfectly
appreciated theme, and which continues his greatest earlier
work, represents much more clearly his present-day full-dress
manner of writing. But to achieve this success, he had to go to a
legendary, Christian past. The war novels show the difficulty of
applying the new mode to the de-Christianized present.

Crouchback, like Helena, is a visionary; he and the secular
world around him are not more at odds than were Helena and
pagan Rome. But while Helena's was a heroic and Homeric fantasy, embraced with epic gusto, Crouchback's contact with the
sources of vitality have wasted away till they are represented by
echoes from childhood adventure stories (Captain Truslove) and
the popular, naive religion of his Italian home (Sir Roger de
Waybroke). Neither can provide the gateway to a larger life.
Both Helena and Crouchback explore their fantasies. But while
Helena's love affair is expansive in its object, Crouchback's flirtation with Army life throws up substitute figures which elbow
him, paralysed, to the wings. Each one is eliminated late, and
with difficulty, and the last is the worst illusion of all. The fantasies to which they, in turn, give rise in his mind, are increasingly remote; the images associated with Ivor Claire (an Eastern Prince, a man withdrawn in prayer), are as decorative and
undynamic as anything in *Brideshead*. The withdrawal of the life
force from these figures leads to no visible enrichment or rise in
stature in the hero himself; his vision is progressively restricted,
from a Crusade to an operation, then to drill on the barracks

square. Chesterton's words about Mr Pickwick are relevant here: 'Pickwick goes through life with that god-like gullibility which is the key to all adventures. The greenhorn is the ultimate victor in everything; it is he who gets most out of life. . . . The whole is unerringly expressed in one fortunate phrase – he will always be "taken in". To be taken in everywhere is to see the inside of everything. It is the hospitality of circumstances. With torches and trumpets, like a guest, the greenhorn is taken in by Life. And the sceptic is cast out by it.' But the greenhorn must be taken in, not in a moment of weakness, but in an impulse of generosity, which compels the hospitality of circumstance. So the pattern sketched by Chesterton fits happily the picaresque mood of Dickens, the fairy-tale tone of *Scoop*, the legendary and poetic style of *Helena*. But Crouchback, in whom generosity was not lacking, but impulsiveness was, is cast out. It is not his religion which isolates him, it is himself.

Presumably, the two volumes now written contain only the stage of dispersion, to be followed by that of re-orientation and of concentration. The Crouchback saga has arrived at the stage when Helena was old, lonely, and forgotten in Dalmatia. The mantle of the Innocent is shared here between the two Crouchbacks, the son and the father. It is Crouchback senior who is 'taken in' by life, and for whom life produces its Mr Baldwins – Major Tickeridge, Colonel Trotter, Major Grimshawe. While his father's presence is effective, Guy's progress is assured. 'Somehow his mind seems to work different than yours and mine,' comments the grasping Mrs Cuthbert, ungrammatically but with perception. Perhaps the continuation will bring the *aristeia* of the father; the spirit of Broome will succeed the illusion of the Crusade.

For this, the stage is already prepared by a development of the City theme, from the point it reached in *Helena*. Her ideal was a Church without a wall, for all mankind ('Instead of the barbarian breaking-in, might The City one day break out?'). This has now happened, in history. But the present age is one in which parody of the Church without walls is the order of the day. The Dreamer, who founded Whispering Glades, built his

University Church as a replica of St Peter's, Oxford, but with a difference. The guide had explained to him that once St Peter's had stood without the city wall. ' " *My* church," said Dr Kenworthy, "shall have no walls." And so you see it today full of God's sunshine and fresh air, bird-song and flowers. . . .' In *Scott-King* the new ultra-national citizenship of the dispossessed is seen as the new Europe taking shape beneath the pattern of the old. The war novels unite these two themes: the parody of the true *civitas* of the Church and of the Nation. The Communion of Saints – Guy and his father – is opposed to the Fellowship of the Damned – Trimmer and Virginia – and to the new Brotherhood of Suspicion created by the Most Secret organizations of the modern State.

Mr Waugh is here using a form of liturgical allegory which can only appeal to a limited audience. But it is precisely this association, within one work, of realistic reflection of the surfaces of contemporary life and religious and mythical symbolism, which has always been present in his writing, and which he will probably be led to develop in the future. It is, after all, a reversion to an ancient technique, and was present in the medieval Mystery Play. The Wakefield Nativity Play contrasts the brotherhood of guilt in just the same way with the birth of our salvation; Mac, the sheep-stealer, and his wife Gill parody the Nativity, as Trimmer and Virginia parody the sacrament of marriage. It is, in Mr Waugh, as it was in the miracle plays, an aspect of the higher burlesque. It is a sphere in which his realism and his allegory can meet on equal terms.

It is in depicting the fantasies of his characters that Mr Waugh exercises most obviously his gifts of literary pastiche. The fantasy of adventure indulged in by Seal, Boot, and Crouchback, exploits the tone of boyhood adventure stories. The allegiance to the City is, for Scott-King, dominated by echoes of Pater, for Helena by a passage in the Homeric style. Tony Last's mental world has both models firmly associated: Hetton Abbey is Tennyson and William Morris, while Morgan le Fay has its 'framed picture of a dreadnought (a coloured supplement from *Chums*), all its guns spouting flame and smoke'. But, apart from these set-piece passages, Mr Waugh's novels, through allusiveness of phrase and title, abound in echoes of his reading of the giants of the past, and especially of the nineteenth century: Homer and Gibbon beside Baudelaire and Proust, Tennyson, Browning, and Pater. It is in these many allusive passages that Mr Waugh pays, in covert fashion, Danegeld to his childhood enthusiasms, and to the literary influences which shaped his youthful interests, which are still prominently represented in his personal literary taste, but which are most distant from the spirit of contemporary movements in literature and pictorial art. The literary influences on the main, realistic current of his writing have been few, mainly those from which, in his first years as an author, he acquired some of his skill in narrative economy and speed, in the conduct of dialogue and the devices of wit: 'Saki', Fitzgerald, Hemingway, Wodehouse. These, though admitted by Mr Waugh himself, are comparatively unimportant. ' "Influence" and "Movements" are convenient inventions for the thesis writer, and also for the hanger-on' (1954) – 'A lecturer in English literature might discern two sources of Dr Wodehouse's art - the light romance of Ian Hay and the social satire of "Saki", but the attribution is quite irrelevant in the world of the imagination' (1956). But his other, more poetic vein, has continued to reflect his own preferred reading of the Victorian and other classics, isolated, as a visionary element, from the main current of the narrative, luxuriating in a kind of nature reserve which is marked by a notice like that which he erected outside Piers Court: 'No admittance on business'. Mr Waugh once said of Mr Betjeman: 'A poet writing prose often has something of the uneasiness of an actor asked to a party after his performance. There are traces of greasepaint behind the ears; the manner is either too vivacious or betrays a studied normality.' Mr Waugh's poetic manner, when it took control in *Brideshead*, was for many too vivacious; they preferred the studied normality of his earlier prose manner – especially when, like that very different writer Franz Kafka, the cool voice enunciated the most preposterous and shocking absurdities.

Mr Waugh omits one way in which the actor at the party can

provide himself with an alibi for the greasepaint adhering behind the ears; he can gently suggest that the histrionic manner is a particularly sophisticated form of self-parody, as the Bright Young People in *Vile Bodies* conversed in self-conscious and affected Cockney. Mr Waugh also uses this method: Paul Pennyfeather approaches King's Thursday past the authentically period lodges and gates, the April sunlight revealing through the trunks of budding chestnuts green glimpses of parkland and the distant radiance of a lake. 'And surely it was the spirit of William Morris that whispered to him . . . about seed-time and harvest, the superb succession of the seasons, the harmonious interdependence of rich and poor, of dignity, innocence and tradition?' Probably, but the house, when revealed, was of ferro-concrete and aluminium, Professor Silenus's interpretation of the instructions received from his gracious employer: 'something clean and square.' Seal's fantasy of a summons to meet a lean, scarred man with hard grey eyes ends with an invitation to lunch with that booby, Sir Joseph Mainwaring. It is Ambrose the butler, announcing to the fevered Tony ' "The City is served".' 'A whole Gothic world had come to grief . . . the cream and dappled unicorns had fled . . .' True, but the author himself has something to do with the collapse. Burlesque is a good alibi for the romantic in an age of dominant realism. It is a secret love affair, and also an excellent private joke against one's contemporaries. That 'whole Gothic world' receives a ritual commemoration each time a novel of Mr Waugh appears, with the piece of Gothic printing, on which he insists, on the title-page. Mr Waugh is a little like Roger Simmonds, in *Work Suspended*, a Marxist with a secret collection of the works of eighteenth-century designers of whimsical architecture. ' "The nucleus of my museum", he explained. "When the revolution comes, I've no ambitions to be a commissar or a secret policeman. I want to be director of the Museum of Bourgeois Art."' He is even, in his more wistful moods, a little like Miles Plastic, the modern Common Man who leaves a penitentiary divided equally between echoes of Tennyson and slaughtered peacocks, to prosecute a sad love-affair with a bearded lady in a cubicle of a

Nissen hut strewn with the delicate bric-a-brac of a vanished culture, two eighteenth-century French pictures, riveted old porcelain, a gilt clock.

Roger Simmonds in turn was not unlike his friend John Plant, the one a Marxist with a taste for bourgeois art, the other a writer of thrillers with an interest in country houses; only Plant is clearer about the roots of this unexpected taste. 'In youth we had pruned our aesthetic emotions hard back so that in many cases they had reverted to briar stock; we none of us wrote or read poetry, or, if we did, it was of a kind which left unsatisfied those wistful, half-romantic, half-aesthetic, peculiarly British longings which, in the past, used to find expression in so many slim lambskin volumes. When the poetic mood was on us, we turned to buildings, and gave them the place which our fathers accorded to Nature – to almost any buildings, but particularly those in the classical tradition, and, more particularly, in its decay. . . . It was a kind of nostalgia for the style of living which we emphatically rejected in practical affairs. The nobilities of Whig society became, for us, what the Arthurian paladins were in the time of Tennyson. There was never a time when so many landless men could talk at length about landscape gardening.'

'. . . buildings, but particularly those in the classical tradition, and, more particularly, in its decay.' Brideshead. '. . . the Arthurian paladins in the time of Tennyson.' Hetton Abbey for Tony Last, the spirit of William Morris introducing Paul Pennyfeather to King's Thursday. 'In youth we had pruned our emotions hard back so that in many cases they had reverted to to briar stock.' There is plenty of briar stock, whether of Nature, buildings or human affairs. in Mr Waugh's private rose garden. The categorical imperative which required this pruning is already fully expressed in Evelyn Waugh's last Editorial in the Lancing College Magazine, in 1921, in which the eighteen-year-old editor writes of the 'Youngest Generation', his own: 'In the nineteenth century the old men saw visions and the young men dreamed dreams. The youngest generation are going to be very hard and analytical and unsympathetic, but they are going to aim at things as they are – and they will not call their aim "Truth".' The programme here proposed has been carried out in twenty-five years of outstandingly successful writing, between *Decline and Fall* and *Love among the Ruins*; no one has ever thought of applying the word 'Truth' to it, they have called it 'Satire'. But all the time the rose plants have been sustained and invigorated by discreet and regular crossing with the briar stock of romantic fantasy.

'. . . a kind of nostalgia for the style of living which we emphatically rejected in practical affairs.' Not only a style of living, but also a taste in literature was rejected. The world of Tennyson was that of Evelyn Waugh's father, Arthur Waugh, who admitted that his main qualification for writing a *Life* of the great Poet Laureate for Heinemann, in 1892, was that 'I . . . was at any rate a frank Tennysonian idolator'. Growing up in this milieu, Evelyn, the younger son, carried out in his personal taste that major re-orientation away from the spirit of late Victorian and Edwardian poetry which English literature as a whole carried out, after the first World War, under the influence of Mr T. S. Eliot and others; biographical records reaching back beyond Lancing, into the days when he frescoed the family nursery in Hampstead with strange Cubist pictures, give abundant evidence of this. But the change of skin was not complete and final. A whole world disappeared from view, but was not destroyed; it only sank, like Lyonnesse in *Brideshead*, below the waters. Arthur Waugh recorded that his *Life of Tennyson* went through six editions 'before it sank into those coral caves, full fathom five below the surface, where a perpetual sleep awaits all the little craft of our imagination and our dreams'. Charles Ryder, emerging at last from the charming, strange world of the Marchmains, reflects: 'I had come to the surface, into the light of common day and the fresh sea-air, after long captivity in the sunless coral palaces and waving forests of the ocean bed. – I had left behind me – what? Youth? Adolescence? Romance? . . . "I have left behind illusion," I said to myself, "Henceforth I live in a world of three dimensions – with the aid of my five senses".' – Again, a categorical imperative, not unlike that pronounced at Lancing in 1921: 'What will the young men of 1922 be? –

They will be, above all things, clear-sighted, they will have no use for phrases and shadows.' Both Anthony Blanche and Sebastian Flyte have laid strong claim to the artistic soul of Mr Waugh; the outcome of the conflict is still undecided. The coral cave, full fathom five, has never properly relinquished its hold. In a dedication of 1919, Arthur Waugh addressed these words to his son Evelyn: 'You are not yet so wedded to what is new that you seem likely to despise what is old. You may copy a Cubist in your living-room, but an Old Master hangs over your bed.'

Evelyn Waugh once said of his father: 'He was a good man, with a beautiful speaking voice.' Voices play a large part in the acoustic imagination of Mr Waugh. An acute sensitivity to their quality, tone, and balance is the secret of his uncanny control of dialogue. They are the bearers of many of his fantasies; they may be the voice of life, or of death. *The Loved One* is full of voices: the voice of the Dreamer in Whispering Glades, drooling of 'the soul of the Loved One who starts from here on the greatest success story of all time'; the voice of the Guru Brahmin, brutally telling Aimée to launch herself on that road from a top-floor window. Once only, in the novelist's earlier work, the voices became hallucinatory and took control of the hero's mind and fate: when Dr Messinger had brought Tony Last to within a sick, feverish man's wanderings of Mr Todd's farm. Tony had loved reading, to Brenda, with little success, to John Andrew in the nursery, and now to Mr Todd, 'a unique audience' – unique because from now on his audience is one and perpetual. In this fantasy of living incarceration, Mr Waugh has judged and condemned a side of himself. The works read are those of Dickens; the voice condemned to perpetual reading is a voice from the past, the link with his father's outlook and taste.

The American critic, Mr Edmund Wilson, has said that Mr Waugh achieved his greatest success by contriving a world which existed by virtue of its audacity. 'Never apologize, never explain' is the title and keynote of his article, an injunction drawn from the repertoire of the great Jowett of Balliol. Mr Waugh has never explained his works; but it is quite baseless to assume that he has never apologized for his audacity. The apology must be sought, not among the roses, but among the briar stock. Paul Pennyfeather did penance for his love affair with Margot by going to prison for white slave dealings of which he was innocent; the Latin-American Entertainment Co. Ltd and Blackstone Gaol follow with the logic of the crazy world into which he has entered on his fall from virtue in Pervigilium Veneris.

Mr Waugh also pays, in those regressive symbols of the artistic personality, the bounders and outsiders Basil Seal, Ambrose Silk, Anthony Blanche, for the audacity of his satirical intent. In a review of 1945, Mr Waugh diagnosed in the author, Mr Connolly, a threefold schizophrenic personality, 'a middle-aged gentleman in reduced circumstances . . . his disorderly Irish valet . . . and the flushed and impetuous figure of a woman novelist.' May we not, on the analogy of these three facets of the one Mr Connolly, distinguish between Mr Waugh the established writer and satirist, Mr Waugh the bounder and Mr Waugh the romantic? Does he not send Tony Last to a grim fate for his selfish concentration on the fortunes of his family and of Hetton Abbey, and for his refusal to emerge from the worlds of Tennyson and Dickens? Does he not, in *Brideshead*, expiate that self-regarding languor, the first flush of artistic inspiration, by condemning the tempter, Sebastian Flyte, to drink and a seedy decline? There can be no doubt, Mr Waugh has passed judgement on many things, but has not excluded himself; for his audacity he has apologized, for his self-regarding romanticism he has atoned. One thing he has not done: he has not given up writing.

His most recent work turns on just this point. All Mr Waugh's voices rise up against him, in a hallucinatory chorus intensely more clamorous than that heard by Tony Last, and give voice to all those negative aspects of the creative personality which have plagued – though also richly rewarded – him throughout his other novels, calling him to account for the crimes of Basil Seal and Ambrose Silk, for the insults to the press in *Scoop*, and the derogation of the plebs in *Brideshead*, for the death of Tony Last and the decay of Sebastian Flyte, challenging his right as an artist to depict those things which he would eschew as a man. For the first time, the hero's ordeal, from the moment when he is first tempted by the irrational to emerge from his refuge to the moment when he is returned, dishevelled but in good shape, to limbo and to sanity, is one which happens wholly and entirely within the mind of the author himself. The voices rise to a babble until, in self-defence, Mr Waugh subjects them to the treatment which he meted out to Tony Last, and by doing just what he has always done – by putting them all in a book. This latest and wholesale judgement of Mr Waugh by Mr Waugh is *The Ordeal of Gilbert Pinfold.*

PORTRAIT OF THE ARTIST, 1957

CHAPTER 10

Portrait of the Artist in Middle Age

THE ORDEAL OF GILBERT PINFOLD

'If you ask me all murderers are mad,' said Scarfield.
'And always smiling,' said Mr Pinfold

NO IMAGINATIVE WRITER is without a great store of personal experience and impressions – the raw material, so to speak, of his craft. What he may lack after the period of his youth is a stimulus sufficiently incisive to bring the molten matter to the surface at a given point where it may take on a shape dictated by the upper topography of the working mind. This is especially so with Mr Waugh, so that an experience which he had in 1954 was as welcome to him as a craftsman as it was distressing to him as a man. Some internal crisis brought on by his manner of life and the passing of his fiftieth year, heightened and made acute by medication, both professional and amateur, caused him for a period to be pursued by hallucinations of voices. 'I went slightly mad.' Such, in fictional form, was, and is, *The Ordeal of Gilbert Pinfold*.

Neither author nor hero, in any proper sense, 'lost his reason'. 'His reason, like mine, worked incessantly and accurately. The trouble was that all the information he had to work on was fallacious and fantastic.' Fallacious, because the voices emanated, not from creatures of flesh and blood, but from his own inner consciousness. Fantastic, because what they said had not passed through the filter of reason, but was presented for the reason to work upon. The result, being based on a false premise, was, like all the delusions of paranoia and persecution mania, nonsense. But the data was far from being nonsensical. Happily Mr Pinfold-Waugh is now cured. But the problem remains how far what the analyst might have said to Mr Pinfold about his case-history may be addressed by the critic to Mr Waugh concerning his novel. Mr Waugh has reduced and shaped the volume of material at his disposal, adding nothing but certain fictional subsidiary characters. 'I have been at pains to edit what was said to me, trying to keep it light and printable.' The critic may formulate what it all means to him, trying to keep his account brief and presentable.

The critic may the more reasonably take heart in this venture, as this new structure appearing on Mr Waugh's private landscape, this new hermitage in the Chinese taste, is raised on the same foundations as many earlier structures. Pinfold's data is fallacious and fantastic. So was that of most of Mr Waugh's heroes, from Paul Pennyfeather to Scott-King. For the Innocent works on the premise, which he shares with no one else, that the world must conform to his own simple preconceptions. Mrs Beste-Chetwynde is a charmer – but also a brothel-keeper. Captain Steerforth smiles – and is a murderer. The reader may say – oh, but Steerforth is *not* a murderer, only Pinfold *thinks* he is, because he has delusions. And delusions are fallacious; but a brothel-keeper as a character in a published work of fiction must be what the author says she is. But does Margot pursue her dark trade by decision of Evelyn Waugh, or by a need in the mind of Paul Pennyfeather? Surely she, and Prendergast, and Grimes and Potts are all in some degree shadows of the hero; the *anima*, beyond good and evil, the clergyman as a moralist, the life force, immoralist to the core, the censor figure, all these gesticulate within the shadow of Paul Pennyfeather, they are like voices thrown by the apparently immobile and impassive ventriloquist. Pinfold is anything but immobile – his reason is racing on, twisting and turning on a number of false premises – but these false premises are produced by himself. Captain Steerforth *is* a murderer, because the voices say so, and the voices are those of Pinfold the ventriloquist, so that Pinfold is a murderer – and Pinfold is the dummy of Evelyn Waugh, who is the real murderer.

'He's quite capable of taking you to the courts,' says someone of Pinfold. So in case the above statement proves to be actionable, it should now be substantiated.

Mr Waugh's legal action would be based on the evidence of character given in the measured and admirably detached *Portrait of the Artist in Middle Age*, with which the book opens. He has written nothing better on his public personality, that of a traditional, country gentleman, of Roman Catholic faith, with fastidious and rather outmoded tastes, 'a combination of eccentric don and testy colonel', of an age when he has learnt to survey with detachment his early literary and social success. He has written nothing at all before which lifted the corner of this acquired mode of life and pattern of tastes, hard and bright as a cuirass, but also somewhat antiquated, to reveal the highly strung, sensitive personality beneath. 'As a little boy he had been acutely sensitive to ridicule. His adult shell seemed impervious.' That it was not impervious is shown by the succeeding chapters. The defence to any action by Mr Waugh, on the statement made in the last paragraph, would rest its case on the evidence provided by Chapters II to VIII, the molten matter of Mr Waugh's sensitivity, poured out over the surface topography of Chapter I, and taking its rough shape.

Mr Pinfold has ordered his life predominantly to safeguard his one desire, privacy – privacy from all those things he dislikes in the modern world, 'plastics, Picasso, sunbathing and jazz', from all expressions of vulgarity or brash vitality. He has regulated as well as had John Plant, in *Work Suspended*, all the channels by which the outside world could get at him. Or almost all, since within his own social circle there is a 'gentle, bee-keeping old bachelor', Reginald Graves-Upton, who is addicted to an entirely spurious contraption for the diagnosing and treating of illness, called 'The Box'. ' "An extremely dangerous device in the wrong hands," said Mr Pinfold.' Mrs Pinfold does not agree. ' "No, no. That is the beauty of it. It can't do any harm. You see it only transmits *Life* Forces. Fanny Graves tried it on her spaniel for worms, but they simply grew enormous with all the Life Force going into them. Like serpents, Fanny said." '
Mr Pinfold was right; the Box *was* dangerous. The Life Force

was only awaiting the opportunity to connect up with his own restrained, parasitical, subconscious fears and apprehensions for them to grow like serpents. The battle of Pinfold-Laocoon with the serpents, and his victory, is related in the succeeding chapters.

For reaction to begin, a catalyst was needed. It was provided by the arrival of a Mr Angel, from the B.B.C., with recording equipment, to conduct an interview to which Mr Pinfold had consented in a moment of weakness. The idea was to emulate a series of interviews, cleverly done in Paris, 'in which informal, spontaneous discussion had seduced the object of inquiry into self-revelation'. Mr Pinfold's conscious control is slipping. The enemy is within the gates. Mr Angel sets about his devilish task, and Pinfold experiences the first distortion of reality, long before his attack of aural hallucination sets in. 'The commonplace face above the beard became slightly sinister, the accentless, but insistently plebeian voice, menacing.' Mr Pinfold presents his cuirass to the enemy, his conscious self answers 'succinctly and shrewdly, disconcerting his adversaries, if adversaries they were, point by point'. The discovery that the next intended victim of Mr Angel's team, the actor Cedric Thorne, has escaped their visitation by committing suicide, does not greatly disturb his composure. The re-broadcast, heard on the cook's wireless, dispells any uneasiness that remained. '. . . "They tried to make an ass of me," he said. "I don't believe they succeeded."' But the B.B.C. Box has taken the wavelength of his Life Force, and further operations are imminent. 'Despite his age and dangerous trade Mr Pinfold seemed to himself and to others unusually free of the fashionable agonies of *angst*.' But fifty is a dangerous age, satire a weapon likely to recoil on the wielder, and *angst* is growing like a serpent. The following chapter, 'Collapse of Elderly Party', relating the physical and medical crisis, the sudden decision to take a health-cruise to a warmer climate, the growing suspicion of the intentions of all with whom Mr Pinfold comes into contact, his parting visit to his mother, all set the stage for the spiritual battle which begins as soon as he walks up the gangway of the S.S. *Caliban*, commanded by Captain Steerforth, bound from Liverpool to Colombo.

The following three chapters represent a drama in three acts, leading to a peak and a peripeteia, the gradual recovery of the hero and his discomfiture of the forces arraigned against him. Two concluding chapters lead the action into calmer waters, and present us with Pinfold the man sane, and Pinfold the novelist in a state of creative disturbance only to be resolved by the writing of the book itself. Each chapter presents the episodes constituting the attack, the rational explanations devised by Mr Pinfold's intensely active mind, his own defence and counter-attack, and the stages by which catharsis is achieved, the self-healing of the confused mind. Mr Pinfold is right in the end when he rejects Dr Drake's explanation of the case as a simple one of poisoning by inexpert and excessive drug-taking. This provided but the occasion of the attacks, the physical predis-position to a state of health in which unacknowledged mental contents can rise uncensored to the surface, there to be exam-ined by the conscious mind ignorant of their proper nature and origin. He is right in assuming that 'he had endured a great ordeal' – of his own making – 'and, unaided, had emerged the victor'. He is wrong in thinking that the indictment itself was so much nonsense. 'I mean to say, if I wanted to draw up an indictment of myself, I could make a far blacker and more plausible case than they' – the voices – 'did.' Far blacker and more plausible, perhaps; but not a poetically truer case. The *examen de conscience* of Mr Pinfold, sane, would no doubt have followed the traditional, moral lines of all such balanced reviews – some of it is evident from the *Portrait of the Artist*. The ordeal from which he has emerged is the confrontation with the other side of his public personality, literary and social; he has raised the boulder for a moment and faced the crawling monsters underneath its 'hard, bright and antiquated cuirass'. An appropriate setting for such a confrontation is the ship S.S. *Caliban*, the monstrous counterpart of the good spirit Ariel.

The prime matter for interpretation is provided by the aural hallucinations. There is an opening process of softening up, taking the form of an assault on Mr Pinfold's most endangered sense, that of hearing. Mr Waugh combines an uncanny power to reproduce the inflections of the spoken voice in print with a confessed insensitivity to music. His conversational passages in all his books are authentic to the point of hallucination, while one of his known aversions is jazz. So it is appropriate that a work which reproduces voices out of the air should also introduce a jazz rhythm from under his feet, maddening in its luscious, vital, savage syncopation. Then, episodes are enacted below, outside, and above his cabin. A self-appointed moralist reproves a sea-man for immodest practices; a lascar is injured in an operation conducted by a bullying officer; a steward is accused of an im-modest approach to the mistress of the Captain, and tortured to death by the fiendish pair; a group of hooligans plan a common assault on Pinfold; a plot is hatched by the Captain and his cronies to sacrifice Pinfold to the marauding Spaniards, who are claiming the right to search Her Majesty's ships in an attempt to lay by the heels a British agent. Wireless sets blare out abuse of Mr Pinfold's published works from a B.B.C. programme. Mr Pinfold is subjected to inquisition on the details of his private life, followed by undetected agents throughout the ship, chal-lenged to throw himself over the side, calumniated by voices emerging from middle-aged ladies, calmly knitting on the promenade deck.

Mr Pinfold's rational mind races on with attempted explana-tions which will save the appearances and serve to maintain his struggling belief in his own sanity. There is, he thinks, an inter-communications system left over from the war, but in a state of disorder, so that wires touch by accident through the movements of the ship, and relay noises and speech to his cabin. There is a plot against him laid by his enemies. It is all a hoax, directed by evil-wishers at the B.B.C. He is pursued by the mephistophelean Mr Angel, on board with his family. The prac-titioners of the Box are directing the waves of the Life Force towards him in pursuance of some practical joke, some ill-con-sidered hoax, some evil plan. He reacts by changing his cabin, leaving the ship at Port Said, flying to Colombo; finally, at the insistence of his wife, who has received two air mail letters with a jumble of rational-irrational explanation, he flies home. The voices are gradually defeated, and leave him. The explanation is given, he is free of them for good.

Free of the voices, certainly, but what of the charges they bring? At one stage, 'Mr. Pinfold's orderly, questing mind began to sift the huge volume of charges which had been made against him'. Stated quite briefly, they alleged him to be a social parvenu, and a literary failure. The latter accusation, initiated by an imagined broadcast from the third programme of the B.B.C., caused him little concern. There was the incontrovertible evidence of the sale of his books, and, in any case, he had always considered it his job to make his books – let others talk about them. But the other group of charges, developed at great length when 'The Hooligans' take over, is more serious: it is nothing less than a direct onslaught on his status in society. Mr Pinfold's orderly mind has no hesitation in finding them in part preposterous, in part inconsistent. He was demonstrably *not* a refugee, a homosexual, a Fascist, a Communist German Jew. He could therefore not have allowed his poor, immigrant mother to die in indigence. But if he had entered England in 1937, since then claiming falsely to be an old Etonian, an ex-Guards officer, he could clearly not have disgraced himself at Oxford many years before.

And yet the charges bite. How can he be an adventurer who cheated the English farmer Hill out of his acres, causing the poor man to hang himself, when Hill is still vulgarly alive, and the truth is so obviously the reverse? How can the voices state that 'his religious profession was humbug, assumed in order to ingratiate himself with the aristocracy'? And yet Pinfold's mind itself runs on to formulate the historical analogy to this false charge . . . 'a reincarnation . . . of the "new men" of the Tudor period who had despoiled the Church and the peasantry'. What truth – what point indeed is there in such 'preposterous' and 'inconsistent' charges? And yet, to judge from the voices, they are put forward by representatives of the landed and military classes living apparently not far from Lychpole, with a disconcerting inside knowledge of his affairs. It is as if Mr Pinfold's country neighbours had banded together, collected the most disreputable gossip of their servants' halls, and deputized Mr Graves-Upton to broadcast it all through the Box as an exquisitely refined form of third degree torture. How this 'gentle, bee-keeping bachelor' would have shrunk from the task, as Mr Pinfold is aghast at the result. It was a task, one would have thought, much more adapted to the fictional personality which the Pinfold family, addicts of nicknames as they were, had assigned to him when they called him, privately, 'the Bruiser'; this, and the variations 'Pug', 'Basher', and 'Old Fisticuffs', all derived from 'Boxer', from his interest in the esoteric doctrine of 'The Box'.

It is, of course, Mr Pinfold broadcasting all the time to himself. The 'refined, fastidious old gentleman' with the sinister sobriquets, is a perfect shadow figure for the ageing, fastidious, bored, and sometimes perhaps rather boring writer, who has struggled hard to transform a difficult temperament into the innocent mask of 'a combination of eccentric don and testy colonel', and to exercise, without danger to himself – here we must assume some knowledge of the nature of Mr Pinfold-Waugh's works, not enlarged upon in the opening chapter – the dangerous métier of social satirist. The Hooligans of Chapter IV, in their hymn of hate against Pinfold, are interrupted by their mother's voice, in yearning tones, which reminded Pinfold of his deceased Anglican aunts. 'Why do all you young people *hate* so much? What has come over the world? You were not brought up to *hate*.' Neither was Mr Pinfold, who may be assumed, like his creator Mr Waugh, to have been brought up in an eminently respectable and conventional late Victorian household, with a family tree which 'burgeons on every twig with Anglican clergymen', and sent to a school of very ecclesiastical temper on the South Downs. The lachrymose reproaches of 'the mother' begin to acquire meaning. Is it so preposterous, the accusation that Mr Pinfold had been ashamed of his illiterate immigrant mother, 'had let her die alone, uncared for, had not attended her pauper's funeral?' He had, of course, said a dutiful farewell to her several days before in Kew, but in terms which showed the emotional link to have been broken. 'In childhood Mr Pinfold had loved her extravagantly. There remained now only a firm *pietas*. "Why does everyone except me find it so easy to be nice?" '

Let us state Mr Pinfold's inner qualms concerning the nature of his foul trade of satirist in the images in which his unconscious mind has chosen to clothe them. The 'dangerous trade' he has elected to ply is the extreme of non-respectability, it is like homosexuality and other disgusting and indecent practices, such as that revealed by the short colloquy between the self-appointed clergyman and the seaman Billy. It is not consonant with the practice of religion. At Oxford 'he accused the Dean of the most disgusting practices'. The attacks to which he is commonly subjected by public critics, B.B.C. commentators and the like, may, at a pinch, be ignored. Mr Pinfold has acquired the lowest view of literary critics, editors of literary magazines, and men who, like Jimmy Lance, are poets and artists by nature but have been untrue to their vocation at the call of the siren voices of the B.B.C., of Bohemian circles and the demands of popularized entertainment. But is his own trade any more creditable than that of the journalist, which a Prime Minister of England once described as 'power without responsibility, the privilege of the harlot throughout the ages'? The privilege of the harlot Goneril, here, is to team up with Captain Steerforth to punish an alleged immodest advance on the part of one of the Goanese stewards by torturing him to death. 'Now, lying in his spruce cabin in this British ship, in the early afternoon', a few yards distant only from simple, clean-living English passengers, Mr Pinfold 'was the horrified witness of a scene which might have come straight from the kind of pseudo-American thriller he most abhorred.' It is a characteristic thriller setting, such as was loved by Mr Waugh's earlier hero John Plant: 'Murder at Mountrichard Castle. . . . Vengeance at the Vatican.' Murderous commands issuing from the esteemed Lord of the Manor of Lychpole, a Roman Catholic drunk with his secret power, tempted by the harlot of unrighteousness, convinced of his own uniqueness. 'There's only one Lychpole . . . and Pinfold is its Lord.'

And all the time Mr Pinfold, the writer, pretends that his murderous designs are a great joke. That is what he is known for, his 'peculiar sense of humour. . . . "He is going to make notes of us",' said the foreign lady. ' "You see, we shall all be in a humorous book".' Humour for some means torture for others, a practice peculiarly repellent when it is exercised by someone in a position of trust, of honour and of responsibility, like Captain Steerforth. Goneril has a peculiar sense of humour ('there broke out not far from him in the darkness peal upon rising peal of mocking laughter – Goneril's. . . . It was devoid of mirth, an obscene cacophany of pure hatred'), a sense of humour hardly distinguished from a blood lust to see others suffer. In maudlin moods, the desire to inflict suffering would seek its acquittal by arguing, with 'the mother' here, that it is merely the other face of love: 'I love you so. All loving is suffering.' But more insistent are the moans and sobs of the victim from which Mr Pinfold, listening, cannot escape, interrupted by 'the more horrific, ecstatic, orgiastic cries of Goneril.' The Captain will dispose of the corpse quietly, secretly, overboard in the dark, thinks Pinfold, and dictate a death-certificate of natural causes. But Pinfold is privy to the horrible secret of his unhappy ship. At dinner, that night, 'Mr Pinfold stared full in the eyes of the smiling Captain' – his own *alter ego*. ' "If you ask me, all murderers are mad," said Scarfield. – "And always smiling," said Mr Pinfold. "That's the only way you can tell them – by their inevitable good humour",' – ' "You see, we shall all be in a humorous book",' said the foreign lady. Not only are *they* all in a book, but Mr Pinfold has liberated for a short while all the negative contents of his creative mind, all the preposterous, agonizing and foul earth spirits of which he, as Captain Steerforth, master of the S.S. *Caliban*, is in command; has offered himself to them as the sacrificial victim, and has thereby in some degree exorcized the monster. And Mr Waugh has put it all in a book – a humorous book, perhaps, but also an intensely moving one.

A brief account can give but a remote impression of the knotted drama of attack and counter-attack, of rising confidence in Mr Pinfold, and of growing weakness and dissension among his imputed enemies, their tone changing from threat to bluster, then to whine, and of the subtlety with which the gradual process of self-healing is indicated. Each chapter brings an attack, varying in its nature, an answer in kind, a peak and a resolution. At first, the injured lascar and the tortured seaman are projections of the sick man Pinfold himself. The web of metal through which the lascar's flesh is lacerated, repeats the theme of the torturing wires of 'The Box' at Lychpole, the wireless set, and the presumed intercommunications system. The sedative injection given to the lascar and the presumed death of the steward brings relief to the harrowed listener as well; Mr Pinfold experiences the benefit of deep sleep, freedom from physical pain, and gains his first conviction that the scenes of which he has been an unwilling witness are unreal. The common assault contemplated by the young hooligans Fosker and friend fades away into irresolution and mutual recrimination as soon as Pinfold is in position, blackthorn stick in one hand, malacca cane in the other, to repel the would-be invaders of his cabin. He invades their territory by citing them to the lounge to answer for their crimes. The plot to ship him over the side into the hands of the Spaniards is met, and defeated, by the resolution of the former Commando. The S.S. *Caliban* then rounds the Rock into the Mediterranean, 'that splendid enclosure which held all the world's history and half the happiest memories of his life', and for six hours Mr Pinfold falls into a deep, natural sleep. Thereafter, his enemies' operations lack any terror for Pinfold; when Angel comes on to the scene, he is almost ineffective from the first.

Critics have doubted whether the case-book record of a delusion can have fictional value; the situation, they say, is brilliantly original, the incidents – some of them, at least, – uproariously funny. But there is no peak to the action; it just tails off when Pinfold reaches home, with a lame explanation of the physiological origin of the voices. This is completely to misunderstand the progress of the engagement. The letter mailed by Mr Pinfold to his wife from Port Said, containing a complete and to him satisfying explanation of the whole series of events, though totally inaccurate, is a mere prelude to complete healing. The inner drama is in the way in which each assault is beaten off with its own chosen weapons: the threat of physical attack by preparedness for physical defence, persecution by counter-persecution. Two episodes call for special comment. The one may be called 'Ordeal by Reading', the other, developed mainly in Chapter VI, is the Margaret episode.

In *Portrait of the Artist* we are told of Mr Pinfold that 'at night his most frequent recurring dream was of doing *The Times* crossword puzzle; his most disagreeable that he was reading a tedious book aloud to his family.' Mr Waugh's heroes have always been made to face the situation which arises when their fantasies materialize in the world of real relationships. In a sense the whole of this book is the facing of a monstrous fantasy; so it is also in miniature. The voices present him with evidence and clues, but no controlling pattern; it is a mammoth crossword puzzle which he has to solve. Having done so to his satisfaction, he proceeds to subject the plaguing voices to a punishment fitted to the crime. If they had his wavelength, so that he could not escape their voices, then they could not escape his. 'He took a copy of *WestwardHo!* from the ship's library and read it very slowly hour by hour . . . making gibberish of the text, reading alternate lines, alternate words, reading backwards until they pleaded for a respite. Hour after hour Mr Pinfold remorselessly read on.' This is not the first time Mr Waugh has used a Victorian classic as the instrument of an Ordeal by Reading; he has placated the shade of Tony Last.

At one point, Mr Pinfold puts on his Brigade tie, and spruces up his personal appearance, sadly neglected in the period of his greatest physical pain and mental confusion; the persecuting party then becomes female, sympathetic, and maudlin, and the voice Margaret is the centre of a scene of erotic invitation, the prospect of which successively offends, intrigues, and bores Pinfold. Delusion bears here a more conciliatory air: 'he's so grand . . . he's so brave . . . often brave people are the most sensitive.' But it is no less delusion; no movement towards integration can proceed from this scene. To all his attempts to see her, question her, face her, she returns consistent refusals. 'It's against the Rules for us to meet . . .'

It *is* against the Rules of the delusional world for the victim to break out of the web of deception which it weaves. So Pinfold breaks their hold by not playing, by throwing his crazy, private world open to real people. A direct approach to the Captain on the matter of the apparent misuse of Mr Pinfold's cable messages is the first stage, his full letter on the presumed Angel plot to Mrs Pinfold the second. Flying across Europe to Mrs Pinfold, home, and release, he rejects the bargain offered by the Angel voices, that they will cease plaguing him if he promises never to reveal his experience. ' "The answer is: no" . . . Angel was a beaten man and knew it.' Later Mr Pinfold realizes that if he had accepted their bargain, he would all his life have lived under the fear that the whole thing might start up again.

To tell the truth, Pinfold, throughout his 'Ordeal', was never quite alone. Going down to dine for the first time by invitation at the Captain's table, in his dinner jacket, 'he noticed a small dark man in day clothes sitting at a table alone'. The small dark man, at first unnamed, is the only person on board whose role in Mr Pinfold's delusioned world is positive and beneficial. He is the anonymous man, with no public role, and therefore no plaguey shadow. Enmeshed in the net of his gallant and despairing attempts to reconcile the horrors revealed by the voices and the superficial chatter of the Captain's table, Mr Pinfold comes to envy him – comes, indeed, to watch his bearing and actions for a good omen of his, Pinfold's progress under ordeal. 'He wondered how without offence he could escape from the Captain's table to sit and eat alone, silent and untroubled, like that clever, dark, enviable little fellow.' A twist in the crazy events of Mr Pinfold's delusional world presents the dark man as a passenger on no list, with no ticket or papers, and of very special importance to H.M.G. 'It's him, of course, that the Spaniards are after.' Mr Pinfold acquiesces, after a struggle, to the plan that he should be sacrificed for the secret agent. 'We've got to see that that man gets through.' Mr Pinfold, after his first, healing talk with the Captain, is allotted the table where the dark man had sat. Mr Murdoch, as he is now, returns Mr Pinfold's service, leaves the ship with him at Port Said, and sees that *he*, Pinfold, gets through – to Colombo and sanity. Who is he, this man who promises release, companionship, and assistance, himself removed from the conflicting jangle of public life? A promise of healing, of integration, in Mr Pinfold's own nature? A benevolent presence, put aboard to look after him on behalf of Mrs Pinfold? A sympathetic analyst, who knows of Mr Pinfold's stony path? Only Pinfold himself could say.

What was wrong with Pinfold? asked Mr Priestley, in the *New Statesman* (31 August 1957), and many a reader may echo this question. The answer is – apart from the false medication which was the physical cause of the voices – nothing. To assume that anything was wrong with Mr Pinfold is rather like assuming that a satirist is just a man with a grievance. A satirist is a man with an infinite possibility of creative irritation when observing the behaviour of his fellow-men; Mr Pinfold was in the same fruitful state when observing the behaviour of his own inner mind. The point of Mr Priestley's article was that Mr Waugh should give up the pretence of living the life of the Catholic country-gentleman, and settle down to being a writer; this was the recipe which would banish boredom, drink, and strain. People have been saying this to Mr Waugh for twenty years. There is by now almost an official form for delivering the minatory message. Mr Priestley says: 'Pinfold must step out of his role as the Cotswold gentleman quietly regretting the Reform Bill of 1832 . . .' Mr Pritchett said in 1954: 'He just wants a club for those who refuse to know the Reformation socially.' Mr Waugh neither wants a club nor need he abandon a personality. He has spent many years creating a private world in which a profusion of personalities, split off from his own, inhabit a rich variety of dwelling-places. Of what importance is Mr Waugh's social persona as long as, in tension with other aspects of his personality, it provides a sufficient number of reflecting facets for the works he wishes to write?

Mr Priestley takes, in passing, a psychological line. Of *Pin-*

fold he says: 'For the benefit of Jungians, it may be added that both the Shadow and the Anima are busily engaged in these spectral intrigues.' He does not add, for the benefit of non-Jungians, who these are. There are at least two shadow figures in the book, Mr Graves-Upton ('the Bruiser') and Captain Steerforth; the anima figure is, of course, Margaret. As there is nothing wrong with Mr Pinfold, we need not worry what he *ought* to do about her; we need only consider what Mr Waugh *has* done with her. She is, of course, at first, the self-regarding principle; Mr Pinfold regains his self-respect, and comes in for some sympathy, when she appears. In this aspect she derives from 'little Julia' in *Work Suspended*. But she is much more than this. The invisible charade played by Margaret, her sentimental military father, and her lachrymose mother, before the proposed erotic assignation in Pinfold's cabin, is in the best tradition of Mr Waugh's romantic and burlesque fantasies. In the term used by John Plant of his own private tastes, it is best briar-stock. All the more strange, then, that when first her voice is heard, it is raised in a maidenly duet to the words of a bawdy song well known to Mr Pinfold. As the lines of the song 'rose now on the passionless, true voices of the girls, they were purged and sweetened; they floated over the sea in perfect innocence'. But perhaps it is not so strange. The horrors, calumnies and suggested obscenities of the book are the projection into imputed speech and imagined scenes of Mr Pinfold's public métier of satirist; but there is also the world of fantasy which, for thirty years, he has used to nourish the surface flora of realistic observation. There all is pure, innocent, self-regarding. At the moment, the passionless, true voices bring no relief; a paradox is no solution.

As the voice of Margaret becomes more frequent and insistent, Pinfold is flattered and intrigued. 'He relished the simple male pleasure, rather rare to him in recent years, of being found attractive, and was curious to see this honey-tongued girl.' Margaret then plays a coy game of leading him on, making him get his hair cut, but refusing finally to meet. Mr Priestley would have no difficulty about this; the conscious mind should make friends with the anima, though it will never properly lose its air of mystery. In critical terms, the briar-stock roots of Mr Waugh's fantasy are there for him to use, but must not be exposed to the light of day. Into this world there is no admittance on business; it would be fatal to pull up the plant to inspect the roots. Above all, one should maintain a discreet silence before the master of the ship; he is one of those nasty, smiling murderers. '. . . she chid him . . . gently for his visit to the Captain. "It's *against the Rules*, darling, don't you see? We *must* all play by the Rules."' If Mr Pinfold will play by the Rules, then Margaret will leave a present in his cabin, to make up for the beastly things the young hooligans are threatening to do to him. ' "After the silly way the boys behaved last night it will show him *we* weren't in it. At least not in it in the way they were."' This is the point: *not in it in the way they were.* Of course, the poor fumbling Pinfold, trying to make sense of all this with his rational mind, finds no present in the cabin. ' "He can't find anything," she said in a soft note of despair. "The sweet brave idiot, he can't find anything."' He could hardly have done so, for the present the poor sweet idiot was to find is this book; *The Ordeal of Gilbert Pinfold* had yet to be written. Mr Pinfold broke the hold of his delusions by telling them to the outside world; but perhaps Mr Waugh will keep the pact with Margaret, after all.

The Works of Evelyn Waugh

JUVENILIA

The Curse of the Horse Race. A 500-word novel, unpublished. 1910.

The Pistol Troop Magazine. Underhill. At the Pistol Troop Press. 1912.

The World to Come. A Poem in three Cantos. Privately printed. 1916.

Conversion. A three-act play on public school life. Produced at Lancing College, 1921.

Antony, who sought the things that were lost. The Oxford Broom, No. 3, June 1923.

The Balance. A Yarn of the Good Old Days of Broad Trousers and High Necked Jumpers.

NOVELS (All first published by Chapman & Hall, London)

Decline and Fall, an Illustrated Novelette. 1928 (DF)[1]

Vile Bodies. 1930. (VB)

Black Mischief. 1932. (BM)

A Handful of Dust. 1934. (HD)

Scoop, a Novel about Journalists. 1938. (S)

Work Suspended. 1942. (WS)

Put out more Flags. 1942. (PF)

Brideshead Revisited. The Sacred and Profane Memories of Captain Charles Ryder. 1945. (BR)

Scott-King's Modern Europe. 1947. (SK)

The Loved One, an Anglo-American Tragedy. 1948. (LO)

Helena. 1950. (H)

---

[1] Abbreviations for titles of novels are given for use in Appendix Three.

Men at Arms. 1952. (MA)

Love among the Ruins, a Romance of the Near Future. 1953. (LR)

Officers and Gentlemen. 1955. (OG)

The Ordeal of Gilbert Pinfold, a Conversation Piece. 1957. (GP)

ADAPTATIONS

Vile Bodies, a play in twelve episodes, adapted from Evelyn Waugh's novel by H. Dennis Bradley. 1931.

Helena, adapted for radio by Evelyn Waugh and Christopher Sykes. Broadcast 1951.

Brideshead Revisited, adapted for radio by Lance Sieveking. Broadcast 1956.

SHORT STORIES

Mr. Loveday's Little Outing, and Other Sad Stories. Chapman and Hall, 1936.

'Tactical Exercise'. *The Strand Magazine*, March 1947.

'Compassion'. *The Month*, August 1949.

ART AND TRAVEL

P.R.B. An Essay on the Pre-Raphaelite Brotherhood, 1847–54. Privately printed. 1926.

Rossetti, His Life and Works. Duckworth, 1930.

Labels, a Mediterranean Journal. Duckworth, 1930.

Remote People. Duckworth, 1931.

Ninety-two Days. Duckworth, 1934.

Waugh in Abyssinia. Longmans, 1936.

Robbery under Law, the Mexican Object-Lesson. Chapman and Hall, 1939.

When the Going was Good (abridged reprint of *Labels, Remote People, Ninety-two Days, Waugh in Abyssinia*). Duckworth, 1946.

RELIGION

Edmund Campion, Jesuit and Martyr. 1935, second edition 1947.

'The Best and the Worst: Mgr Ronald Knox'. *Horizon*, May 1948.

A Selection from the Occasional Sermons of the Rt. Rev. Mgr. R. A. Knox. Dropmore Press (limited edition), 1949.

'Come Inside', in *The Road to Damascus,* ed. John O'Brien, pp. 9–12. W. H. Allen, 1949.

'A Literary Opinion on Mgr. Knox's Old Testament'. *The Month,* July 1949.

'The American Epoch in the Catholic Church'. *The Month,* November 1949.

The Holy Places, with wood engravings by Reynolds Stone. Queen Anne Press, 1952. (Contains the two articles next following.)

'St. Helena, Empress'. *The Month,* January 1952.

'The Defence of the Holy Places'. *The Month,* March 1952.

'Goa: The Home of a Saint'. *The Month,* December 1952.

MINOR WORKS, ARTICLES, LETTERS

An Open Letter to H.E. the Cardinal Archbishop of Westminster, unpublished MS. dated May 1953.

'Fan-Fare', *Life,* 8 April 1946.

'Half in Love with Easeful Death', An Examination of Californian Burial Customs. *The Tablet,* 18 October 1947.

Wine in Peace and War, with Decorations by Rex Whistler. Privately printed by Saccone and Speed, Ltd, London, n.d. (1949).

Electoral Address as Candidate for the Lord Rectorship of Edinburgh University. Flysheet, n.d. (1951).

Writers at War. Unpublished typescript, 1952.

'Frankly Speaking', a Wireless Interview, 16 November 1953.

An Open Letter to the Hon[ble] Mrs. Peter Rodd (Nancy Mitford) on A Very Serious Subject, in *Noblesse Oblige,* ed. by Nancy Mitford, illus. by Osbert Lancaster, Hamish Hamilton, 1956, pp. 63–82.

Select Bibliography

BIOGRAPHICAL

ACTON, H. *Memoirs of an Aesthete*. London, 1948.

BALFOUR, P. (Lord Kinross). *Society Racket*. London, n.d. (1933)

BIRKENHEAD, LORD. *Lady Eleanor Smith*, A Memoir. London, 1953.

CAREW, D. The *House is Gone*, A Personal Retrospect. London, n.d. (1949).

CHAMBERLIN, C. L. De Mortuis Nil Nisi Bonum. Lancing College Magazine, October 1942. (On the Corpse Club). *Lancing College Magazine*, 1919–22, especially November, December 1921.

LINKLATER, E. See below.

PAKENHAM, LORD. *Born to Believe*. London, 1953.

SAUNDERS, H. ST. GEORGE. *The Green Beret*, The Story of the Commandos, 1940–5. London, 1949.

WAUGH, A. *One Man's Road*. London, 1931.

CRITICAL

BETJEMAN, J., Evelyn Waugh, in *Living Writers*, critical studies broadcast in the Third Programme, 1946, London, n.d. (1947), pp. 137–50.

BOYLE, A. Contemporary Novelists, IV. Evelyn Waugh. *Irish Monthly*, lxxviii, 1950, pp. 75–81.

DENNIS, N. Evelyn Waugh and the Churchillian Renaissance. *Partisan Review* (New York), x, 1943, pp. 350–61.

DE VITIS, A. A. *Roman Holiday*, The Catholic Novels of Evelyn Waugh. Bookman Associates, New York, 1956. 88 pp.

GORE ALLEN, W. Evelyn Waugh and Graham Greene. *Irish Monthly*, lxxvii, 1949, pp. 16–22.

HOLLIS, C. *Evelyn Waugh*. Longmans, for the British Council and National Book League, 1954. 38 pp.

LINKLATER, E. Evelyn Waugh, in *The Art of Adventure*, London, 1947, pp. 44–58.

MACAULAY, R. The Best and the Worst, II. Evelyn Waugh. *Horizon*, December 1946, pp. 360–76. Reprinted in *Writers of Today*, second series, ed. D. V. Baker, London, 1948, pp. 135–151.

MCCORMICK, J. *Catastrophe and Imagination*, An Interpretation of the recent English and American Novel, London, 1957, pp. 286–89.

MENEN, A. The Baroque and Mr. Waugh. *The Month*, April 1951, pp. 226–37. (Mainly on *Helena*.)

MIKES, G. *Eight Humorists*, London, 1954, Chapter 6.

NEAME, A. J. Black and Blue, A Study in the Catholic Novel. *The European*, April 1953, pp. 25–36. (On Evelyn Waugh and Graham Greene.) Cp. also N. MOSLEY, A New Puritanism, *ibid.*, May 1953. pp. 28–40.

O'DONNELL, D. *Maria Cross*, Imaginative Patterns in a Group of Modern Catholic Writers, London, 1953, Chapter 5 and *passim* in Chapter 9. (Mainly on *Brideshead Revisited*.)

O'FAOLAIN, S. *The Vanishing Hero*, Studies in the Novels of the Twenties, London, 1951, Chapter 2. (On Huxley and Waugh.)

SAVAGE, D. S. The Innocence of Evelyn Waugh, in *The Novelist as Thinker* (=Focus Four), ed. B. Rajan, London, 1947, pp. 33–46.

SPENDER, S. *The Creative Element*, A Study of Vision, Despair, and Orthodoxy among some Modern Writers, London, 1953, Chapter 9.

STOPP, F. J. Grace in Reins, Reflections on Mr. Waugh's *Brideshead* and *Helena*. *The Month*, August 1953, pp. 69–84.

STOPP, F. J. The Circle and the Tangent, An Interpretation of Mr. Waugh's *Men at Arms*. *The Month*, July 1954, pp. 17–34.

STOPP, F. J. End of an Illusion, *Renascence* (Milwaukee), Winter, 1956, pp. 56–67. (On *Officers and Gentlemen*.)

SYKES, C. The Pocket Waugh. *The Tablet*, cxcviii, 1951, pp. 9–10, 7 July 1951. (On the Penguin Edition of the Novels.)

Times Literary Supplement, 20 November 1948. Review of *The Loved One*, with a survey of the earlier novels.

VOORHEES, R. J. Evelyn Waugh Revisited. *South Atlantic Monthly* (Durham, New Carolina), xlviii, 1949, pp. 270–80.

WILSON, EDMUND. Never Apologize, Never Explain. *New Yorker*, 4 March 1944. Reprinted in *Classics and Commercials*, London, 1951, pp. 140–6.

Persons and Places in the Novels of Evelyn Waugh

(Titles of Novels are abbreviated as shown in Appendix 1, *p.* 235–7)

APTHORPE. Employed by tobacco company in Africa, then commissioned into Royal Corps of Halberdiers. School: Staplehurst House, Southsand. Two aunts, one real, one imaginary. Ops.: Battle of the Thunder-box. Died in hospital, Freetown, of fever and whisky. MA, OG.

ATWATER, ARTHUR. Sponger, various aliases. Claims descent from Henry VII. War service: unstated. Postwar: C.C.G. (B.E.). Club: Wimpole. WS

BARLOW, DENNIS. Poet, one volume. War service: Transport Command, R.A.F. Then as script-writer to Hollywood (Life of Shelley). Pet's mortician at Happier Hunting Ground. Club: Cricket, Hollywood. LO

BEAVER, JOHN. Only son of Mrs Beaver, decorator, dealer, house-agent, and general provider, of Sussex Gardens. Occupation: spare man in society. '. . . wrote a large, school-girlish hand with wide spaces between the lines.' To California with mother. HD

BELLORIUS. Poet. Born, died (1646) Simona (then Hapsburg Empire, now Neutralia). Works: Poem describing an island Utopia in 1500 Latin hexameters. Tercentenary celebrations, University of Simona, 28 July – 5 August 1946. SK

BESTE-CHETWYNDE, MARGOT, V. Metroland, Lady.

BESTE-CHETWYNDE, PETER, V. Pastmaster, Earl of.

BLANCHE, ANTHONY. 'A nomad of no nationality'. Oxford (Chr. Ch.), 1922–3, then Munich. Otherwise, movements uncertain. BR

BLOUNT, NINA. Daughter of Colonel Blount of Doubting Hall (v.). Engaged to Adam Fenwick-Symes (v.), sold by him for £78 16s. 2d. to 'Ginger' (Captain Eddy) Littlejohn, whom she marries. VB

BOOT, JOHN COURTENEY. Author of fashionable novels and works on history and travel. Member of cadet branch of Boots, of Boot Magna Hall. Receives K.C.B. for Services to Literature. S

BOOT, WILLIAM. Countryman, owner of Boot Magna Hall, where reside numerous relatives and retainers, invalid and active. Edits *Lush Places* for *Daily Beast*. Special war correspondent for *Beast* in Ishmaelia; on return, life contract of £2,000 p.a. S

BOX-BENDER, ARTHUR, M.P. Married (1914) Angela, eldest child of Mr Crouchback (v.). Three daughters, one son (Tony). Home: Lowndes Square, house in Gloucestershire. MA, OG

BRIDESHEAD, LORD. Eldest son and heir to Lord Marchmain (v.) '. . . the Flyte face, carved by an Aztec.' Knight of Malta; Joint-Master of the Marchmain. Marries Beryl, widow of Admiral Muspratt (three children). Hobby: collecting match-boxes. BR

COPPER, LORD. Newspaper magnate, owner of Megalopolitan Newspaper Corporation, Fleet Street, publishing *Daily Beast, Clean Fun, Home Knitting*, etc. Features Trimmer in the *Beast* after Op. Popgun. Pre-occupations: banquets, super-tax, death duties. S, OG

CORNER, JAMES PENDENNIS ('Chatty'). Son of Bishop; Eton, Oxford; violinist, traveller. Ref.: any book on gorillas. War service: jungle warfare school, then instructor in rock-climbing. Inherits Apthorpe's kit. MA, OG

CROUCHBACK, MR. Son of Gervase and Hermione Crouchback,

and father of Angela (m. A. Box-Bender, v.), Gervase (Downside, Irish Guards, killed in France), Ivo (d., mad, 1931), and Guy (v.). Temporary master, Our Lady of Victory's Preparatory School, evacuated Matchet. Home: Broome, Somerset (v.), then Matchet. MA, OG

CROUCHBACK, GUY. Youngest son of Mr Crouchback, of Broome (v.). Settled Kenya, married Virginia, who left him (1931); lived on family property Villa Hermione (Castello Crouchback), Santa Dulcina delle Rocce, Italy. War service: commissioned 1939 into Royal Corps of Halberdiers, Lieut., then Capt. Att. X Commando, Hookforce. Ops.: Dakar, Crete. Club: Bellamy's. MA, OG

CRUTTWELL, TOBY. Safe-breaker, then Major (V.C., Dardenelles), and M.P. (Cons.) for various constituencies. DF, BM

CRUTTWELL, MR. Bone-setter. HD

CRUTTWELL, GENERAL, F.R.S. Soldier and traveller ('Cruttwell's Folly', a waterless and indefensible camp near Salonika). Employed by firm of tropical outfitters. S

DIGBY-VANE-TRUMPINGTON, SIR ALASTAIR, V. Trumpington, Alastair.

FAGAN, DR AUGUSTUS. Headmaster, Llanabba Castle School, N. Wales. Two daughters, Florence and Diana ('Florrie', 'Dingy'). As Augustus Fagan, M.D., Proprietor of Cliff Edge, Worthing, High-Class Nursing and Private Sanatorium. DF

FENWICK-SYMES, ADAM. Writer, Only son of the late Professor Oliver Fenwick-Symes. Engaged to Nina Blount (v.). Writes Mr Chatterbox column for Lord Monomark's *Daily Excess*. VB

FLYTE, LADY CORDELIA. Youngest child of Lord Marchmain (v). Convent school, then ambulance work in Spanish Civil War. BR

FLYTE, LADY JULIA. Eldest daughter of Lord Marchmain (v.),

who left her Brideshead Castle at his death (1939). Married (1925), Rex Mottram (v.), divorced (1939). BR

FLYTE, LORD SEBASTIAN. Second son of Lord Marchmain (v.). Dipsomaniac. Oxford (Chr. Ch.), 1922–4. Travels in Levant (with Mr Samgrass), N. Africa and Greece (with Kurt, ex-Foreign Legionary). Taken in at monastery near Carthage. BR

GRIMES, CAPT. EDGAR. Assistant master at Llanabba Castle. Harrow (Podger's), Marries (bigamously) Florence Fagan for which receives three years penal servitude. Escapes from Egdon Heath Penal Settlement, reported drowned in Egdon Mire. DF

HELENA, SAINT. Youngest daughter of Coel, Paramount Chief of the Trinovantes, Colchester. Marries Constantius Chlorus, by whom becomes mother of Constantine, Emperor. Becomes Christian, and finds timbers of the True Cross in rock-cistern near Mt. Calvary. Died 18 August 328. H

HINSLEY, SIR FRANCIS. Script-writer for Megalopolitan Pictures Inc., Hollywood. Passed over by own hand. Publication: A Free Man greets the Dawn. Club: Cricket, Hollywood. LO.

LAST, ANTHONY (TONY). Owner of Hetton Abbey (v.). Marries Brenda, née Rex (v.); one son, John Andrew, killed in riding accident. Lost, reported dead, on expedition to hinterland of Brazil, Dutch Guiana, in search of the City. Clubs: Bratt's, Greville. HD

LAST, BRENDA, née Rex. Daughter of Lord St. Cloud (whose children: Reggie, Brenda, Marjorie). Marries: (1) Tony Last (v.), then, after his reputed death, (2) Jock Grant-Menzies, M.P. HD

LYNE, ANGELA. Only child of Glasgow millionaire. Marries Cedric Lyne (v.). Occupation: her appearance. BM, PF

LYNE, CEDRIC. Dilettante architect. Marries Angela (v.); one son (Nigel). Occupation: collecting grottoes (Naples, S. Germany, etc.). Killed in action, Norway, 1940. PF

MANNERING (or MAINWARING), SIR JOSEPH. Politician, adviser to Lady Seal on treatment of Basil. '. . . a self-assured old booby.' PF, BM

MARCHMAIN, MARQUIS OF, of Brideshead Castle, Wiltshire (v.), and Marchmain House, St James's. Became Catholic on marriage. Served yeomanry in World War I, after which left Lady Marchmain and settled Venice with mistress, Cara. Returns to Brideshead (January 1939) and dies reconciled to Church (July). BR

MARCHMAIN, LADY. Member of old Catholic family. Three brothers, killed between Mons and Passchendaele. Eldest (Ned, Oxford, Grenadier Guards), left literary remains, which edited for Lady Marchmain by Mr Samgrass (History don, genealogist and legitimist, of All Souls), and published as Memorial Book. Died 1926. BR

METROLAND, LADY (MARGOT). Society woman. As Mrs Beste-Chetwynde, buys and rebuilds King's Thursday (v.). Engaged to marry Paul Pennyfeather. Marries Sir Humphrey Maltravers, Minister of Transportation, later Home Secretary, who becomes Viscount Metroland. Owns the Latin-American Entertainment Co. Ltd, for which engages Chastity and Divine Discontent, two Angels of Mrs Melrose Ape, Evangelist. One son, Peter, who becomes Earl of Pastmaster (v.). DF, VB

MONOMARK, LORD. Owner of many newspapers, including the *Daily Excess.* BM, PF

MOTTRAM, REX. Financier and politician. Service in World War I: Canadian Army (M.C.). M.P. for North Gridley, then (in World War II) Minister. Married: (1) Sarah Cutler (Montreal, 1915), divorced (1919); (2) Lady Julia Flyte (London, 1925), divorced (1939). Occupations: Politics and Money. BR

PARSNIP AND PIMPERNELL. Left-wing poets, friends and collaborators. Left England for New York, 1939. Successively patients of the Euthanasia Service. Publication: Parsnip, *Guernica Revisited*. PF, LR

PASTMASTER, EARL OF (PETER). Son of Mrs Beste-Chetwynde (v. Metroland, Lady), School: Llanabba Castle. Oxford (Scone). Marries Lady Mary (Molly) Meadowes, second daughter of Lord Granchester. War service: commissioned, seconded to Special Service Forces. Clubs: Bratt's, Bollinger. DF, VB, PF

PENNYFEATHER, PAUL. Reading theology at Oxford (Scone). Assistant master, Llanabba Castle School. Engaged to Mrs Beste-Chetwynde; seven years' penal servitude for white slave traffic; serves part at Blackstone Gaol and Egdon Heath Penal Settlement. Escapes under arrangements made by Home Secretary, returns to Scone. DF

PHILBRICK, SOLOMON. Butler at Llanabba Castle School, Probably son of 'Chick' Philbrick, boxer, one-time associate of Toby Cruttwell (v.), safe-breaker, and landlord of 'Lamb and Flag', Camberwell Green; but many other identities. Marries Diana Fagan. Sentenced for false pretences and impersonation; reception bath cleaner at Blackstone Gaol. DF

PINFOLD, GILBERT. Successful author. Married, numerous children. Occupations: writing, reading, managing own affairs. Tastes: pictures, books, furniture. Negative tastes: plastics, Picasso, sunbathing, jazz. Politics: an idiosyncratic Toryism. War service: Guards. Home: Lychpole. Club: Bellamy's. GP

PLANT, JOHN. Son of Academician. Writer of detective stories: Vengeance at the Vatican, Death in the Dukeries, The Frightened Footman, Murder at Mountrichard Castle (in progress). Tastes: English domestic architecture. War service: regimental soldiering. WS

PLASTIC, MILES. The Modern Man. Burns down Air Force Station, sentenced for Antisocial Activity, sent to Mountjoy (v.), discharged and posted to Euthanasia Service, Satellite City, meets and loses Clara, ballet-dancer, burns down Mountjoy, marries the gruesome Miss Flower and lectures on the new Mountjoy, a packing-case. LR

PRENDERGAST. Assistant master at Llanabba School. Formerly incumbent of living (Anglican) at Worthing, till Doubts began. Becomes Modern Churchman, Chaplain at Blackstone Gaol, where murdered by convict with religious mania. DF

RAMPOLE AND BENFLEET, publishers. VB

RAMPOLE AND BENTLEY, publishers, *inter alia* of novels by Ruth Mountdragon (Mrs Parker), and the *Ivory Tower* (ed. Ambrose Silk, v.). Senior partner, 'old Rampole', interned Brixton Gaol for security reasons. PF

RITCHIE-HOOK, BRIGADIER BENJAMIN (BEN), Royal Corps of Halberdiers, 'the great Halberdier *enfant terrible* of the first World War'. Often wounded, often decorated, often in difficulty with authority. Exponent of art of offensive warfare. Commander Hookforce, Special Service Forces. MA, OG

RYDER, CHARLES. Artist. Oxford (1922–4), then Paris, to study art; speciality: architectural painting. Travels in Mexico, C. America. Marries Celia, daughter of Lord Mulcaster, divorced (1939); two children (John, Caroline). Early work included decorations at Brideshead Castle (v.) and four canvases of Marchmain House, St James's. Publications: Ryder's Country Seats, Ryder's English Homes, Ryder's Village and Provincial Architecture, Ryder's Latin America. War service: regimental soldiering. Club: Bratt's. BR

SCOTT-KING. Classical master at Granchester School since 1925. Works: Translation of Bellorius (v.) into Spenserian stanzas, with introduction and notes (unpub.). The Last Latinist, essay on Bellorius for tercentenary of death (1946) Attended tercentenary celebrations at Simona, Neutralia. SK

SEAL, BASIL. Son of Lady Seal (v.). Many occupations, incl. High Commissioner and Comptroller General of Modernization, Azania; Parliamentary candidate (Cons.);

leader-writer for *Daily Beast*; champagne salesman; expedition to Afghanistan, etc., etc. Tastes: girls. War service: irregular. BM, WS, PF

SEAL, LADY (CYNTHIA). Widow of Sir Christopher Seal, Chief Conservative Whip for twenty-five years. Three children: Tony (Foreign Service), Basil (v.), Barbara (married Freddy Sothill of Malfrey, v.). Occupation: dealing with Basil. BM, PF

SILK, AMBROSE, Half-Jewish aesthete. Editor and sole contributor to the *Ivory Tower* (Rampole and Bentley, 1940), incl. esp. *Monument to a Spartan*. Escapes to Ireland as Fr Flanagan, S.J. Tastes: Love and Art. PF

SIMMONDS, ROGER. Marxist writer, author of ideological play *Internal Combustion*. Oxford (New). Member Socialist Party. Married Lucy (fortune: £58,000); one son (b. 25 August 1939). War service: Office of Political Warfare. Tastes: collecting works of Batty Langley and William Halfpenny. Aim: to be director of Museum of Bourgeois Art. WS

STITCH, JULIA. Wife of Algernon Stitch, politician and Cabinet Minister. House by Nicholas Hawksmoor, St James's. Protectress of X Commando, Alexandria. Occupation: varied, the Stitch Service. S, OG

THANATOGENOS, AIMEE. Cosmetician at Whispering Glades, Hollywood. Father Four Square Gospeller, mother (alcoholic) New Thought. College: Diploma in Beauticraft, with special mention for Psychology and Art. Thesis: Hairstyling in the Orient. Passed over by own hand on instructions from the Oracle. LO

TRIMMER. The People's Hero. Formerly Gustave, hairdresser on the *Aquitania*. Later Major (then Colonel) Alistair McTavish, Argyll Highlanders. War service: Op. Popgun. MA, OG

TRUMPINGTON, ALASTAIR (Sir Alastair Digby-Vane-Trumpington). Nephew of Lady Circumference. Eton and Oxford (Scone). Marries Sonia. War service: mortar-man, then

Special Service Forces. Clubs: Bratt's, Bollinger. DF, BM, PF

YOUKOUMIAN, KRIKOR. Armenian. Owner of Amurath Café and Universal Stores and other establishments at Matodi and Debra Dowa, Azania. Under Seth, Financial Secretary to Minister of Modernization. BM

ANCHORAGE HOUSE. Home of Lady Circumference, last survivor of the noble town houses of London; 'a "picturesque bit" ending in a ravine between concrete skyscrapers'. VB

AZANIA. 'A large, imaginary island off the East Coast of Africa, in character and history a combination of Zanzibar and Abyssinia.' Capital: Debra Dowa. Autonomous Empire under Amurath and Seth, then Anglo-French Protectorate. BM

BRIDESHEAD CASTLE, WILTSHIRE. Built late seventeenth century, with stones from original castle near village. English Baroque (period of Inigo Jones). Special points: Great Hall, Chinese Drawing Room (note the Queen's Bed), Terrace with Fountain (brought in Nelson's time from Naples area), Chapel (art nouveau). Home of Marquis of Marchmain, since 1939 owned by Lady Julia Flyte. BR

BOLLINGER (OR BULLINGDON) CLUB. Oxford Club, membership largely aristocratic. Annual dinner (when not suspended). Memorable occasions: ducking of Anthony Blanche in Mercury (1923), debagging of Paul Pennyfeather (1928). Club activities: drink and destruction. DF, BR

BROOME, SOMERSET. Home of Crouchback family, Catholic recusants, by whom held in uninterrupted male succession since reign of Henry I. Special point: North turret of forecourt where Blessed Gervase Crouchback lodged when taken on information given by a spy from Exeter. MA, OG

DOUBTING HALL, near Aylesbury. Home of Colonel Blount. Palladian façade. Setting for 'Life of John Wesley' (Wonderfilms). VB

GRANCHESTER. Public school, 450 boys. Classical and Modern Sides, Army Class. Annual cricket match at Lord's. SK

HAPPIER HUNTING GROUND. Pet's Cemetery, Hollywood. Proprietor: Mr Schultz. Unequalled between San Francisco and Mexican border. Services of non-sectarian clergyman available. LO

HETTON ABBEY, HETTON. Formerly home of Anthony Last Explorer (d. 1934, note memorial in local stone), now of Richard Last (see silver-fox farm behind stables). Entirely rebuilt in 1864 in the Gothic style (article in Architectural Review more percipient than note in County Guide Book). Special points: battlements, clock-tower, great hall, bedrooms. HD

ISHMAELIA. Republic in N.E. Africa. The Presidential office has descended in the family of the first President, Mr Samuel Smiles Jackson, of Alabama. Capital: Jacksonburg. Foundation member of the League of Nations. S

KING'S THURSDAY. From sixteenth century till recently, country mansion in pure domestic Tudor and seat of the Earls of Pastmaster, but twice rebuilt by Lady Metroland, the present owner, and now devoid of interest. DF

LLANABBA CASTLE, N. Wales. Unique combination of medieval and Georgian. Llanabba House, Georgian, till 1860's, when rebuilt in the feudal style. Special points: main gates, towered and turreted, heraldic animals, portcullis in working order. DF

MALFREY. Home of Freddy and Barbara Sothill, née Seal. Early seventeenth century. Special points: Grinling Gibbons saloon, orangery (rare tropical plants), PF

MARCHMAIN HOUSE, St James's, S.W.1. Site of former town residence of Marquis of Marchmain, demolished 1926. BR, OG

MEGALOPOLITAN NEWSPAPER CORPORATION, 700–853, Fleet Street. v. Copper, Lord. S

MEGALOPOLITAN PICTURES INC., Hollywood. LO

MOUNTJOY CASTLE. Ancestral seat of maimed V.C. of World War II, then gaol and penitentiary of the new Penology, then burnt down. Model for the new Mountjoy: a standard packing case on end. LR

NEUTRALIA. An imaginary and composite Mediterranean Republic representing no existing state. Neutral in World War II. Capital: Bellacita. SK

WHISPERING GLADES. 'Happy Resting Place of Loved Ones', of Caucasian race only, Hollywood. Founded by Dr Wilbur Kenworthy, The Dreamer. LO

Index

INDEX

* *The more important sections on each novel are italicized.*